Decolonising Australian History Education

This book is the first of its kind to showcase a range of fresh and expert perspectives on decolonising history education in Australia. The research-informed chapters by First Nations and non-Indigenous educators and scholars provide guidance on applying practical strategies for decolonising learning and teaching, and moving beyond the 'history wars'.

History has long been the most contentious area of education in Australia. This book tackles the narrow and overtly politicised 'history wars' debates and foregrounds the need to re-examine impacts of settler-colonialism on Australia's history. First-hand knowledge and much-needed teaching practices are presented, demonstrating how decolonisation can be put into action through Australian history education. The chapters present a range of perspectives from the early years right through to higher education settings and argues that there is an increased need for greater awareness, appreciation, and willingness to explore and engage with multiple narratives of truth-telling that are so often contested. Readers are guided to discover how this translates to classroom practice through unique, provocative, and research-informed strategies that foreground applied decolonising approaches.

Combining theoretical perspectives and practical ideas, this book is an essential resource to support pre- and in-service teachers, in all education contexts, in navigating the decolonisation of Australian history education. This makes it an important contribution to local, as well as global, decolonising efforts.

Rebecca Cairns lives and works on Wadawurrung Country as a non-Indigenous researcher and senior lecturer at the Deakin University School of Education. Prior to this, she taught in secondary schools. Her curriculum inquiry research examines the complexities of how we *do* curriculum, focusing on history education, studies of Asia, and decolonising practices.

Aleryk Fricker is a proud Dja Dja Wurrung academic. His research focus is on Indigenous Education and decolonising education practices in Australia to enable all students in Australia to benefit from accessing the oldest pedagogies and teaching knowledges in the world.

Sara Weuffen is a teacher-researcher expert in cross/intercultural education between First Nations Peoples and non-Indigenous people in Australia. As a non-Indigenous woman born on Gundijtmara Country (Warrnambool) and living on Wadawurrung Country (Ballarat), she specialises in supporting other non-Indigenous people to develop critical consciousness via curriculum analysis and pedagogical enhancement.

Decolonising Australian History Education

Fresh Perspectives from Beyond the 'History Wars'

Edited by Rebecca Cairns, Aleryk Fricker, and Sara Weuffen

LONDON AND NEW YORK

Designed cover image: © Aleryk Fricker

First published 2024
by Routledge
4 Park Square, Milton Park, Abingdon, Oxon OX14 4RN

and by Routledge
605 Third Avenue, New York, NY 10158

Routledge is an imprint of the Taylor & Francis Group, an informa business

© 2024 selection and editorial matter, Rebecca Cairns, Aleryk Fricker and Sara Weuffen; individual chapters, the contributors

The right of Rebecca Cairns, Aleryk Fricker and Sara Weuffen to be identified as the authors of the editorial material, and of the authors for their individual chapters, has been asserted in accordance with sections 77 and 78 of the Copyright, Designs and Patents Act 1988.

All rights reserved. No part of this book may be reprinted or reproduced or utilised in any form or by any electronic, mechanical, or other means, now known or hereafter invented, including photocopying and recording, or in any information storage or retrieval system, without permission in writing from the publishers.

Trademark notice: Product or corporate names may be trademarks or registered trademarks, and are used only for identification and explanation without intent to infringe.

British Library Cataloguing-in-Publication Data
A catalogue record for this book is available from the British Library

ISBN: 978-1-032-56455-5 (hbk)
ISBN: 978-1-032-56454-8 (pbk)
ISBN: 978-1-003-43561-7 (ebk)

DOI: 10.4324/9781003435617

Typeset in Galliard
by SPi Technologies India Pvt Ltd (Straive)

Contents

List of contributors		*vii*
Foreword		*x*
Acknowledgements		*xii*
1	The thin veneer of 'the history wars' on unceded lands ALERYK FRICKER, REBECCA CAIRNS, AND SARA WEUFFEN	1
2	Truth commissions, transitional justice, and history education MATI KEYNES	16
3	"Peeling off the final scab of thinking that everything's fine": Exposing the poison of Australian education's colonising history through drama-based learning DANIELLE HRADSKY	31
4	Challenging the *Great Australian Silence* ALERYK FRICKER	53
5	Positionality: The foundational threshold concept for decolonising practices SARA WEUFFEN	69
6	Learning, unlearning, and relearning history in early childhood education CAROLYN BRIGGS, KAREN ANDERSON, AND ANN SLATER	87
7	"Mummy, what did YOU do in the history wars?" White teachers decolonising Australian curriculum...and themselves LUCINDA MCKNIGHT	107

8 Acknowledging First Nations perspectives in primary
schools 123
KATE HARVIE

 9 *Doing* intercultural history: A framework for history
teachers 141
KERRI ANNE GARRARD

10 Examining invasion and possession narratives through
Asia-related history 159
REBECCA CAIRNS

11 Decolonising the teaching of local history using
cinematic virtual reality 176
WILL KING

12 Decolonial futures for history in Australian schools 193
SARA WEUFFEN, REBECCA CAIRNS, AND ALERYK FRICKER

Index *211*

Contributors

Karen Anderson has a Bachelor of Education: Early Childhood. Karen teaches at Balnarring Preschool where she has a strong belief in children connecting with nature and learning from First Nations Peoples.

Dr Carolyn Briggs is a descendant of the First Peoples of Melbourne, the Yullukit Willum clan of the Boon Wurrung. She is an Elder in research for the College of Design and Social Context at RMIT.

Dr Rebecca Cairns works on Wadawurrung Country as a non-Indigenous researcher and senior lecturer at the Deakin University School of Education. Prior to this, she taught in secondary schools. Her curriculum inquiry research examines the complexities of how we *do* curriculum, focusing on history education, studies of Asia, and decolonising practices.

Dr Aleryk Fricker is a proud Dja Dja Wurrung academic. His research focus is on Indigenous Education and decolonising education practices in Australia to enable all students in Australia to benefit from accessing the oldest pedagogies and teaching knowledges in the world.

Dr Kerri Anne Garrard is a non-Indigenous lecturer in education in the Deakin University School of Education on Wurundjeri Country. She has a strong background in History and Humanities education, having taught in secondary schools for over 20 years. Part of her work now with pre-service teachers includes intercultural approaches to teaching history. Kerri's research interests include the status of history education in Australia, the development of culturally safe resources in schools, relational and pedagogical uncertainty in schools, and intercultural education.

Dr Kate Harvie has 30 years of education experience in teaching, research and leadership. She has local and international teaching experience in Australian and UK schools, as well as 12 years lecturing pre-service teachers at Deakin University. Kate's passion for including First Nations perspectives in all Australian schools stems from her PhD titled *Indigenous Perspectives, Teacher Practice and Australian Curriculum: The Dynamic Interplay*

(2021). Kate is currently employed at the Department of Education: Teaching and Learning Branch as a senior project officer in the "Koorie Curriculum Clusters Project." She works alongside First Nations colleagues, Registered Aboriginal Parties, and cluster schools to lead improvement in teacher capability and confidence through resource co-design and partnerships.

Dr Danielle Hradsky is an early career researcher and educator who is passionate about the power of embodied learning, particularly about engaging with the supercomplex spaces of teaching for reconciliation and de/colonising education. Danielle strongly believes in the importance of exposing the poisons of the past if we are to have any hope of understanding the present and changing the future. Danielle completed her PhD at Monash University in 2023. She currently teaches at the Melbourne Graduate School of Education and the National Gallery of Victoria.

Dr Mati Keynes is a McKenzie Postdoctoral Research Fellow in the Faculty of Education, University of Melbourne. Mati's research explores connections between historical justice and education in comparative international perspective.

Will King is a former secondary school teacher with 20 years of experience in the Humanities classroom. He is a filmmaker whose credits include the cinematic virtual reality documentary *The Crossing* and the documentary *Am I Enough?*, which is currently in post-production. Will is a doctoral student at Deakin University, and his thesis *How Can the Process of Designing a Virtual Reality Simulation of Local Indigenous History Be Practiced as Acts of Truth-Telling and Reconciliation?* examines how his cross-cultural collaboration with an Indigenous Elder in designing a cinematic virtual reality film can become a site for truth-telling, healing, reconciliation and transitional justice.

Dr Lucinda McKnight is a former secondary Australian History teacher and studies of Asia project manager, now senior lecturer in pedagogy and curriculum, interested in inclusive education and curriculum design. Her research draws on arts-based methods, using black theory to tell narratives of whiteness, published, for example, in the edited collection *Black Women Theorizing Curriculum Studies in Colour and Curves* (2019). She wrote, chaired, and lectured in Deakin University's *Culture, Diversity and Participation in Education* unit, providing an introduction to principles of decolonisation for students across the university. Lucinda is currently an Australian Research Council Discovery Early Career Research Fellow.

Ann Slater has a Master of Early Childhood Education. Ann has worked with Karen at Balnarring Preschool for the past ten years and has a strong commitment to reconciliation in practice.

Dr Sara Weuffen is a teacher-researcher expert with a PhD in cross/intercultural education research between First Nations Peoples and non-Indigenous people in Australia. As a non-Indigenous woman born on Gundijtmara Country (Warrnambool) and living on Wadawurrung Country (Ballarat), she specialises in supporting other non-Indigenous people to develop critical consciousness via curriculum analysis and pedagogical enhancement. Dr Weuffen critiques dominant structures and ideologies, interrogate binary discourses, and push educational boundaries for emancipatory and success-orientated shared-learning outcomes and positive social progress. She currently works as a postdoctoral research fellow on the Culturally Nourishing Schools project at the University of New South Wales.

Foreword

I love the old stories of my Uncles and Aunties. Of them growing up. Of them, in their youth, finding ways to have fun despite being involved in an age of oppression. Growing up on Missions, the bush was their playground. They found magic in their environment. They were somewhat oblivious to the struggles of their parents, i.e., to put rationed food on their table. Not far from these tin shanties, on the edge of town, was a road called *Boundary Road* which they were forbidden to cross. One of their games was just that, darting across Boundary Road. As innoxious as the game may seem, they were actually breaking the law, an early form of apartheid in this country. Many towns still bear such legacies of apartheid by having Boundary Roads. The residents of today transverse them daily, never giving a thought to why the name exists. They are seemingly a relic of our past.

But the vestiges of 'colonisation' flow broader and wider than land. On Sunday, 15 October 2023, the nation woke with a cloud having descended upon it. The 43rd constitutional referendum, *A Voice to Parliament*, had come and gone, and with it, the opportunity for a reconciled Australia was delayed and postponed.

From a First Nations perspective, it is hard to see anything positive in the result. It was unequivocally a resounding success for those of the 'No' campaign. However, in the run-up, we, the nation, did have conversations around Voice, Treaty, Truth that should have taken place five decades ago. Those conversations were about telling the full and accurate history of the nation. Yet, the 'No' campaign ran an unencumbered campaign with imbued scare tactics which ignited uninformed minds that sheltered in the shadows of the dark history of the country rather than be drawn to the light of a reconciled people. It was essentially a plebiscite on the heart and soul of the nation. At the centre of these arguments was the concept of egalitarianism. It was as if the nation had found its own Boundary Road.

In the dawn after the referendum, I struggle with how I might look young Indigenous People in the eye with optimism and say, while the nation deems you equal, they do not want to hear your opinions about your future, despite knowing that you and your loved ones will die 10 years younger, and some of you are 17 times more likely to go to jail than university.

That is why it is so important, in the aftermath of the constitutional referendum, to return to progressing a reconciled Australia.

The insidious nature of colonisation means that effects are felt much further than land. It is transgenerational and indiscriminate in its effect. The worst aspect of which is the 'colonisation of the mind' to which every Australian is susceptible.

By picking up this book, you are now standing at the edge of your own Boundary Road. Decolonisation is not about compliance or conversion but about crafting a mature nationhood, one with balance-informed insights about its full history. Decolonisation is not about guilt but recognising that living in a hologram society, where if you hold the picture one way, you are presented with a first-world image, but if you hold it another, you see a juxtaposition to the other side and third-world conditions for some, is unacceptable.

As you stand there on the edge of Boundary Road recognise the boundaries of your paradigms and the sources and intentions of your tacit assumptions. Be prepared to experience the exhilaration of going to a brave space. Be prepared to have your mind stretched and your spirit stirred. Read each chapter with intention and leap across Boundary Road. Stride purposely in your work to deliver a reconciled Australia.

Uncle Professor Mark Rose
Gundijtmara Elder
Pro Vice Chancellor, Indigenous Strategy and Innovation
Deakin University

Acknowledgements

We begin by acknowledging the First Nations Peoples and Traditional Owners of the unceded lands and waters on which this edited collection was created. As editors located on Countries of the Kulin Nations, we pay our respects to the Wadawurrung and Wurundjeri Peoples, their Elders past and present, and their vital and enduring cultural practices.

Connection to Country and culture is beautifully evoked by the Possum Skin Cloak on the cover. Possum Skin Cloaks have been an important part of First Nations cultures in the southeastern regions of the Australian continent for millennia. On a practical level, these garments were used to keep people warm, dry, and safe during the cold and damp winter months. Beyond the utility of the garment, these cloaks held great importance as a record of the Dreaming of a person, their family and extended kin, and their wider community. This was a practice that was almost completely destroyed as European colonisation spread across the Australian continent but has been revived in recent times through the work of dedicated community members and Elders.

The cloak pictured was created in 2019 at RMIT University's Bundoora campus over three days by an estimated 70 First Nations and non-Indigenous staff and students. The image burnt into the skin reflects the natural landscape and waterway that used to flow freely across the land, prior to the colonisation of Victoria in 1835. The image was created by using burning tools to etch the design onto the skin and coloured using red, yellow, and orange ochres. A waterhole takes prominence in the centre. The large and small U shapes represent old and young people coming together to be present, to play, to celebrate, to learn, and to care for Country. The three lines extending from the waterhole represent waterways and the flow of knowledge, as we learn at university, we take this learning to share with our communities. It was co-designed by Dr Aleryk Fricker (Dja Dja Wurrung) and Mr Mitch Mahoney (Boon Wurrung).

As the editors we of this collection are very grateful for the support of the people in our professional and personal lives who helped bring this book to fruition. We have had the privilege of working together as an editorial team, and with esteemed colleagues, and relished the opportunity for co-learning.

We acknowledge the courageous work of the contributing authors and their commitment to leading important conversations about the future of history education in Australia. A big thank you goes to Professor Mark Rose, Pro Vice Chancellor Indigenous Strategy and Innovation, at Deakin University, for his profound and poignant foreword. It is a provocative call to action. Thank you to the anonymous reviewers who provided critical feedback and support for the collection. We are greatly appreciative of Professor Fred Cahir at Federation University for his positive and supportive endorsement. And finally, we wish to extend our thanks to the Routledge team, especially Vilija Stephens, who recognised the need for this scholarship.

Lastly, we wish to acknowledge the work of the History pre-service and in-service educators who are already seeking to decolonise Australian history education. We hope this collection will further inspire, provide guidance, and challenge educators to take some practical steps towards ensuring First Nations histories take their rightful place in the education of current and future generations.

Chapter 1

The thin veneer of 'the history wars' on unceded lands

Aleryk Fricker, Rebecca Cairns, and Sara Weuffen

Authors' positioning statements

As editors, we have drawn on our cultural and research contexts to support the authors of each chapter to present high-quality research which plainly articulates that, at any age and stage of a professional education, there are possibilities for engaging with the complexities and prospects of decoloniality.

Aleryk Fricker

I am a proud and sovereign Dja Dja Wurrung man and a lecturer in Indigenous education. I was grown up on unceded Wurundjeri land, and my research focus is Indigenous education and decolonising education systems in Australia. My research is a strengths-based approach that challenges the neo-colonial deficit positioning of First Nations pedagogies and teaching knowledges[1] that have been a crucial element in First Nations cultures being the oldest continuous cultures in the world.[2]

Rebecca Cairns

I am a non-Indigenous settler of mostly Irish and Scottish ancestry. I recognise I have experienced history education and settler colonialism from a comfortable and unearned position of privilege while living on the unceded, ancestral lands of the Boonwurrung, Wurundjeri, Wadawurrung, and Gimuy-walubarra Peoples. My curriculum inquiry research seeks to understand the sociopolitical complexities of how we *do* curriculum and focuses on contributing understandings of the ways curricular practices can be enhanced by decoloniality, multiperspectivity, and relationality.

Sara Weuffen

I am a non-Indigenous woman of German, Scottish, and Welsh descent who grew up on Gunditjmara Country in Warrnambool and currently lives on Wadawurrung Country in Ballarat. I champion the need to find new and

DOI: 10.4324/9781003435617-1

integrated ways of working with First Nations and non-Indigenous knowledges in Australian education. Coming from a low socio-economic background, and over the past 13 years, I have continued my social justice efforts by listening and learning from First Nations Peoples and colleagues, and non-Indigenous comrades, to unpack the ongoing conditioning effects of settler colonialism and adopt decolonial ways of thinking, being, and doing.

From review to referendum

In the recent 2021–2022 review of the Australian Curriculum, calls from federal education ministers for a more 'patriotic,' 'optimistic,' and 'decluttered' national History curriculum revived familiar debates of previous rounds of the so-called 'history wars.'[3] For over two decades, the education provided to the next generation of Australian citizens about Australia's nation-making story has been at the centre of nationalistic disputes divided by a black armband or white blindfold viewpoint.[4] More recently, the imperative to decolonise history education has gained momentum in response to the *Uluru Statement from the Heart's*[5] call for Truth, Treaty, Voice. While social directives for change have had a limited impact on curriculum, on-the-ground evidence suggests that little has changed for successive generations in relation to the re/telling of Australia's history.[6] In this chapter, we problematise Australian history in its contemporary context, explore conceptualisations of decolonising history, and provide a warrant for moving beyond the 'history wars.' Finally, we consider how decolonising approaches may impact Australian History curriculum applications and theorising in a post-'history wars' context to decolonise the thin veneer of the 'history wars' on unceded lands and enable First Nations histories their rightful place in the Australian history classroom.[7]

The recent debate and campaigning about the Voice to Parliament referendum has indicated that we are still well and truly mired in the 'history wars' and feel as though the nation remains locked in a struggle for the very soul of Australia. On the one hand, there have been calls to reform the Australian Curriculum: History F–10 to make space and better engage with the necessary truth-telling that will help us mature as a nation. On the other, there have been fervent calls to ensure that the colonial narrative remains unchallenged and, in many ways, memorialised to enable young people to 'love their country.'[8] This struggle was no more visible and public than in the lead-up to the historic vote for a First Nations Voice to Parliament. During this campaign period, there was a significant increase of instances of racism and bigotry being reported by First Nations Peoples, and in the media, across the length and breadth of the Australian continent and adjacent islands.[9]

Much of the recent debates have been driven by the online and social media revolution, which has moved discussions about Australian history from the dusty shelves of libraries—demonstrated within black and white lithographs, grainy monochrome footage, and hastily written explorers' notes in their journals—to pithy 140-character comments and brief sound bites amplified through algorithmic curation and conservative traditional media into vast echo chambers of outrage and division. Compounding this phenomenon has been the hostility and unceasing attacks on First Nations Peoples through traditional media channels and even from within the Australian Parliament itself. Within this context, on 14 October 2023, Australians voted about whether or not to change the Constitution to recognise the First Peoples of Australia by establishing a body called the Aboriginal and Torres Strait Islander Voice.[10] Overall, they voted no.

In the backdrop of all this controversy, the groundbreaking book *Dark Emu*[11] by Yuin, Bunurong, and Tasmanian man Bruce Pascoe has almost single-handedly reframed the entire discussion of how pre-colonial and First Nations history has been viewed and discussed. Despite some of the spurious opposition,[12] this work has illuminated First Nations land management practices, a hitherto neglected part of Australian history. It has provided compelling counter-knowledge that warrants a re-evaluation of the teaching of Australian history. To deny this evidence is unfathomable in Australia in the twenty-first century.

Beyond the referendum and Voice to Parliament debates, more broadly, within and beyond the echo chambers of division and outrage, the instances of Australian history being weaponised as an emotive force are frequent. Where this was largely the domain of academics and politicians, it seems now that everyone has at least some 'skin in the game.' This has left us pondering, in the context of an almost supercharged interest in First Nations issues and histories in Australia, in the aftermath of the failed referendum, what are the roles and responsibilities of History educators and other stakeholders across the sector, and how might they impact this national discourse? This is critically important to shifting classroom practices to move past the 'history wars' that have been resurrected after 20 years.

Decolonising approaches

As underscored by the book's title, decolonising approaches to Australian history education are the key focus throughout this collection. Decolonisation is a process that aims to remove the oppressive control of a colonising power over a specific territorial area and, in doing so, also emancipate the indigenous [sic] peoples[13] of that area to reassert their sovereign rights to power, economic prosperity, and cultural expression, and, importantly, to have control over their own education systems.[14] We note that Australia is still a long way from full First Nations education sovereignty despite ratification of the *United Nations Declaration for the Rights of Indigenous People*,[15] and this is something to be negotiated as part of a national treaty or treaties. Until then, there is a significant amount of work required to educate students of today, who will be the adults and active citizens of the future and who will vote on campaigns relating to a treaty.

The working definition of decolonisation that provides the conceptual foundation for this collection has been framed by the influential work of Frantz Fanon.[16] Fanon's compelling arguments suggest that all decolonial struggles are unique to the context in which they are occurring, but one aspect that all decolonial struggles share is the application of violence to re-establish 'indigenous' [sic] humanity to overthrow colonial power.[17] In more contemporary scholarship, Tuck and Yang discuss decolonisation as that which unsettles the colonial or neo-colonial context.[18] Aware of the distinction between physical and non-physical violence, the contributors of this edited collection have sought to convey experiences of non-physical discomfort in their respective educational contexts as part of the process of applying decolonial approaches to contemporary education practices. In addition to the application of non-physical violence, the authors have written about decoloniality with an acknowledgement that to do so authentically requires intersectional analysis and approaches. As such, we acknowledge all the ways that different groups are marginalised as colonial constructions and need to be challenged as part of the wider decolonial struggle.

The final aspect of decolonisation represented in this collection is the requirement to remove conversations and explorations from the abstract halls of the academy to the complex interface of contemporary Australian schooling. As Mingno and Walsh highlight, place and positionality are essential to how we understand what it means to decolonise:

> "What does it mean to decolonize?" cannot be an abstract universal. It has to be answered by looking at other W questions: Who is doing it, where, why, and how?[19]

In Australia, asking these questions begins with recognising that sovereignty was never ceded by First Nations Peoples. These questions, therefore, need to be uniquely formulated for Australian contexts, to History as a discipline based on western-centric knowledge-making traditions, and as a curricular domain with national and state-based idiosyncrasies.

Given that we have envisaged the main audience of this collection as Australian history educators—almost all of whom are non-Indigenous—the collection asks, What does it mean to take a decolonising approach as an Australian history educator living and working on unceded lands? How do educators undertake decoloniality in relation to the Country and communities of the diverse places in which they are located? How do history educators decolonise according to the affordances of specific curricular contexts? And, importantly, what are some strategies Australian history educators can use to begin or continue this work with their students and school communities? Reinforcing Tuck and Yang's[20] assertion that decolonisation should never be a metaphor and should always be focused on outcomes, each chapter includes practical ideas and suggestions to support History teachers and their classroom practice in addition to the detailed theory and research that has contributed to their scholarly rigour.

While we believe this to be the first Australian collection dedicated to decolonising Australian school history, we stand on the shoulders of scholars and activists who have strived for educational transformation to build critical theoretical foundations, such as indigenous studies, postcolonial theory, feminist theory, southern theory, and critical race theory, to name a few. The broader project of decolonising curriculum that has gathered momentum internationally over the last decade has also been spurred by student-led campaigns and protests. These include the *Why Is My Curriculum White?*[21] movement begun at University College London in 2014 and the *Rhodes Must Fall* campaign initiated at Cape Town University in 2015.[22] Perhaps as these movements were launched by university students, there has been considerably more literature about decolonising curriculum and History in the higher education sector.[23] Colleagues working towards decolonising history curriculum in other settler colonial societies, including Canada[24] and Aotearoa/New Zealand,[25] have also contributed to this emerging area of literature.

Although international scholarship has been tackling the topic of decoloniality, its application in the Australian education space has been emerging. This is not to say that Australia-based history education researchers and historians have not made progress in this area; rather, the sort of language, theoretical orientations, and socio-political conditions have shifted in recent years. In particular, scholarship from Robert Parkes,[26] Tony Taylor,[27] and Anna Clark and Stuart Macintyre[28] has critically analysed the implications of politicisation and race nationalism on history education over the last few decades. Indigenous and non-Indigenous scholarship focused on First Nations education and the Aboriginal and Torres Strait Islander cross-curriculum priority in the Australian Curriculum has also informed discussions about decolonising Australian education systems. However, there remains a need for more explicit interrogation of what decolonising approaches mean for the Australian history education community, especially as we face urgent questions about who we think we are as a nation in the wake of the nationally divisive Voice to Parliament referendum.

Fresh perspectives

Committed to supporting future scholarship in this discipline, the editors made the conscious decision to invite and encourage mostly early career educators and researchers to contribute fresh perspectives in this edited collection. Their voices, perspectives, and experiences will be crucial to guiding and navigating the complex contexts of a post-'history wars' period and the challenges that will no doubt arise in the future. To ensure that this collection moves beyond theory, there are practical ideas for the classroom to support educators navigating the complexities of what history education could be.

In Chapter 2 of this collection, Mati Keynes takes readers on an exploration of the importance and role of truth-telling. Keynes contextualises this via the Voice to Parliament and international contexts of truth-telling as part of global efforts to advance reconciliation with their respective colonial pasts. This chapter explores manifestations of power as it shapes and impacts decolonial actions to advance its aims or, in some cases, inhibit them. To address the politicised curriculum, readers are guided in considering the role of a liberal view that interrogates the impact of transnational justice to 'reset' the relationship between Indigenous and non-Indigenous Australia, especially around issues relating to land and reparations. Analysis of the current History curriculum in Australia is undertaken to expose how it upholds a limited curriculum to the detriment of truth-telling and student outcomes. In conclusion, the chapter considers the potential of a decolonial view of the curriculum as supporting courageous and profound changes in the History curriculum as a means of actively contributing to a more equitable future in Australia.

Chapter 3 provides in-depth discussions around the discomfort of decolonial praxis through drama-based professional learning. Danielle Hradsky takes readers on a journey exploring the unease of truth-telling that comes from decolonising history through verbatim theatre. The use of vignettes evocatively demonstrates how educators may use immersion to step into the vulnerability of coming to terms with Australia's dark past. For the participants of their study, the opportunity to feel the impact of colonisation enabled participants to experience the 'unsafe' in a safe environment through the uncensored reading of historical texts.

Chapter 4 explores the role of education publishing in the future of History teaching. In the context of acute teacher shortages,[29] which has resulted in an increasing number of secondary educators teaching subjects outside of their usual discipline areas,[30] there has never been a greater requirement to produce curriculum resources that are of high quality and fit for purpose. This is because discipline-specific knowledge is critical to engaging with decoloniality and unpacking neo-colonial ideologies and agendas. In this chapter, Aleryk Fricker applies the decoloniality outlined in Hughes and Fricker[31] to discuss processes undertaken in the creation of a history textbook chapter relating to First Nations content. It details how the publishers leveraged their power and privilege to provide space and encouragement that allowed for self-determination to occur. This, in turn, enabled the First Nations author to actualise truth-telling, share First Nations stories, and elevate First Nations perspectives to the same level as western knowledges to create an accurate and authentic resource for the study of Australian history.

Chapter 5 focuses on the topic of threshold concepts and theorises the knowledges required for non-Indigenous educators to appropriately engage with First Nations content. Sara Weuffen considers the varied transformational processes that begin with a willingness to engage in critical self-reflection and understanding of the interplay of power and privilege in neo-colonial educational settings. The aim of the chapter is to hypothesise an answer to the 'disabling reluctance and hesitation' often reported by non-Indigenous educators when engaging with First Nations content. While proposing that personal/professional growth by educators is an integral component to moving beyond the 'history wars,' they acknowledge that reform, multiple factors, and truth-telling of the History curriculum could impact this process.

Chapter 6 shifts the focus of the collection to the early childhood education space. In this chapter, Boon Wurrung Elder Carolyn Briggs and non-Indigenous educators Karen Anderson and Ann Slater articulate how teaching and learning about culture on Country has been facilitated for both young children and their educators. In many ways, this chapter highlights the power of First Nations stakeholders leading education programmes, and the importance of non-Indigenous stakeholders taking on the labour, which is directly related to decolonial praxis. In doing so, this chapter details what truth-telling may look like in the early childhood learning context and how the children and educators co-navigate their ways around confronting topics. It provides a powerful illustration of how leadership of First Nations stakeholders is prioritised as a key part of imagining a future that previously has been denied to and constructed without them.

Chapter 7 begins with a provocation challenging readers to consider what they did during the 'history wars'—namely, whether they supported or inhibited truth-telling and reform of history education. In this chapter, Lucinda McKnight demonstrates how memory work may support educators' processes of critical self-reflection. The chapter provides examples of how providing space for memory writing can support and encourage ongoing professional development. McKnight argues that memory work provides an avenue for creating narratives that are a bricolage of memories that illustrate a variety of neo-colonial themes that have impacted and continue to impact how history is understood, taught, learned, and experienced in Australian schooling. In a similar vein to other chapters in this collection, this chapter focuses on the intellectual labour required by history educators as they undertake decolonial process.

Chapter 8 considers how decolonising history may be achieved in a primary school setting. Kate Harvie explores how many primary educators are still unquestioningly teaching the same content they learned as students progressing through the Australian schooling system. To address this limitation, Harvie introduces readers to the Maroondah Framework, which prioritises yarning, Dadirri (deep listening), and Ganma (knowledge sharing) for the purpose of shaping whole-school strategic implementation of First Nations contexts. The chapter also contains practical advice for implementing this framework, such as the importance of relationship building with local First Nations communities, researching and understanding local placenames, using local language in teaching resources, undertaking a full school curriculum audit to locate and expand First Nations content, making commitments to using First Nations resources, holding a zero-tolerance attitude toward, cultural appropriation, and, finally, sharing teacher memories to combat uncritical perceptions of Australian history that educators may bring to the discipline.

Chapter 9 provides insight into ways of decolonising the history classroom by focusing on curriculum. In this chapter, Kerri Anne Garrard guides readers to navigate the complex and diverse histories of the Australian continent without risking further entrenchment of colonial and Eurocentric paradigms. Engagement with the four stages of the Intercultural History Framework is proposed to support decolonial teachings of History. These stages include the traditional stage as an exploration of History, as it has been a taken-for-granted homogenising story; the second stage, which implores educators and students to create tangible bridges from the past to the present; the third stage as a moment of critical exchanging and respecting of different histories; and the final stage of transformative learning using insights from the previous stage to directly challenge traditional knowledges. Ultimately, this chapter provides a compelling and valuable framework which supports history educators and students in speaking back to a Eurocentric view and neo-colonial historical narratives that for so long have shaped Australia's history curriculum.

Chapter 10 maintains the decolonial focus but examines the impact of such practices on another minoritised cultural group in Australia that has undoubtedly been impacted by the Eurocentric portrayal in Australian history. From the colonial period, Asian migrants have directly contributed to the contemporary success of the Australian nation-state but are often overlooked, stereotyped, or marginalised in the construction and teaching of Australian history. In this chapter, Rebecca Cairns explores various invasion narratives and examines how these have been manipulated to construct a false sense of ownership and possession in non-Indigenous contexts. The concept of possessive logics is used in dialogue with the notion of Asia as method to provide an analytical framework for rethinking Asia-related Australian Curriculum descriptions and commonly used historical sources.

Chapter 11 demonstrates the power of storytelling. Will King shares their experience of working alongside Peek Wurrung Elder Uncle Rob Lowe in the retelling of his story, which provides insights into the silencing of First Nations Peoples experiences in southwest Victoria. The chapter vividly illustrates the possibilities for decolonising local history through building relationships with First Nations communities and utilising new technologies. The potential of using cinematic virtual reality for perspective-taking and developing historical empathy is set out as a model for history teachers to use in other contexts. This chapter provides readers with both inspiration and concrete steps for enacting the advice provided by First Nations educational organisations to *start local*[32] and use contemporary technology to support students' learning of Australian history. In doing so, it calls attention to ways of localising history education to subvert previously silenced narratives and recentre First Nations People as historical agents ever present on Country.

Chapter 12 considers why and how decolonising approaches in this collection are beneficial, and perhaps, arguably, essential, to the future of history education in this country and what could be achieved if education practices are shifted towards decoloniality. As the authors of this final chapter also, we argue that decolonising history is an opportunity for empowering teachers, enacting truth-telling, and breaking down the fallacy of assumed European centricity in the nation's story. The chapter draws on Yunkaporta and Shillingworth's[33] work to demonstrate how the approaches taken throughout this collection embody the spirit of decoloniality through hearts, heads, and limbs. This points to the multifaced nature of doing decolonial history in schools but also the importance of an ethic centred on self-reflexivity and the interface between self and the neo-colonial systems that maintain hegemonic power within education systems and beyond. Ultimately, this chapter argues that while the disciplinary traditions of History have helped sustain Eurocentric narratives, they can also be used to disrupt the status quo and support the development of critical consciousness.

Beyond the 'history wars?'

Here in Australia, the so-called 'history wars' describe the intellectual and ideological sparing initiated in the context of the late twentieth century. The reality is that despite some significant reforms in the Australian Curriculum: History, the same polarisation and intellectual and political debate seem to mire this reform in arguments that have already run their course and are now only capable of disrupting the progress and expectations in contemporary Australia. We suggest that it is time to distance Australian history education from the deliberately divisive discourse of the 'history wars.' The ongoing contestation of Australian history will, and should continue to, be one of its inherent features. This is because such debates shape what, and how, content gets taught in schools and remind educators to critically reflect on the ways in which perspectives are positioned by the politics of history[34] and the rhetorical façade created by political stakeholders invested in simplifying national narratives. Such professional engagement is critical to unpacking the militaristic and hyperbolic language used to describe 'new fronts,' 'battlegrounds,' 'causalities,' and things getting 'reignited' or 'enflamed,' which only seek to sustain a facile metaphor to simplify the teaching of Australian history.

The origins of the 'history wars' are usually traced back to the mid-1990s, when the Labor government, with Paul Keating as prime minister, was replaced by the Coalition and John Howard in 1996. Prior to this, in 1993, the conservative historian Geoffrey Blainey had argued that the overly negative and mournful view of Australian history represented a 'black armband' view which contrasted starkly with the more positive 'three cheers' view. Although Blainey notes that neither are accurate, John Howard repeatedly used the term 'black armband' to elevate his preferred conservative and white supremacist national narrative and distance himself from the Keating government's position on recognising First Nations dispossession and the Stolen Generations. In 1996, Prime Minister Howard said,

> This "black armband" view of our past reflects a belief that most Australian history since 1788 has been little more than a disgraceful story of imperialism, exploitation, racism, sexism and other forms of discrimination. I take a very different view. I believe that the balance sheet of our history is one of heroic achievement and that we have achieved much more as a nation of which we can be proud than of which we should be ashamed.[35]

Views such as this came to represent what was criticised as a 'white blindfold' perspective because it implied a historical blindness and whitewashing of other perspectives. Historians were also politicised as stakeholders in a public debate that was split between the liberal left and radical right, with each side accusing the other of distorting and misusing history.[36] This is exemplified by Henry Reynold's 1999 book *Why Weren't We Told?* critiquing the ongoing silence about violence against Aboriginal people and the idealised version of Australian history that people of his generation had grown up with. In contrast, Keith Windshuttle's 2002 book *The Fabrication of Australian History* sought to rewrite history by arguing that the violence towards Aboriginal people in Tasmania was exaggerated—a revisionist position that has been thoroughly repudiated by most Australian historians.[37] Historical scholarship drawing on postcolonial and postmodern theory also shaped historiographical debates during this period. The 2003 *History Wars*—a critical examination of the political polarisation of Australian history by Stuart Macintyre and Anna Clark[38]—further cemented the term and the power of such nomenclature to stimulate debate. Publicly, the intellectual complexity associated with the 'history wars' was reduced to "questions of national pride versus national guilt over the nation's past,"[39] which exacerbated division and national anxieties about Australian history, particularly around the treatment of First Nations Peoples.

In 1997, Don Watson, Prime Minister Keating's former speech writer, warned, "[T]he employment of this black armband's charge is probably quite dangerous. It will be a very sad thing if it begins to affect school curricula."[40] Two and a half decades later, we can indeed see how the study of History in Australian schooling continues to be affected by those who champion a more celebratory approach to colonialism, or what Parkes describes as the *celebratory reconstructionist* approach to remembrance and commemoration.[41] The legacies of John Howard's interference with history education[42] continue to reverberate through Coalition-led reviews in recent years. During the 2014 review of the Australian Curriculum, conservatives expressed fears that the achievements of 'western civilisation' were in danger of being overlooked, and during the 2021 review, then Education Minister Alan Tudge claimed that the revised history curriculum "paints an overly negative view of Australia."⁴³ During this review, media headlines reinforced the discourse that the "history wars flare again over revised national curriculum"⁴⁴ and "old curriculum chapter reopens as 'history wars' erupt."⁴⁵

The continued mobilisation of this discourse points to the willingness of politicians and commentators to prolong circular divisive debates in order to retain the status quo. In a similar vein to emotive slogans used in the *Voice to Parliament* referendum, 'if you don't know, vote no', failure to move beyond tropes associated with the 'history wars' impedes the capacity of educators in working with the complexities and truth-telling of Australian history. Furthermore, rehearsal and (re)enactment of traditionalist tropes acts to invalidate the strength of First Nations cultures and their contributions to legacies associated with 'pioneers', as well as the intergenerational traumatic experiences and memories of First Nations Peoples that have been stalled, stifled, and silenced in wider recognition of multiple past truths and colonial injustice.⁴⁶

If the history of education in Australia has indicated anything to date, it is that the study of the story associated with the making of 'the nation' will continue to be the most controversial area of the curriculum. As stated earlier, this is because it brings forth an undercurrent associated with the 'soul' of the country, one that is arguably restless and hurting from truths that have been largely stuffed away. Yet, we can choose to resist the *thin veneer* of the 'history wars' rhetoric and its use of simplistic binaries—'black armband' and 'white blindfold'—or us versus them—that disguise and occlude the historical realities of the long (pre-1770) and short (post-1770) histories of the nation. In advocating for moving beyond the 'history wars,' the premise of this collection inadvertently echoes the 2009 sentiments of former Prime Minister Kevin Rudd, who said,

> [It's] time to leave behind us the polarisation that began to infect our every discussion of our nation's past. To go beyond the so-called "black armband" view that refused to confront some hard truths about our past.⁴⁷

Regardless of the headlines, we argue that it is time for everyone in the history community—educators, students, researchers, historians, journalists, etc.—to roll up their sleeves and get on with the business of decolonising history education in Australian schools so that we can not only achieve moving beyond the 'history wars' but in doing so finally establish a place for First Nations histories in Australian classrooms.

The contrast between the chapters in this book and the previous scholarship dominated by the 'history wars' is one of absence—that is, the absence of First Nations voices in the discussions and debates relating to the 'truth' of the history in Australian classrooms. Without exception, the scholarship in this collection has either been led by First Nations People, in partnership with First Nations Peoples, or significantly influenced and inspired by First Nations

Peoples. Unlike the aforementioned politicians and historians who all had a significant impact on the 'history wars,' in a post-'history wars' engagement with Australian history in the classroom, we argue that a post-'history wars' classroom will only be able to exist with the presence of uninhibited and sovereign First Nations voices and that it is the decolonial focus and process which will enable this to occur, just like it has in this collection.

Ultimately, the scholarship in this book provides a compelling argument that decolonising history will be a key process for History educators, and more broadly the nation, to finally begin moving beyond divisive positioning to take up mature perspectives of the nation, of which First Nations contexts and voices ought to be prominent. While it is generally accepted and celebrated that First Nations cultures are the oldest continuing practicing cultures on earth, it's fascinating to observe how their perspectives, stories, and voices, are silenced in the education of the nation's citizens. While we can teach about colonisation practices that have occurred elsewhere, and while we can educate about genocide acts that have caused devastation elsewhere, when it comes to home soil contexts on the Australian continent, significant discomfort is experienced.

What has proven to be successful in assisting in processing discomfort is leaning into it, processing it, and forming new practices based on new knowledge. In the study of History, we would argue that this boils down to a recognition that contemporary society is built on dispossession and injustice. By scratching through the thin veneer of colonisation that has shaped curriculum discourses in Australia, we take the brave step towards decolonising ways of knowing, being, and doing associated with such history.

Notes

1 Griffin, L., & Trudgett, M. (2018). 'Everybody's talkin' at me: A review of literature about deficit discourse and deficit thinking in relation to Indigenous Australian learners. *Journal of Australian Indigenous Issues, 21*(3), 2–19.
2 Rasmussen, M., et al. (2011). An Aboriginal Australian genome reveals separate human dispersals into Asia. *Science, 334*(6052), 94–98. https://doi.org/10.1126/science.1211177
3 Hurst, D. (2021). Alan Tudge says he doesn't want students to be taught 'hatred' of Australia in fiery Triple J interview. *The Guardian*. https://www.theguardian.com/australia-news/2021/sep/08/alan-tudge-says-he-doesnt-want-students-to-be-taught-hatred-of-australia-in-fiery-triple-j-interview
4 Macintyre, S., & Clark, A. (2004). *The history wars*. Melbourne University Press.
5 First Nations National Constitutional Convention & Central Land Council (Australia), issuing body. (2017). *Uluru: Statement from the heart.* http://nla.gov.au/nla.obj-484035616
6 Fricker, A. (2017). Indigenous perspectives: Controversy in the classroom? *Agora, 52*(4), 4–12.
7 Throughout the collection the authors distinguish between lowercase history and uppercase History. In most cases, History is capitalised when it is referred to a subject area and is in lower case when referring to history more generally.

8 Hurst (2021). Alan Tudge says he doesn't want students to be taught 'hatred' of Australia in fiery Triple J interview.
9 Karp, P. (2023). In the aftermath of the voice referendum how can we unbork a polarised Australia? Here are three ways forward. *The Guardian*. https://www.theguardian.com/australia-news/2023/oct/16/in-the-aftermath-of-the-voice-referendum-how-can-we-unbork-a-polarised-australia-here-are-three-ways-forward
10 Australian Government. (2023). *Referendum on an Aboriginal and Torres Strait Islander Voice*. National Indigenous Australians Agency. https://www.niaa.gov.au/indigenous-affairs/referendum-aboriginal-and-torres-strait-islander-voice
11 Pascoe, B. (2018). *Dark Emu*. Scribe Publications.
12 Please see: Sutton, P., & Walshe, K. (2021). *Farmers or hunter-gatherers? The Dark Emu debate*. Melbourne University Press. This response to Dark Emu is limited to an analysis of the use of the historical sources Pascoe used in the original book, the semantic loading of the terms hunter-gatherer, farmer, and agriculturalist, and exception taken to the alleged implication that the specific land management practices detailed in specific regions were applicable across the continent and adjacent islands. The main issue with this text is the seeming lack of engagement with First Nations people directly. It is a simple matter to engage with the many First Nations communities across Australia to speak with the Elders and those tasked with caring for Country to observe and learn about the agricultural practices that have kept Country and people healthy for millennia and have these confirmed based on the descriptions in *Dark Emu*.
13 For the purposes of this collected work, we have conformed with an Australian style guide when making distinctions between local and international indigenous contexts. This style guide requires us to use a capital 'I' when referring to Australian Indigenous contexts, and a lowercase 'i' when referring to indigenous subject matter in an international context. Furthermore, while there is no universally accepted collective noun for Aboriginal and Torres Strait Islander people in Australia, we have used a variety of terms for First Nations people and do so with respect.
14 Tuck, E., & Yang, K. (2012). Decolonization is not a metaphor. *Decolonization: Indigeneity, Education & Society, 1*(1), 1–40.
15 United Nations (General Assembly). (2007). *Declaration on the rights of Indigenous people*.
16 Fanon, F. (1961). *The wretched of the earth*. Grove Press.
17 *Ibid*.
18 Tuck & Yang (2012). Decolonization is not a metaphor.
19 Mignolo, W. D., & Walsh, C. E. (2018). *On decoloniality: Concepts, analytics, praxis*. Duke University Press. p. 18.
20 Tuck & Yang (2012). Decolonization is not a metaphor.
21 UCL. (2014). *Why is my curriculum white?* YouTube. https://www.youtube.com/watch?v=Dscx4h2l-Pk
22 Fairbanks, E. (2015). The birth of Rhodes must fall. *The Guardian*. https://www.theguardian.com/news/2015/nov/18/why-south-african-students-have-turned-on-their-parents-generation
23 For example, Bhambra, G. K., Gebrial, D., & Nişancıoğlu, K. (Eds.). (2015). Decolonising the university. Pluto Press; D'Sena, P. (2021). Decolonising the curriculum: Contexts and strategies. In A. Nye & J. Clark (Eds.), *Teaching history for the contemporary world: Tensions, challenges and classroom experiences in higher education*. Springer pp. 29–41.
24 For example, Collishaw, R. (2022). Decolonising the curriculum: A Canadian perspective. *Agora, 57*(3), 36–38; Cutrara, S. (2020). *Transforming the Canadian history classroom: Imagining a new "we."* UBC Press.

25 Davison, M. (2021). Teaching decolonised New Zealand history in secondary schools. *Historical Encounters, 8*(2), 90–106. https://doi.org/10.52289/hej8.205; Sheehan, M. (2020). Historical thinking, 'difficult histories,' and Māori perspectives of the past. In C. Berg & T. Christou (Eds.), *The Palgrave handbook of history and social studies education.* Palgrave Macmillan pp. 497–510.
26 For exampe, Parkes, R. J. (2011). *Interrupting history: Rethinking history curriculum after 'the end of history.'* Peter Lang; Parkes, R. J. (2007). Reading history curriculum as postcolonial text: Towards a curricular response to the history wars in Australia and beyond. *Curriculum Inquiry, 37*(4), 383–400.
27 For example, Taylor, T. (2019). Historical consciousness in the Australian curriculum. In T. Allender, A. Clark, & R. Parkes (Eds.), *Historical thinking for history teachers.* Allen & Unwin pp. 3–17; Taylor, T. (2012). Under siege from left to right: A tale of two Australian history wars. In T. Taylor & R. Guyver (Eds.), *History wars and the classroom: Global perspectives.* Information Age Publishing pp. 25–50.
28 For example, Macintyre & Clark (2004). *The history wars*; Macintyre, S. (2019). Understanding the Australian curriculum: History. In T. Allender, A. Clark, & R. Parkes (Eds.), *Historical thinking for history teachers.* Allen & Unwin Pp.18–30; Clark, A. (2008). *History's children: History wars in the classroom.* NewSouth Books; Clark, A. (2006). *Teaching the nation: Politics and pedagogy in Australian schools.* Melbourne University Press.
29 Australian Government Department of Education. (2022). *Teacher workforce shortages—Issues paper.* https://ministers.education.gov.au/sites/default/files/documents/Teacher%20Workforce%20Shortages%20-%20Issues%20paper.pdf
30 See Hobbs, L. & Porch, R. (Eds.) (2022). *Out-of-field teaching across teaching disciplines and contexts.* Springer.
31 Hughes, R. & Fricker, A. (2024). Decolonising practice in teacher education in Australia: Reflections of shared leadership. *Australian Educational Researcher.* https://doi.org/10.1007/s13384-023-00670-4
32 VAEAI. (2016). *Protocols for Koorie education in Victorian primary and secondary schools.* http://www.vaeai.org.au/wp-content/uploads/delightful-downloads/2020/01/Protocols-for-Koorie-Education-in-Victorian-Primary-and-Secondary-Schools-2019.pdf
33 Yunkaporta, T., & Shillingsworth, D. (2020). Relationally responsive standpoint. *Journal of Indigenous Research, 8*(1), 1–14. https://digitalcommons.usu.edu/kicjir/vol8/iss2020/4.
34 See Parkes R. J. (2019). Developing your approach to teaching history. In T. Allender, A. Clark, & R. Parkes (Eds.), *Historical thinking for history teachers* (pp. 72–87). Allen & Unwin.
35 Howard, J. (1996). *Robert Menzies lecture.* https://pmtranscripts.pmc.gov.au/release/transcript-10171
36 McKenna, M. (1998). *Different perspectives on Black armband history.* Research paper. http://www.aph.gov.au/About_Parliament/Parliamentary_Departments/Parliamentary_Library/pubs/rp/RP9798/98RP05
37 Mann, R. (2003). *Whitewash: On Keith Windschuttle's fabrication of Aboriginal history.* Black Inc.
38 Macintyre & Clark (2004). *The history wars*
39 Munro, D. (2021). *History wars.* ANU Press. https://library.oapen.org/bitstream/handle/20.500.12657/51552/1/book.pdf
40 As cited by McKenna (1998). para. 64.
41 Parkes (2019). Developing your approach to teaching history.
42 Howard (1996). *Robert Menzies lecture.*

43 Hurst (2021). Alan Tudge says he doesn't want students to be taught 'hatred' of Australia in fiery Triple J interview.
44 ABC. (2022). History wars flare again over revised national curriculum. YouTube. https://www.youtube.com/watch?v=sfj1CtAtuJc
45 Baker, J. (2021). Old curriculum chapter reopens as history wars erupt. *The Age*. https://www.smh.com.au/education/old-curriculum-chapter-reopens-as-history-wars-erupt-20211104-p5965g.html
46 Mencevska, I. (2020). Truth telling in Australia's historical narrative. *NEW: Emerging Scholars in Australian Indigenous Studies*, 5(1), 1–6; Maddison, S. (2019). The limits of the administration of memory in settler colonial societies: The Australian case. *International Journal of Politics, Culture & Society*, 32, 181–194. https://doi.org/10.1007/s10767-018-9303-0
47 Rudd, K. (2009). *Launch of first volume of Tom Keneally's Australians*. Australian Government. https://pmtranscripts.pmc.gov.au/release/transcript-16778

Chapter 2

Truth commissions, transitional justice, and history education

Mati Keynes

Author positioning statement

My ancestors were English and German settler colonisers, and I was born and grew up on Whadjuk Noongar Boodjar (Perth, WA). I have since lived on Ngunnawal, Nambri, Wurundjeri, Gadigal, and Noongar lands, and South Sápmi, Sámi territory (Sweden). In doing so, I have walked over other peoples' histories while simultaneously studying and writing 'history.' Settler ways of knowing are intimately connected with settler ways of being on stolen land. For settler subjects, history education can only begin once we give a truthful account of our origins as those who dwell in a place belonging to another and when we acknowledge and take full responsibility for that world.

Introduction

In May 2017, after an unprecedented series of regional dialogues across Australia, more than 250 Aboriginal and Torres Strait Islander delegates issued the *Uluru Statement from the Heart*—a proposal for substantive, sequenced reform known as 'Voice Treaty Truth.'[1] The proposal called for a First Nations 'Voice' to parliament to be enshrined in the Australian constitution to oversee subsequent nation-to-nation processes of treaty-making and truth-telling about the past.[2] A 2023 national referendum on the 'Voice' is also a litmus test on subsequent processes of truth and treaty. Meanwhile in Victoria, a truth-telling process about the injustices experienced by First Peoples since invasion—the Yoorrook Justice Commission (YRJC)—has been underway since 2020. Its findings and recommendations, to be delivered in 2025, will inform the treaty process in Victoria. Victoria is the first jurisdiction to have actioned the Treaty and Truth elements of the Uluru Statement, although there are now treaty processes which incorporate truth-telling underway or proposed in numerous other Australian jurisdictions.[3] Together, these processes of truth and justice signal the growing momentum of First Nations–led movements for substantive, structural, legal, and political reform.

DOI: 10.4324/9781003435617-2

History education is poised to play a crucial role in that project. Throughout the regional dialogues that shaped the Uluru Statement, the promise of truth-telling was repeatedly connected with hopes of changing how Australian history is taught in schools.[4] During first-stage treaty consultations in Victoria, changing the school curriculum to include a compulsory and more comprehensive view of Aboriginal history emerged as a clear desire. A 2021 report from the First Peoples' Assembly called for the "overhauling of history education" while recent reforms to the Australian Curriculum include a focus on "truth-telling" within the broader history of Australia.[5] Telling the truth about and through education is a core imperative of recent truth commissions in Australia and other Western states.[6] This context raises new questions and imperatives for history teachers who are tasked with negotiating complex ethical relations between past, present, and future. How should history teachers engage in truth-telling? As new histories come to light through truth-telling processes, how should these be included in history education? Does truth-telling demand new frameworks for historical understanding and pedagogical skills?

History education in Australia has a complex and chequered past. Since its inception in the nineteenth century, history education has been a potent tool of settler nation-building and state legitimation. It has actively obscured the truth of dispossession and colonial violence, and promoted narratives of settler legitimacy to construct a particular sense of shared history and allegiance to empire and then nation-state.[7] In more recent times, the idea of Australian history as a settler-national story has been challenged. Subsequent reforms, however, such as the Aboriginal and Torres Strait Islander cross-curriculum priority, have not alleviated the concerns of Aboriginal and Torres Strait Islander leaders, academics, activists, and educators, who have continued to assert the failures of history education to convey the full truth of the past.[8]

Around the world, history education has long been a focus for researchers interested in how contested understandings of the past can incite, exacerbate, and transform conflict. Today, there is general recognition that "understandings of history are crucial to a society's ability to reckon with the difficult past for the sake of a more just future," as human rights scholar Elizabeth Cole has noted.[9] In recent decades, history education has emerged as a vital site and instrument of *transitional justice*, defined by the United Nations as: "the full range of processes and mechanisms associated with a society's attempts to come to terms with a legacy of large-scale past abuses, in order to ensure accountability, serve justice and achieve reconciliation."[10] However, most work in this field has concentrated on post-conflict societies emerging from civil war or dictatorship rather than Western democracies. Yet, liberal democracies such as Australia have been founded on large-scale abuses (e.g., genocide, dispossession), and injustices against Indigenous Peoples are continuing.[11] Settler colonialism, as explained elsewhere in this book, is a specific political formation where settlers "come to stay" and claim territory by seeking to eliminate and replace the existing owners. Settler colonialism is both historically specific but also an ongoing structure—an enduring web of relations and process of domination.[12]

This chapter outlines liberal and decolonial perspectives on truth commissions, truth-telling, and transitional justice in Western settler colonial contexts. It draws out key tensions, implications, and strategies for history educators who are poised to play a crucial role in interpreting commission findings and mediating civic dialogue.

Truth commissions in Western settler states

Truth commissions are a defining feature of the contemporary political landscape. A truth commission is a non-judicial, temporary inquiry set up to investigate a pattern of violations over a period of time that concludes with a final report and recommendations for reforms.[13] Truth commissions were pioneered in non-Western contexts.[14] Since the first widely recognised truth commission in Argentina (1983–1984), there have been at least 40 truth commissions globally. Since the flagship South African Truth and Reconciliation Commission (1996–2002), they have become more common in countries of the Global North, including in Australia and Canada, and in Nordic welfare states like Norway, Sweden, and Finland.

In Canada, the landmark Truth and Reconciliation Commission of Canada (2008–2015) grew out of an influential Royal Commission on Aboriginal Peoples (1991–1996) and was followed by the National Inquiry into Missing and Murdered Indigenous Women and Girls (2015–2019). In Norway (2017–2023), Sweden (2021–2025), and Finland (2021–2025), truth commissions dedicated to documenting injustices experienced by Indigenous Sámi populations have been ongoing. In Australia, there have been more than 100 Royal Commissions since Federation in 1901, and in recent times, two prominent inquiries detailing injustices experienced by Aboriginal and Torres Strait Islander Peoples: the 1987–1991 Royal Commission into Aboriginal Deaths in Custody (RCIADIC) and the 1995–1997 National Inquiry into the Separation of Aboriginal and Torres Strait Islander People from their families (Bringing Them Home report). The Yoorrook Justice Commission is investigating injustices experienced by First Peoples in Victoria (2020–2025); there are truth-telling processes underway or proposed in numerous other states, and, as mentioned earlier, the referendum on the 'Voice' is slated for late 2023.

The promises of 'truth'

'Truth-telling' in the Australian context is not the same as truth commissions, despite their recent prominence. From the earliest decades of British invasion, First Nations Peoples have called for a more truthful and historically accurate account of both First Nations histories on the continent, as well as histories of colonial violence and Indigenous-settler relations. Sovereign First Nations political activity and movements for self-determination are long-standing, and First Nations Peoples have consistently articulated repatriation of lands, treaty, civil and political rights, and truth-telling as key demands.[15] Many commissions, including the 1881 Coranderrk Inquiry and the RCIADIC were established after sustained campaigning and political activism by First Nations communities. The idea of truth-telling is more complex and far greater than the structured and finite model of a truth commission.

The truth commission phenomenon is a recent innovation. Its emergence should be understood within the broader rise of transitional justice, which, over the last three decades, has become the established international framework for addressing legacies of past violence.[16] In recent years, transitional justice has expanded exponentially to become a global industry embedded in the United Nations. Transitional justice is both a suite of tools (e.g., criminal trial, truth commission, apology, reparations) and a set of assumptions about what constitutes 'transition' and 'justice' and how best to achieve it. Classically, transition was from a conflict situation to liberal democracy, and justice was retributive. The truth commission is arguably the most recognisable 'tool' of transitional justice. Its foundational idea—to overcome a period of violence it is necessary to tell the truth about what happened—remains a powerful assumption in the field and beyond. Scholars have traced the rise of a 'right to truth' in international law and have argued that conveying truthful knowledge of the past is now an expectation of belonging to the liberal international community.[17] In the context of transitional justice, truth-telling has been linked to a range of outcomes, including national healing, reconciliation, justice, the prevention of future harm, and social transformation.[18]

However, the question of what truth-telling can achieve, including how it might support or contribute to processes of social transformation in settler colonial states, remains unclear. In Australia, truth-telling has been explicitly linked to processes of negotiated political transition, such as treaty making, but there is considerable conjecture among First Nations political leaders and scholars about how sovereignty will be meaningfully addressed in those processes.[19] Some have argued that the sequencing of truth-telling prior to treaty in many Australian jurisdictions will serve only to delay and obstruct political momentum for meaningful reform.[20] In lieu of the implementation of recommendations from previous commissions, such as the RCAIDIC and Stolen Generations inquiries, the promises of truth-telling for some First Nations People and communities remain unfulfilled.

For history educators and researchers specifically, the discourse of truth-telling presents a paradox. Both scholars and teachers have been trained to mediate *plural* narratives about the past, and the idea of 'historical truth' has been the subject of politicised debates that have undermined teachers' and historians' expertise. Nonetheless, in the field of transitional justice, historical discourses and methods carry authority, and the skills of historians (detecting bias, weighing evidence, knowledge of historical contexts) are seen to be beneficial. Importantly, these are the same kinds of 'skills' embedded in discipline-based models of history education and hence, history education has increasingly been linked to processes of transitional justice, to which I now turn.

Truth commissions and (history) education

Truth commissions in Western contexts are inherently fraught, including in their relationship to education. One reason for this is the complicity of educational systems in perpetuating injustice, a fact that has been systematically exposed through recent commissions. Official inquiries into the historical abuse of children in out-of-home institutional care, abuse in religious institutions, and harms caused to Indigenous Peoples through colonial, segregated, and assimilatory schooling practices, policies, and systems have been undertaken in Australia, Canada, Ireland, the United Kingdom, Sweden, Norway, Denmark, Germany, and the Netherlands.[21] Despite this, truth commissions tend to recommend forward-looking educational reforms and vest responsibility for social transformation in education. Often, the education sector is tasked with resolving the damage it has been responsible for creating, as was the case in Canada's Truth and Reconciliation Commission, which identified education as the "key to reconciliation."

The education sector clearly has an important role to play in carrying the findings of truth-telling processes into schools, classrooms, and communities. How should teachers and researchers interpret and implement truth-telling findings and recommendations? Is wide-scale reform of curricula, policy, teacher education, and pedagogy required as was recommended by Canada's Truth and Reconciliation Commission (TRC) process? Both the RCIADIC and Stolen Generations inquiries engaged closely with the school education sector, including curriculum. RCIADIC recommendation 290 stated "that curricula of schools at all levels should reflect the fact that Australia has an Aboriginal history and Aboriginal viewpoints on social, cultural and historical matters," and the Bringing Them Home (BTH) report recommended "that State and Territory Governments ensure that primary and secondary school curricula include substantial compulsory modules on the history and continuing effects of forcible removal." However, in Victoria, it took until the implementation of the national curriculum in 2012, more than 20 years after RCAIDIC and 15 after BTH, for colonial injustices to be systematically included in history curriculum.[22] Other reforms, including the 2011 reform of the Australian Institute for Teaching and School Leadership (AITSL) professional standards for teachers and the 2010 inclusion of the Aboriginal and Torres Strait Islander cross-curriculum priority in the Australian Curriculum, have been subject to sustained critique by First Nations scholars.[23]

History education has been repeatedly criticised by First Nations People and communities for its failure to accurately represent histories on the Australian continent. This was reflected in the dialogues that preceded the Uluru Statement, where delegates across the country called for "the history of Aboriginal people taught in schools, including the truth about murders and the theft of land, Maralinga, and the Stolen Generations, as well the story of all the Aboriginal fighters for reform," and an acknowledgement of Australia's "true history. Not Captain Cook. What happened all across Australia: the massacres and the wars," for example.[24] Despite countless curricular reforms, history education continues to be linked to failed social transformation and identified as a key area of reform by First Nations Peoples. Yet, questions remain as to how history education might be meaningfully revised. Does it require an "overhaul," as the First Peoples' Assembly has suggested? Or can history education embrace agendas of truth and justice in its current form, and if so, how?

Both local and international experience suggests a circumspect assessment of the possibilities of systemic change emerging from truth-telling processes. History education is not an easy or natural partner for truth-telling, truth commissions, or transitional justice more broadly. Their growing relationship represents a coming together of complex and contrary agendas. This chapter surveys some of those tensions, considers their implications, and signals possibilities for future scholarship and processes of reform.

Liberal and decolonial perspectives in Western settler states

There are two broad views on the suitability of transitional justice in settler colonial societies, such as Australia. One sees transitional justice instruments, like truth commissions, as being complicit in a broader settler colonial logic that asserts settler dominance, marginalises structural harms, and dismisses Indigenous sovereignties and nationhood. The other sees transitional justice as presenting promising opportunities for advancing goals such as justice, healing, truth-telling, and more legitimate state-building that might exceed those contained by prevailing policies of 'reconciliation.' Lately, there has been expanding engagement in settler states with transitional justice as a framework for redressing settler colonial violence and for facilitating meaningful reform. Transitional justice has increasingly been used to address past human rights violations against Indigenous Peoples, and transitional justice as a framework has begun to engage more directly with Indigenous perspectives. Key examples of this have occurred in Canada, which has explicitly adopted a transitional justice framework for redressing mass harms committed against Indigenous Peoples. In this section, I outline two basic views—hereafter 'liberal' and 'decolonial'—drawing out key insights and implications for history educators, policymakers, and researchers tasked with navigating this changing and charged landscape.

The liberal view

Transitional justice is bound up with a progressive narrative of Western liberalism. In that story, the origins of transitional justice are plotted at key moments of the West's victory over various opponents—World War One war reparations; World War Two criminal trials; the post-1970s waves of political transition in formerly authoritarian states in Southern Europe, Latin America, and Asia; and the fall of the Iron Curtain. Understood in this frame, the rise of transitional justice forms part of a mythic narrative of Western-style liberalisation.[25] When legal scholar Ruti Teitel coined the term 'transitional justice' in the 1990s, she had in mind the specific circumstances of a political transition from a period of conflict to a rule-of-law situation.[26] At the time, transitional justice was viewed largely as an instrument for supporting the uptake of the rule of law and democracy in post-conflict countries of Eastern Europe and Latin America.[27] Upholding human rights, the rule of law, free elections, and other indicators of legitimate liberal statehood, as well as coming to terms with the history of recent conflict, are the traditional markers by which societies undertaking transition have been measured.

However, as transitional justice norms and practices have been taken up in contexts where liberal democracy is already established and where there is no recent history of dictatorship or war, scholars have advocated for the widening of its remit to include a broader range of circumstances and goals.[28] This includes Australia, where scholars have argued that transitional justice offers a promising framework for moving beyond the political project of 'reconciliation', which has produced limited substantive reforms for First Nations Peoples and continues to neglect their own proposals for reform. Transitional justice, supporters argue, provides an internationally recognised set of norms and instruments for addressing legacies of past violence as the basis for a re-founding of political legitimacy.[29]

But why should Australia's political legitimacy need re-founding? Australia's political system was illegitimately established through colonisation and upon the fictional claim of *terra nullius*. On that basis, large-scale harms were inflicted upon Indigenous Peoples. According to liberal theorists, this has undermined the legitimacy of the Australian state. For instance, in the ongoing legacies of systemic violence such as policies of forced child removal, stolen wages, police violence, and other wrongdoings sanctioned through state policies, legislation, and institutions. Liberal theorists have argued that "established democracies can and do undergo transitional processes in the form of radical change to their legitimating regimes."[30] Australia is also the only Western settler state that does not have a treaty with the First Nations polities of the continent. In the continuing absence of a treaty and a human rights framework, such as a bill of rights, the state's authority to govern First Nations People remains contested.

Transitional justice is a response to restore political legitimacy. It affords the state an opportunity to re-evaluate and re-establish its foundation. In Australia, transitional justice takes the form of a series of 'negotiated' or protracted transitions, using tools such as truth-seeking, recognition, acknowledgement of past injustice, and institutional reform. This, liberal theorists claim, will move Australia gradually towards a more just and legitimate social contract.

The decolonial view

The central decolonial critique of truth commissions, and transitional justice more widely, is that they are generally silent on questions of land repatriation and Indigenous sovereignty. Let's take the liberal view explained in the prior section—that transitional justice seeks to create a more just social contract—as an example. Decolonial critics might argue that without *decolonising land* as justice or acknowledging Indigenous sovereignties, the aim of transitional justice is to preserve and rehabilitate the liberal settler state. Transitional justice is usually focused upon legal accountability and civil and political rights. This focus has tended to isolate acute violence (torture, murder, sexual abuse) from structural violence (colonialism, racial capitalism, patriarchy). Decolonial critics have argued that this has resulted in limited regard for the long-term legacies of colonisation in transitional justice processes and for the "underlying root causes of […] crimes against humanity, namely systemic and structural inequities," as Brinton Lykes and van der Merwe have explained.[31] Another focus of decolonial critique is the colonial dynamics at play in the global transitional justice industry, where Western states and actors serve as 'support agents' for post-conflict societies undergoing transition.[32] Often, these societies are coming to terms with histories of exploitation and violence inextricably connected to the imposition of Western colonial systems.[33]

Decolonial scholars have argued that transitional justice can be understood as a "settler move to innocence." In "Decolonization is Not a Metaphor," Unangax̂ scholar Eve Tuck and K. Wayne Yang explained that "moves to innocence" are a set of strategies where non-Indigenous Peoples attempt to reconcile settler guilt and complicity in colonialism.[34] Building on this, Jennifer Matsunaga argued that transitional justice focuses energies "on change at the level of thoughts, beliefs, and perceptions" rather than on the more uncomfortable task of returning stolen land.[35] For example, in truth commissions and political apologies, there is a focus on acknowledging historical wrongs and then moving those difficult histories into the past as a way of beginning a new chapter. In this way, liberal democracies undertaking transitional justice manufacture a point of rupture, or an "artificial" transition, according to Yellowknives Dene scholar Glen Coulthard, by "isolating the abuses of settler colonialism to the dustbins of history."[36] In the context of truth-telling specifically, Cherokee scholar Jeff Corntassel and Cindy Holder have warned that processes of truth-telling can be used to "neutralise a history of wrongs" and to legitimate state sovereignty by closing over a history of oppression.[37] A related critique was voiced by Audra Simpson, Mohawk anthropologist from the Kahnawake community in Quebec, who critiqued the Canadian TRC process, which, she argued, positioned Indigenous Peoples as "incapacitated sufferers."[38] Tanana Athabascan scholar Dian Million powerfully argued that the appropriation of Indigenous trauma in truth-telling can often become part of a settler nation-building project, directed ultimately towards settler-national healing.[39]

These critiques echo experiences in the Australian context. The RCIADIC and Stolen Generations inquiries created an extensive public record of systemic colonial injustices. But the subsequent failure to implement many of their recommendations has been linked to the continuation of both Indigenous deaths in custody and child removals at rates higher than at the time of the inquiries.[40] Other acts of redress, such as the 2008 National Apology to the Stolen Generations, have done little to engage Indigenous-led movements for treaty and land repatriation, and they have been criticised for prioritising settler nation-building and social harmony.[41] In terms of education, subsequent reforms to curriculum have largely worked to incorporate Aboriginal and Torres Strait Islander Peoples' claims for truth, justice, and self-determination *within* the framework of settler-national sovereignty rather than being understood as the actions of distinct sovereign nations with their own aspirations. This is part of a long-standing failure. Recent research has shown that for more than 100 years, history curriculum in the state of Victoria failed to accurately represent Indigenous political movements and aspirations. Misleading and inaccurate history curricula have contributed to large gaps in public understanding of the depth and diversity of Indigenous aspirations.[42]

Implications for history education

History curriculum in its current form is well-suited to support a *liberal* vision of transitional justice in Australia, understood as a series of negotiated transitions aimed at coming to terms with a history of wrongdoing and restoring political legitimacy. Since the development of the national curriculum, history curriculum has included more explicit representations of colonial violence and wrongdoing. Revisions to the history curriculum since 2010 have sought to revise the national story as one replete with minoritised struggles for human rights and inclusion, for instance, in campaigns for rights and freedoms and inclusion of diverse contributions to the national story. Finally, the consolidation of a discipline-based framework for history curriculum focuses on methods for taking historical perspectives, using historical evidence, and challenging biases, all skills which have been linked (though not well evidenced) to building peace and democracy.[43] These reforms align with liberal visions of transitional justice: that coming to know more about the unjust past and developing skills to mediate plural historical narratives can contribute to gradual social transformation. In these ways, history education might contribute to liberal ideas of 'justice' understood as developing more just relations, supporting more legitimate state-building, and rebuilding citizens' trust in state institutions.

If we take a *decolonial* perspective, we might instead see a "move to innocence" through history education. In other words, these reforms seek individualised change in beliefs and attitudes rather than genuine structural reform, such as those which would centre First Nations sovereignty and engage First Nations knowledge systems. If we take seriously decolonial critique of transitional justice in relation to history education, it becomes clear that the current framework for history education in Australia is more likely to hinder even the most expansive idea of transitional justice. There are several reasons for this. One is that any agenda for meaningful change in Australia must take account of not only the originary violence of colonisation but also the enduring colonial inequities and harms that continue to shape and limit the lives of both dominant and minority groups. Do historical thinking concepts grounded in Western ways of knowing provide adequate opportunities to engage the complex relations between past, present, and future that are central to truth-telling?[44] In recent research on history education in South Africa, for instance, scholars found that "Apartheid was placed firmly in the past, with rigid lines drawn around that time as distinct from the present." In positioning the South African 'post-conflict' present as a rupture from the conflicted past, discussion of ways in which present inequalities might be informed by or explained by past injustices was highly limited.[45] A curricular framework which cannot easily accommodate enduring injustices or Indigenous knowledges and ways of knowing history represents a considerable barrier to the capacity of history education to contribute meaningfully to truth-telling and transitional justice processes.

Another reason that the current framework for history education in Australia is more likely to hinder meaningful change relates to curricular reforms since the 2010s. As I mentioned earlier, these have incorporated histories of colonial violence and moments when the settler state accommodated First Nations political demands and/or extended rights to First Nations People more systematically. On the surface, this looks like steps towards a more historically accurate curriculum. Yet when we step back and look at the story curriculum as a whole, those two gestures have the effect of preserving the integrity of the national story and reframing it as a story of progress towards tolerance. Past injustices are cleaved away from the present and positioned as errors on the pathway to greater freedom. The political unit of 'Australia'—the settler nation—remains the unquestioned frame of reference, giving sense to the story, and both historical injustice and First Nations self-determination get enclosed in ways that do not disrupt or decolonise that organising unit. This echoes Million's decolonial critiques of truth-telling as processes that appropriate Indigenous trauma and incorporate it into a settler nation-building project.

Ultimately, decolonial critique, whether in the context of transitional justice or not, prompts a comprehensive rethinking of both the content and the form of history curriculum, and history education broadly. While the project of articulating a decolonial history education should be led by First Nations

Peoples, settlers in this space have a responsibility to first, listen, and second, decentre settler stories and ways of knowing. While I am deeply sympathetic to the sustained efforts of history teachers and historians to embed historical thinking approaches in curriculum, in "moving beyond the history wars," we now have an obligation to engage the epistemological and ethical limits of that framework. This includes laying the groundwork to resituate the story of the settler nation as but one chapter in a much longer Indigenous story.[46]

Ideas and strategies

- **Actively listen** to First Nations scholars, educators, leaders, and young people about how history education continues to fail, as well as their ideas for how those failures should be addressed. You might like to read pages 17, 19, and 32 of the "Final Report of the Referendum Council" for extracts from the Uluru Statement regional dialogues regarding school history education.[47] You might also read First Nations autobiographies and oral histories. A useful guide can be found in Beth Marsden's entry on "Aboriginal and Torres Strait Islander Peoples" experiences of schooling and education' in the *Dictionary of Educational History in Australia and New Zealand*.[48]
- **Reflect** on how Aboriginal and Torres Strait Islander understandings of 'history' might differ from Western conceptions of history. What about other cultural, language, or ethnic groups? How might these reflections shift your own understandings of history and history teaching?
- **Explore** the plural conceptions of nationhood and sovereignty on the Australian continent. While the political unit of 'Australia' is a fairly recent invention (1901), Aboriginal and Torres Strait Islander jurisdictions on the continent are ancient and continuing. Since British invasion, First Nations People have always sustained their own distinctive political demands and aspirations—e.g., the 1880s Coranderrk campaign, 1938 Day of Mourning protest, 1963 Yirrkala bark petitions, 1965 Freedom Rides, 1966 Wave Hill Walkoff, 1972 Tent Embassy, 1988 Barunga Statement.
- **Actively unsettle** the idea of 'Australia' and 'Australianness' through the teaching of history. Draw attention to moments in history when that idea was being contested, fought over, and imposed through physical and epistemic force.
- **Investigate** how history education has been used as a tool for constructing settler possession and belonging on stolen land. Since invasion, the education of settler children has aimed to create a loyal, cohesive population that believed its claims to the land were permanent, natural, and immutable rather than tenuous and recently accumulated at the expense of Indigenous Peoples. You can get a sense of this history by looking at historical teaching materials such as the *School Paper* (1896–1971), which are available in state libraries and via Trove.[49]

Notes

1 In this chapter, I use "Aboriginal and Torres Strait Islander Peoples" and where appropriate, "First Nations" or "First Peoples" as general descriptors for the more than 250 language groups living on the Australian continent for millennia. I use "Aboriginal" to refer to Aboriginal Peoples on the Australian mainland. Where possible, I follow specific naming conventions by referring to language group or a community's chosen names, for example "Whadjuk Noongar." I use "Indigenous" to refer to Indigenous People globally or fields such as "Indigenous Studies." See Australian Institute of Aboriginal and Torres Strait Islander Studies. *Australia's first peoples.* https://aiatsis.gov.au/explore/australias-first-peoples. Accessed June 30, 2023.
2 Referendum Council. (2017). *The Uluru Statement from the heart.* https://www.referendumcouncil.org.au/sites/default/files/2017-05/Uluru_Statement_From_The_Heart_0.PDF
3 Treaty processes are now underway in four states or territories: Victoria, Queensland, the Northern Territory and Tasmania.
4 Appleby, G., & Davis, M. (2018). The Uluru Statement and the promises of truth. *Australian Historical Studies, 49*(4), 501–509. https://doi.org/10.1080/1031461X.2018.1523838
5 First Peoples' Assembly of Victoria. (2021, June). *'Tyerri Yoo-Rook' (seed of truth): Report to the Yoo-Rrook Justice Commission.* https://www.firstpeoplesvic.org/wp-content/uploads/2021/09/Tyerri-Yoo-rrook-Seed-of-truth-Report-2021_Final.pdf; *Australian Curriculum: History*, version 9, Australian Curriculum, Assessment and Reporting Authority, 2023.
6 Paulson, J., & Bellino, M. J. (2021). Education and truth commissions: Patterns, possibilities and implications for historical justice. In M. Keynes, H. Åström Elmersjö, D. Lindmark, & B. Norlin (Eds.), *Historical justice and history education* (pp. 67–83). Springer International Publishing. https://doi.org/10.1007/978-3-030-70412-4_4
7 Keynes, M., Marsden, B., & Thomas, A. (in press). Does curriculum fail Indigenous political aspirations? Sovereignty and Australia history and social studies curriculum. *Nordic Journal of Educational History.*
8 Heiss, A. (Ed.). (2018). *Growing up Aboriginal in Australia.* Black Inc., pp. 14, 88, 117, 122, 137; Referendum Council. (2017). *Final report of the Referendum Council*, pp. 17, 19, 32; Paton, D. (2012). Walking in two worlds. *Independent Education, 42*(1), 8–10.
9 Cole, E. A. (2007). Transitional justice and the reform of history education. *The International Journal of Transitional Justice, 1*(1), 123. https://doi.org/10.1093/ijtj/ijm003
10 United Nations, Secretary General. (2004, August). *Report of the Secretary-General on the rule of law and transitional justice in conduct and post-conflict societies.* United Nations.
11 Hobbs, H. (2016). Locating the logic of transitional justice in liberal democracies: Native title in Australia. *University of New South Wales Law Journal, 39*(2), 526.
12 Kēhaulani Kauanui, J. (2016). A structure, not an event: Settler colonialism and enduring indigeneity. *Lateral, 5*(1). http://csalateral.org/issue/5-1/forum-alt-humanities-settler-colonialism-enduring-indigeneity-kauanui/; Eve Tuck, E., & Gaztambide-Fernández, R. A. (2013). Curriculum, replacement, and settler futurity. *Journal of Curriculum Theorizing, 29*(1), 74.
13 There is some conjecture about what constitutes a 'truth commission' as opposed to a commissioned inquiry. For a discussion of this, see Priscilla, H. (2011). *Unspeakable truths: Transitional justice and the challenge of truth commissions.* Taylor and Francis.

14 Gibney, M. (Eds.). (2008). *The age of apology: Facing up to the past*. University of Pennsylvania Press.
15 Lorena, A. (2019). 'Like writing in the sand': Media discourse, the Barunga Statement and the Treaty '88 campaign. In A. Thomas, A. Jakubowicz, & H. Norman (Eds.), *Does the media fail Aboriginal political aspirations?: 45 years of news media reporting of key political moments* (pp. 87–98). Aboriginal Studies Press; Foley, G., Shaap, A., & Howell, E. (Eds.). (2013). *The Aboriginal tent embassy: Sovereignty, Black power, land*, (pp. 84–97). Routledge; Maynard, J. (2007). *Fight for liberty and freedom: The origins of Australian Aboriginal activism*. Aboriginal Studies Press.
16 Nagy, R. (2008). Transitional justice as global project: Critical reflections. *Third World Quarterly, 29*(2), 275–289. https://doi.org/10.1080/01436590701806848
17 Priscilla, H. (2011). *Unspeakable truths: Transitional justice and the challenge of truth commissions*. Taylor and Francis. p. 24; Barkan, E. (2001). *The guilt of nations: Restitution and negotiating historical injustices*. JHU Press.
18 Zunino, M. (2019). *Justice framed: A genealogy of transitional justice*. Cambridge University Press. pp. 29–34.
19 Khawaldeh, K. A. (2023, June 4). Indigenous voice crucial to treaty, Uluru Statement co-author Megan Davis says. *The Guardian*. https://www.theguardian.com/australia-news/2023/jun/04/indigenous-voice-crucial-to-treaty-uluru-statement-co-author-megan-davis-says; Johnson, P. (2023, January 30). "Ready to chuck it in": Q+A audience member's passionate speech leads to call for treaty. *ABC News*. https://www.abc.net.au/news/2023-01-31/lidia-thorpe-wants-treaty-and-seats-not-voice-qa/101909286; Ore, A. (2023, May 3). Indigenous rights activist Gary Foley warns voice will be ignored by government. *The Guardian*. https://www.theguardian.com/australia-news/2023/may/03/indigenous-rights-activist-gary-foley-warns-voice-will-be-ignored-by-overnment
20 This has been termed "procrastination politics." See Thomas, A., Jakubowicz, A., & Norman, H. (2019). *Does the media fail Aboriginal political aspirations? 45 years of news media reporting of key political moments*. Aboriginal Studies Press.
21 Sköld, J., & Swain, S. (2015). *Apologies and the legacy of abuse of children in "care". International Perspectives*. Palgrave Macmillan; Sköld, J., & Markkola, P. (2020). History of child welfare: A present political concern. *Scandinavian Journal of History, 45*(2), 143–158. https://doi.org/10.1080/03468755.2020.1764383
22 Keynes, M., & Marsden, B. (2021). Ontology, sovereignty, legitimacy: Two key moments when history curriculum was challenged in public discourse and the curricular effects, Australia 1950s and 2000s. *History of Education Review, 50*(2), 130–145. https://doi.org/10.1108/HER-07-2020-0043
23 Moodie, N., & Patrick, R. (2017). Settler grammars and the Australian professional standards for teachers. *Asia-Pacific Journal of Teacher Education, 45*(5), 439–454. https://doi.org/10.1080/1359866X.2017.1331202; Maxwell, J., Lowe, K., & Salter, P. (2018). The re-creation and resolution of the 'problem' of Indigenous education in the Aboriginal and Torres Strait Islander cross-curriculum priority. *The Australian Educational Researcher, 45*, 161–177. https://doi.org/10.1007/s13384-017-0254-7
24 Referendum Council. (2017). *Final report of the Referendum Council*, p. 17, 19, 32.
25 Together with Fukuyama's 'end of history' and Huntington's 'third wave' theses, for instance. See Fukuyama, F. (2012). *The end of history and the last man*. Penguin Books; Huntington, S. P. (1991). *The third wave: Democratization in the late twentieth century*. University of Oklahoma Press.
26 Teitel, R. G. (2000). *Transitional justice*. Oxford University Press.

27 Sharp, D. (2018). *Rethinking transitional justice for the twenty-first century: Beyond the end of history*. Cambridge University Press. pp. 2–3.
28 McMillan, M., & Rigney, S. (2018). Race, reconciliation, and justice in Australia: From denial to acknowledgment. *Ethnic and Racial Studies, 41*(4), 759–777. https://doi.org/10.1080/01419870.2017.1340653; Henry, N. (2015). From reconciliation to transitional justice: The contours of redress politics in established democracies. *International Journal of Transitional Justice, 9*(2), 199–218. https://doi.org/10.1093/ijtj/ijv001; Balint, J., Evans, J., & McMillan, N. (2014). Rethinking transitional justice, redressing indigenous harm: A new conceptual approach. *International Journal of Transitional Justice, 8*(2), 194–216. https://doi.org/10.1093/ijtj/iju004
29 A state's legitimating regime consists of the reasons justifying the exercise of political authority. See Krasner, S. D. (1982). Structural causes and regime consequences: Regimes as intervening variables. *International Organization, 36*(2), 185–205. https://doi.org/10.1017/S0020818300018920; Winter, S. (2014). *Transitional justice in established democracies. A political theory*. Palgrave Macmillan.
30 Winter, S. (2013). Towards a unified theory of transitional justice. *International Journal of Transitional Justice, 7*(2), 224–244. https://doi.org/10.1093/ijtj/ijt004
31 Lykes, M. B., & Van Der Merwe, H. (2017). Exploring/Expanding the reach of transitional justice. *International Journal of Transitional Justice, 11*(3), 371–377. https://doi.org/10.1093/ijtj/ijx026
32 Cunneen, C. (2011). State crime, the colonial question and Indigenous peoples. In A. Smuelers & R. Haveman (Eds.), *Supranational criminology: Towards a criminology of international crimes* (pp. 159–180). Intersentia Press, 2008, UNSW Law Research Paper No. 2011-2.
33 Matsunaga, J. (2016). Two faces of transitional justice: Theorizing the incommensurability of transitional justice and decolonization in Canada. *Decolonization: Indigeneity, Education & Society, 5*(1), 24–44.
34 Tuck, E., & Yang, K. W. (2012). Decolonization is not a metaphor. *Decolonization: Indigeneity, Education & Society, 1*(1), 1–40.
35 Matsunaga (2016). Two faces of transitional justice: Theorizing the incommensurability of transitional justice and decolonization in Canada; Tuck & Yang (2012). Decolonization is not a metaphor.
36 Coulthard, G. S. (2014). *Red skin, White masks. Rejecting the colonial politics of recognition*. University of Minnesota Press.
37 Corntassel, J., & Holder, C. (2008). Who's sorry now? Government apologies, truth commissions, and Indigenous self-determination in Australia, Canada, Guatemala, and Peru. *Human Rights Review, 9*(4), 465–489. https://doi.org/10.1007/s12142-008-0065-3
38 Cited in Matsunaga (2016). Two faces of transitional justice: Theorizing the incommensurability of transitional justice and decolonization in Canada.
39 Million, D. (2013). *Therapeutic nations: Healing in an age of Indigenous human rights*. University of Arizona Press.
40 Taylor, J. (2022, December 19). Indigenous deaths in custody rises to 516 since the 1991 royal commission, report says. *The Guardian*. https://www.theguardian.com/australia-news/2022/dec/20/indigenous-deaths-in-custody-rises-to-516-since-the-1991-royal-commission-report-says; Bhathal, A., Chamberlain, C., Krakouer, D. J., Beaufils, J. C., Gray, P., & Corrales, T. (2021, November 26). First Nations children are still being removed at disproportionate rates. Cultural assumptions about parenting need to change. *The Conversation*. http://theconversation.com/first-nations-children-are-still-being-removed-at-disproportionate-rates-cultural-assumptions-about-parenting-need-to-change-169090.

41 Henry (2015). From reconciliation to transitional justice: The contours of redress politics in established democracies.
42 Keynes, M., Marsden, B., Thomas, A., & Hand, S. (2023, October 12). 3 key moments in Indigenous political history Victorian school students didn't learn about. *The Conversation*. https://theconversation.com/3-key-moments-in-indigenous-political-history-victorian-school-students-didnt-learn-about-213756
43 Paulson, J. (2015). "Whether and how?" history education about recent and ongoing conflict: A review of research. *Journal on Education in Emergencies, 1*(1), 115–141. https://doi.org/10.17609/N84H20
44 Smith, B. (2020). The disciplined winds blow in from the west: The forgotten epistemic inheritance of historical thinking. *Historical Encounters, 7*, 21–32.
45 Dryden-Peterson, S., & Robinson, N. (2023). Time, source, responsibility: Understanding changing uses of the past in 'post-conflict' South African history teaching, 1998 and 2019. *Compare: A Journal of Comparative and International Education*, 1–19. https://doi.org/10.1080/03057925.2023.2212111
46 Mahuika, N. (2023). What is transformative, decolonial or Māori about the new history curriculum reset? *Te Pouhere Kōrero, 10*, 19–35.
47 Referendum Council. (2017). *Final report of the Referendum Council.*
48 Marsden, B. (2022). Aboriginal and Torres Strait Islander peoples' experiences of schooling and education: Oral histories, autobiographies, and life writing. *ANZHES.* www.dehanz.net.au
49 Deakin University. (2023). *Learning to read–A sample from the Australian schools textbook collection.* https://fusion.deakin.edu.au/exhibits/show/textbook/19throyal

Chapter 3

"Peeling off the final scab of thinking that everything's fine"

Exposing the poison of Australian education's colonising history through drama-based learning

Danielle Hradsky

Author positioning statement

I am a non-Indigenous Australian with ancestral ties to the Netherlands, Czechia, and Britain. My ancestors came to these lands now called Australia over the past 180 years as convicts, miners, economic migrants, and refugees and settled on the lands of the Wadawurrung, Dja Dja Wurrung, Wurundjeri Woi Wurrung, and Bunurong/Boon Wurrung Peoples. While my ancestors found relative peace and prosperity, the First Peoples of these lands were forcibly displaced, murdered, segregated, and assimilated. Today, I live and work on the lands of the Wurundjeri Woi Wurrung Peoples. In my work as an educator, arts practitioner, and researcher, as well as in my daily life, I seek to grapple with this complex, uncomfortable history—and present.

Introduction

> *The TEACHERS examine posters showing excerpts from Australian textbooks and policies from 1872 to 2007, as well as quotes from contemporary First Nations activists and educators. The TEACHERS' strong gestures and facial expressions show their emotional responses to the content. JAZ stretches out her arms towards the posters, fingers clenched. NITA gestures towards the posters, fingers interlocking. LALI clutches her fingers in her mouth, eyes widening. Hands on hips, ELLA holds her belly as if nauseated. JONAH wraps one arm around his body, the other over his face. STAN holds his hands in front of his chest.*
>   *JAZ gradually lowers her fists to beside her face*: Jesus! It's just wrong.
>   *NITA holds her hands to her throat as if choking*: Such bullshit. So much fear.
>   *LALI flings her arms out*: How do I not know this story?
>   *ELLA shakes her head*: Oh my God. What? How?
>   *JONAH still hides his face*: Awful.
>   *STAN pushes his hands away from his chest*: Blegh!
> Adapted from *Connections*, Act II, Scene 1[1]

For better or (mostly) worse, Australian education has played a crucial role in the ongoing business of colonisation through policies, curricula, and pedagogical practices.[2] Currently, policies require Australian teachers to promote reconciliation[3] and teach Aboriginal and Torres Strait Islander histories and cultures.[4] While many teachers support these requirements in principle, in practice, there is widespread fear, anxiety, discomfort, shame, and even resentment.[5] Embedded in colonising systems and inheritors of generations of misinformation, many teachers lack the knowledge, skills, and confidence required to challenge colonising narratives and engage students appropriately with First Nations texts and contexts. Widespread professional learning is essential if teachers are to contribute to de/colonising Australian education.[6] I purposefully interrupt 'decolonise' and 'decolonising' with a slash '/', a practice adopted from Dr Spy Dénommé-Welch (Algonquin-Anishnaabe) and Professor Kristiina Montero,[7] to recognise the ongoing need for questioning and scrutinising terminology that can too easily disguise *re*colonising education.

The teacher professional learning programme discussed in this chapter was my attempt to understand how embodied, drama-based professional learning could support teachers to engage with the supercomplexities of teaching for reconciliation.[8] *Supercomplexity* describes challenges that occur when multiple conceptual frameworks, or ways of understanding the world, collide. These challenges cannot be resolved through more resources because more time, money, and people bring new insights, ideas, and controversies.[9] For example, reconciliation is a controversial concept that can be co-opted by colonising agendas.[10] I acknowledge these complexities but maintain that reconciliation still holds de/colonising possibilities. To explore these possibilities, I focus on the five dimensions of reconciliation envisioned by Reconciliation Australia: historical acceptance, race relations, equality and equity, institutional integrity, and unity.[11] Embodied learning, or multimodal, holistic ways of exploring, experiencing, and reflecting, is increasingly used in programmes with de/colonising goals.[12] This study sought to understand how teachers experience engaging with reconciliation through embodied professional learning and the aspects of embodiment that support or hinder transformative learning. In this chapter, I focus particularly on how *verbatim theatre*, or drama drawn directly from real-life,[13] can support teachers, both First Nations and non-Indigenous, to engage with the colonising history of Australian education. Besides discussing what occurred in this specific context, I offer ideas and strategies for other educators seeking to de/colonise Australian history education through drama-based learning.

Methodology

For this study, 12 primary and secondary drama teachers from Victoria, Australia participated in a professional learning programme that occurred over six weekly sessions in October-November, 2020. The participants self-identified as being (a) not confident with teaching First Nations concepts and content and (b) interested in developing their understanding and abilities. Drama teachers were recruited with the aim of reducing participant discomfort with the drama-based pedagogical approach in order to focus on participants' (dis)comfort with the content. I facilitated the programme together with Kisal,[14] a Mabuiag Island/Wuthathi artist and educator. The professional learning content was not drama specific, instead centring the five dimensions of reconciliation outlined earlier. These dimensions were interpreted through a Victorian lens; for example, the second session, which explored historical acceptance, focused on understanding and accepting the wrongs of past education policies, curricula, and pedagogical practices, and their impact on Koorie[15] Peoples. Emphasising place aligned with the study's supercomplex understanding of reconciliation as dynamically affected by a swirl of ideas, institutions, and historico-spatial contexts.[16] The programme was underpinned by critical race and critical Whiteness theories, which offer ways to understand, unpack, and challenge how race and Whiteness are constructed and maintained in Australia and around the world.[17] I also drew on transformative learning theory,[18] which offers possibilities for transforming problematic frames of reference, such as racism and Whiteness. Due to COVID-19, the programme occurred online via Zoom. Some participants joined from Wurundjeri Woi Wurrung Country, as did I. Kisal and the other participants joined variously from Bunurong/Boon Wurrung, Wadawurrung, Gunditjmara, Yorta Yorta, and Bpangerang lands. One of the participants identified as Gunaikurnai, and the others with various non-Indigenous cultural heritages, including Assyrian, British, Cambodian, Jewish, Korean, Irish, and Italian.

Although not the focus of this chapter, large quantities of embodied data were created or collected, including audio-visual recordings, artefacts, and observations. These data were analysed using dramaturgical coding and monologue writing, with findings written up as an *ethnodrama*, or research-based work of theatre.[19] I intersperse my writings in this chapter with excerpts from this ethnodrama, entitled *Connections*, with the aim of providing a visceral window into the participants' experiences. In these excerpts, characters' names, including when they are referred to as a group, are written in capital letters (e.g., 'TEACHERS'). There are six teacher characters (JAZ, NITA, LALI, ELLA, JONAH, and STAN), who are composites of the 12 participants. There are also two facilitator characters, representing myself (ELOISE) and KISAL. Stage directions (descriptions of actions) are written in *italics*. Speech is written without quotation marks unless the characters are themselves quoting another source. Although this is an artistic representation of reality, the words and descriptions of actions are drawn directly from the data. Where relevant, I have also included some quotes from the data that are not present in *Connections*.

Introducing the 'TEACHERS'

I pause now to allow the TEACHERS to introduce themselves. They are about to perform and are feeling rather nervous. This is their first time performing as a group, and some will be playing First Nations roles. While it is inappropriate for professional non-Indigenous actors to play First Nations roles, current advice for teachers in Victoria states that when "there are clear educational reasons for doing so, non-Indigenous…students should be allowed to explore and present First Nations characters."[20] As part of this, students should begin performances by introducing themselves and their roles to the audience. Here, the TEACHERS share a little about their own cultural backgrounds, as well as the role(s) they are about to play:

LALI: I'm Lali. First and foremost, I consider myself to be Australian. I was born here. My heritage is Jewish-Italian. I'll be playing Australia's education system over time.

NITA: I'm Nita. I identify as Italian-Assyrian. Those cultures are more part of me than being Australian. English was my second language growing up. But I think that that's Australian too. Today, I'll be representing Yiman/Bidjara Professor Marcia Langton, and the voices of other First Peoples.

ELLA: I'm Ella. I've never been asked to say my cultural identity before. I'm a First Fleeter, on my father's side. On my mother's side, I'm a first-generation Australian. My mother always called Scotland home. I'm a dual citizen of Britain and Australia. I'll be playing the roles of non-Indigenous or settler school children.

STAN: I'm Stan. I'm getting more comfortable with saying, "I'm part Indigenous, part Korean, and part convict." I'll be speaking the words of Yorta Yorta activist and journalist Jack Patten and Wiradjuri leader Will Ferguson, as well as representing other First Nations voices.

JAZ: I'm Jaz. I get asked this all the time. People always assume I'm international, but I identify myself firstly as Australian. I am of Cambodian and English descent. I'll be speaking the voices of First Nations Peoples, particularly Mandawuy Yunupingu, a Gumatj man of the Yolngu People which is in the Northern Territory nowadays.

JONAH: I'm Jonah, I'd probably say I'm Australian. That question rarely comes up for me. Culture is something I find tricky to understand. I come from two lines of colonial Australian backgrounds. I'll be playing the roles of Burke and Wills, and past prime ministers and Ministers of Education of Australia.

Connections, Act II, Scene 2[21]

Engaging with 'historical acceptance' through embodied, drama-based professional learning

The performance on which this scene is based occurred during the second of six two-hour workshops. The first session focused on building a community of praxis:[22] setting up trusting, respectful relationships, and establishing protocols and practices such as Acknowledging Country, collaborative yarning,[23] embodied learning, and reflecting strategies. De/colonising education is inherently unsettling,[24] as are the postcolonial rights[25] and justice-based[26] approaches to reconciliation taken in this study. Establishing safe spaces for learning was not intended to remove this sense of discomfort but rather to respect participants' emotions and to encourage critical ways of thinking, feeling, and acting.[27] Thus, by the second session, certain learning routines had been established, and most participants already felt part of a community.

All sessions began with an Acknowledgement of Country. As the main facilitator, I led the acknowledgements; however, each participant also shared their own Acknowledgement of Country. During the week prior, participants had been asked to reflect on a personal connection between themselves and First Nations histories. This connection could be familial, related to the Country they live on, or another personal connection. During their acknowledgements, each participant briefly shared some of their learnings and reflections. For example,

> I would like to acknowledge the land that I live on...the land of the Wurundjeri. I quite literally live on the land that Coranderrk is on. I've done a lot of research about that this week...that's been a bit of an emotional journey for me to be honest.

> I'd like to acknowledge the land of the Wathaurong and Eastern Maar People that I live on. But I'd also like to acknowledge the Gurindji People that my partner is a descendant of...they are the freshwater people. I'm researching them, because when or if we have children, I'd like to help that culture continue.

> I acknowledge the Country that we're on today. I'm on Bunurong land. I'm aware that genocide and massacres have a cascading effect in terms of generational trauma. I relate to this due to my family's history with the Pol Pot genocide.

This exercise, like most strategies employed in the programme, was guided by a *Heart, Head, and Hands Arts-Based Pedagogical Framework for Transformative Learning* (Figure 3.1), which I developed for this project drawing on similar frameworks.[28] Beginning with place aligns with First Nations ways-of-knowing[29] and supports learners to find personal meaning and relevance.[30] Encouraging participants to draw personal connections between themselves and First Nations histories highlighted emotionality as a way of knowing[31] (*Heart*).

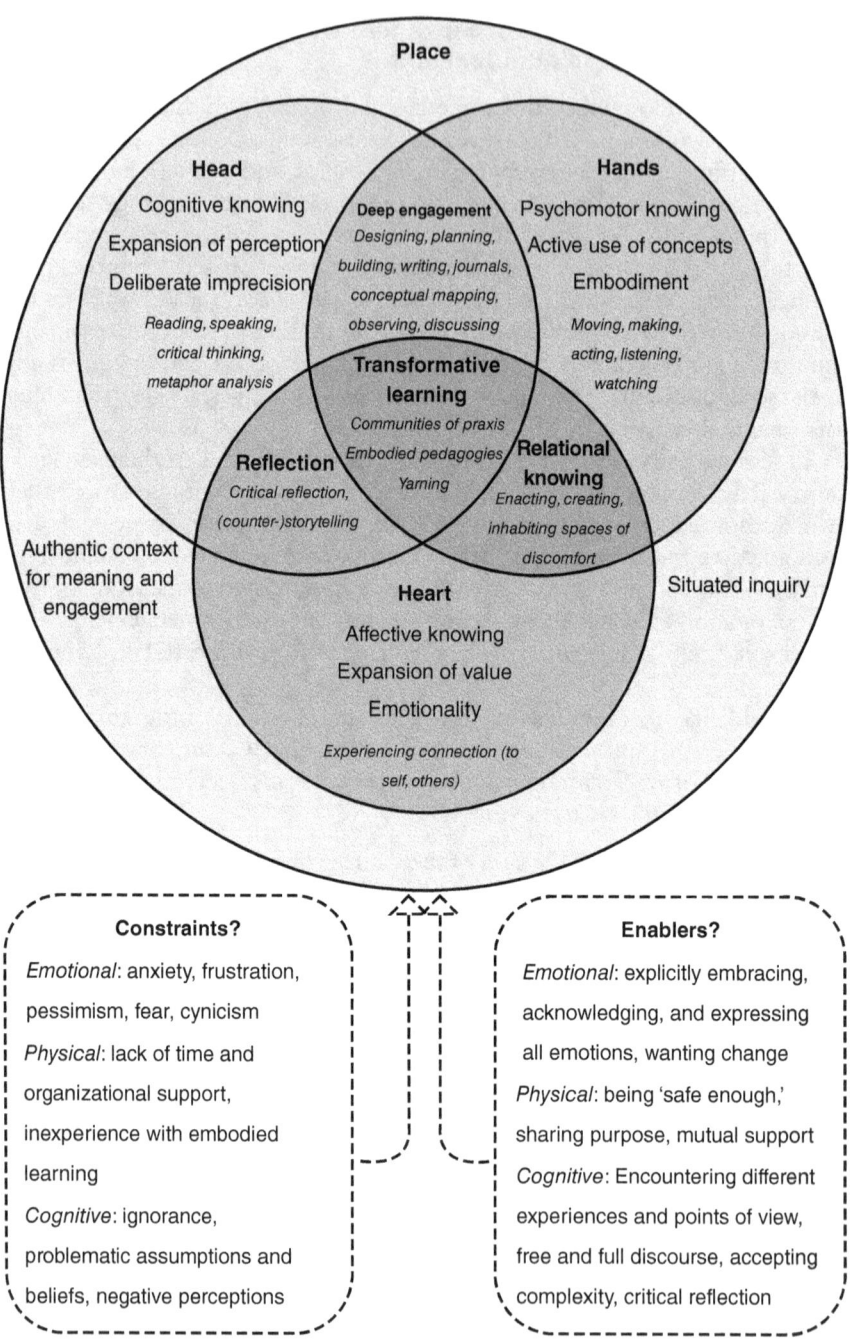

Figure 3.1 Heart, head, and hands arts-based pedagogical framework for transformative learning

Linking the acknowledgement to the session's topic was intended to expand participants' perceptions of reconciliation in general and historical acceptance in particular (*Head*). Having each participant contribute their own acknowledgement was intended to increase their active use of the concept[32] (*Hands*): some had previously never acknowledged Country before. With 12 participants and two facilitators, this section of each session took approximately 10 minutes. During individual interviews following the six-week programme, the practice of Acknowledging Country each week was selected by two participants as their most powerful experience of the entire programme:

> I realised that I have a role to play... I realised that there's a long way to go with the Acknowledgement of Country. It can be tokenistic, but it can also be incredibly significant and meaningful.

> Working on the Acknowledgements of Country each week felt powerful. Obviously, I understood what they were for before. But researching my Country, finding people that lived...or worked on Country, helped strengthen that relationship for me. Now, when I acknowledge Country there's a lot more weight to it. It's not, "We need to do this, because it's the correct thing to do." It's, "I genuinely feel this needs to be paid respect to."

After the acknowledgements, we explored Reconciliation Australia's definition of historical acceptance:

> All Australians understand and accept the wrongs of the past and their impact on Aboriginal and Torres Strait Islander Peoples. Australia makes amends for past policies and practices [and] ensures these wrongs are never repeated...There is truth, justice, healing and historical acceptance.[33]

Participants were asked to create *freeze-frames* (still images using the entire body) expressing their understanding of the key concepts: history, education, truth, justice, healing, and acceptance. After each freeze-frame, participants were given a prompt to reflect on how they had positioned themselves within their freeze-frame. These prompts included the following:

- Where is history?
- What was your personal experience of education? Was it enabling or constraining?
- What emotions are associated with truth?
- Are you giving or receiving justice?
- Where/what is the wound that is being healed?
- What emotions are associated with acceptance?

Following the prompt, participants could change their freeze-frames if they wished to more accurately reflect their understanding of the concept. Figure 3.2

Figure 3.2 Participants embodying "education"

shows four participants embodying "education": the top image shows the participants' original freeze-frames, while the bottom image shows how some participants have altered their freeze-frames after considering their personal experiences of education.

The main body of the session explored the history of education in Victoria from 1835 to 2007. Utilising prior research,[34] I told participants the story of the first 37 years of colonisation, when education was optional and frequently unavailable for most young persons. I then divided participants into four groups, with each group choosing a different era of education:

- 1872–1910: Education during Federation
- 1910–1966: Education as national identity formation
- 1965–1989: Education and independent reform
- 1989–2007: Education as a political agenda

Each group was given a poster (created by myself) containing a timeline of relevant events, excerpts from contemporary textbooks and educational policies, and quotes from First Nations activists and educators of the time. An example poster can be seen in Figure 3.3.

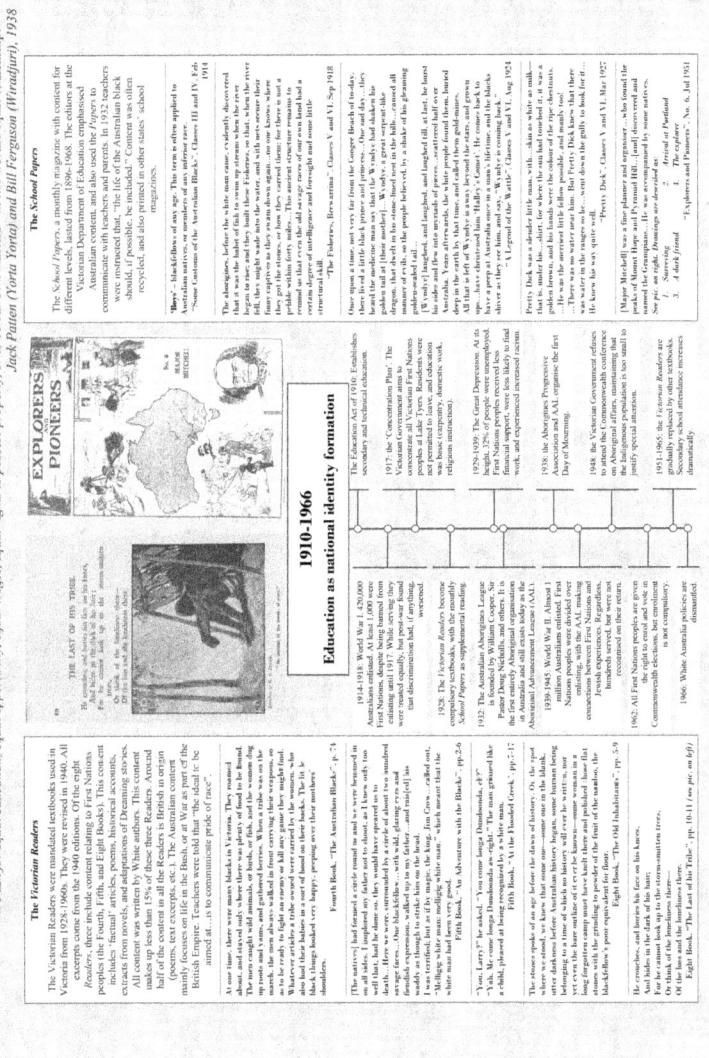

Figure 3.3 Poster for 1910–1966: Education as national identity formation

Participants were asked to spend 20 minutes reading through these posters and discussing the following questions:

1 What First Nations content was being taught?
   a What was being taught about First Nations Peoples?
   b What was being taught about non-Indigenous Australians?
2 Who controlled the content?
3 Why was this content being taught?
4 How was this content positioned in the curriculum?
5 What does this complex history mean for us as educators today?

Each group then had 15 minutes to develop a short, verbatim theatre performance, demonstrating their responses to the questions. Verbatim theatre draws on real-life stories, with performances developed using direct quotes.[35] Participants were instructed to draw only on the words that they had been given and to select keywords and phrases rather than large chunks of text. Participants were also asked to include both First Nations and non-Indigenous characters, and follow current advice for playing First Nations roles in educational contexts.[36] They were given permission to use satire to critique the powerful if they wished. The following vignettes from *Connections* show how each group interpreted their era:[37]

Vignette 1   Education during Federation (1872–1910)

The PARTICIPANTS begin frozen in position. NITA, STAN, and JAZ symbolise Country. LALI, ELLA, and JONAH represent ships. They gradually change into humans, moving forward, staring at each other with wide eyes and wrinkled foreheads. The Education System [LALI]'s face begins to show disgust through curled lips and narrowed eyes. The Settler Child [ELLA], observing, imitates them. Burke/Wills [JONAH] fall to their knees, starving. The Yandruwandha People [NITA, STAN, and JAZ] mime offering Burke/Wills nardoo (a type of fern with edible seeds). Burke/Wills takes it but rudely ignores the Yandruwandha People's instructions on how to eat it. Burke/Wills are dying but refuse to listen. The Education System and Settler Child observe the Yandruwandha People scornfully but lift Burke/Wills up, heroising them.

Burke/Wills [JONAH]:   "Primitive."[38]
Education System [LALI]: "Relic."[39]
Settler Child [ELLA]:   "Savages."[40]

Vignette 2 Education as national identity formation (1910–1965)

JAZ and NITA form the Brewarrina fish traps. The Education System [LALI] shows them to the Settler Child [ELLA]. The Education Minister [JONAH] looks on approvingly but directs the Settler Child's attention away from Patten/Ferguson [STAN].

Education System *[LALI]*:	"This ancient structure remains to remind us that even the old savage races of our own land had a certain degree of intelligence and foresight and some little structural skill."[41]
Education Minister *[JONAH]*:	"The ideal to be aimed at is to communicate pride of race."[42]
Settler Child *[ELLA]*:	"Whose race?"
Education *[LALI & JONAH]*:	"The Empire!"
Patten/Ferguson *[STAN]*:	"We ask for equal education, equal opportunity, equal wages, equal right to possess property, or to be our own masters. In two words, equal citizenship."[43]

Vignette 3 Education and independent reform (1965–1988)

The Voices of First Nations Peoples [JAZ, NITA and STAN] stand together. The Settler Child [ELLA] moves away from the Education System [LALI] and Politicians [JONAH] but is gradually drawn back.

First Nations Voice *[JAZ]*:	"Not enough."
Settler Child *[ELLA]*:	"Beginning of the wave of awareness."
First Nations Voice *[STAN]*:	"Lukewarm."
First Nations Voice *[NITA]*:	"Not enough."...
Education System *[LALI]*:	"Had a chapter."
Politician *[JONAH]*:	"Hope that the anger goes away."
Education System *[LALI]*:	"We feel good."
Settler Child *[ELLA]*:	"We feel important."
Education System *[LALI]*:	"There's nothing to see here."
First Nations Voice *[JAZ]*:	"But the screams of the Black voices."
First Nations Voice *[NITA]*:	"Are haunting us."
First Nations Voice *[STAN]*:	"And they want to be heard."

> **Vignette 4 Education as a political agenda (1989–2007)**
>
> *Yunupingu [JAZ] takes centre stage to speak, but the Education System [LALI] and Prime Ministers [JONAH] cover their ears. The Settler Child [ELLA] imitates them but removes one hand to listen.*
>
> Yunupingu *[JAZ]*: "What about schooling now? Have schools stopped being the instrument of assimilation? European type knowledge is just one sort of knowledge among many. Governments and students need to see."[44]
>
> *The Prime Minister [JONAH] moves in front of Yunupingu [JAZ], silencing them.*
>
> PM Howard *[JONAH]*: "We talk too negatively about our past."[45]
>
> *Yunupingu [JAZ] tries to speak but is interrupted by the Education System [LALI], moving busily about the stage, writing down notes. The Settler Child [ELLA] trails after the Education System [LALI], confused.*
>
> Education System *[LALI]*: "We've gotta tick a box, so…we're going to be an ideology. Next, we'll be a framework, and then an objective."
>
> PM Howard *[JONAH]*: "I sympathise with Australians who are insulted when they're told we have a racist, bigoted past."[46]
>
> *The Voices of First Nations Peoples [JAZ, NITA, and STAN] throw up their hands in frustration…*
>
> *Connections*, Act II, Scene 2[47]

As these vignettes show, the participants did not necessarily follow the instructions, with Group Three drawing on words from their discussion rather than their poster and Group Four creating a new satirical character ('the Education System') that drew on words from the posters (e.g., 'strategy', 'vision', and 'values') but with added words and phrases from their discussion. While not strictly verbatim theatre, these changes did not fundamentally change the exercise. After each performance, the audience was invited to respond to the performance through the Zoom chat, and the performing participants had an opportunity to clarify or discuss aspects of their scene.

The final half hour of the session was spent reflecting on the session. Participants were asked to create another freeze-frame expressing the word 'education', this time specifically thinking about teaching First Nations content in their classes. The group was split in half, with one half asked to hold their freeze-frame, while the other half had an opportunity to observe and write in the chat what they saw in other people's images, and vice versa. Finally, the participants were given three prompts:

- The history we've just been exploring
- Our role as teachers within that historical trajectory
- Helping to build truth, justice, and healing within our classrooms

They were asked to share emotions they were feeling in response to each prompt, thoughts or questions that occurred to them, and actions that they might take. The final scene in Act II of *Connections* brings together participants' reflections, both from this session and from later interviews reflecting back on this particular workshop. This section is written in poetic form, intended to emphasise the emotional nature of these stories:[48]

> STAN *(building anger/outrage and a growing sense of injustice)*:
> Things aren't fair!
> Hurts me in the heart.
> ELLA *(humiliated and self-disgusted)*:
> What a kick in the guts!
> Peeling off the final scab
> of thinking that everything's fine…
> LALI *(rubbing her heart as if feeling a conflict there)*:
> What is my place as an educator?
> How much can I do to change
> when our system is so broken?…
> JAZ *(overwhelmed by frustration)*:
> The history we've just explored,
> I sort of knew it,
> didn't really understand…
> NITA *(overwhelmed by shame)*:
> My school is tokenistic.
> Have I been paying attention?…
> JONAH *(numb with anger and disgust)*:
> Why has this taken so long?
> We're dragging our heels even now.
>
> *KISAL stands and walks softly amongst the TEACHERS, drawing them towards her. ELOISE creates space for and supports KISAL and the TEACHERS…*

KISAL: There is so much work to be done.
    Although it seems impossible
    I will fight to my death to smash down these walls.
    Come along on the journey!
    Going alone is dangerous.
    We need protection.
    Just remember:
    You are realising and dealing with this for the first time.
    Imagine being an Indigenous person who knows this history—any Indigenous person.
    You say, "I've just found this out!"
    We say, "Would you hurry up and catch up?"
    Catch up!
    Time's going
    Time's wasting.

ELLA *(shocked)*: "Catch up!"
    I'm shaken to my bones.
    I needed to hear that…

LALI *(still struggling)*: I feel so much shame about my ignorance,
    but ignorance is not an excuse.
    (Blood boiling) Yeah, you're right,
    I've got to catch up…

ELLA takes LALI's hand, sharing her feelings.

NITA *(love coming through)*: "Catch up!"
    No-one ever says it to your face.
    It's always a world issue:
    "This is happening. Why don't you care?"
    Say it to my person, to my soul.
    I feel my responsibility.
    It's not this big thing out there,
    it's in my every day…

NITA joins ELLA and LALI, making a continuum between generations of teachers.

JONAH *(coming alive, connecting to the others' hope)*:
    Listen, hear, let stories be told.
    Teach the truth.
    (Excitement overcoming fear) If we don't do it,
    it won't happen.

JAZ *(spurred on)*: I know my students really care.
    I'm hopeful for change.

JAZ takes her place in the continuum. The older TEACHERS welcome her.

STAN *(motivated)*: I'm ready,
> don't have to sit back anymore.
> I can be part of that cultural change.

KISAL takes STAN's hand. The TEACHERS, KISAL, and ELOISE stand together, connected, as the lights fade.

Connections, Act II, Scene 3[49]

Exposing the poison of Australian education's colonising history

This session powerfully impacted the participants, evoking strong emotions such as anger, humiliation, self-disgust, fear, frustration, and shame but also love, hope, empowerment, and motivation. As will be discussed, Kisal's request that participants "Catch up!" with history was particularly impactful, with half the participants mentioning this moment again in later reflections. Some participants struggled emotionally in this session, but connected to the others' hope, spurred on and motivated to "be part of that cultural change" (STAN).

The drama-based pedagogies utilised in this session emphasise what Kainai/Blackfoot scholar Ramona Big Head describes as "exposing the poison"[50] of colonising histories in order to heal and move forward.[51] The participants interrogated and creatively challenged textbooks that characterised First Nations Peoples as primitive, relics, and savages,[52] and prime ministers who rejected the possibility of Australia having a "racist, bigoted past."[53] They also engaged with the words of contemporary First Nations activists and educators, such as Patten and Ferguson.[54] Drama on its own neither taught, exposed, nor transformed the participants.[55] Rather, drama was "a medium"[56] for drawing the participants in, allowing them to holistically experience, share, and reflect upon new truths.

As a medium, drama can expose or conceal poison. Big Head[57] links drama and theatre to Indigenous storytelling practices, seeing potential for theatre to support reclamation, de/colonising, and healing. However, with different source texts, or without careful guidance, the participants might have created theatre that indoctrinated, colonised, and wounded. This risk is represented by ELLA who, playing the Settler Child, questions whose race is being referred to in the quote, "The ideal to be aimed at is to communicate pride of race."[58] This quote confused some participants, who misread it as supporting First Nations Peoples to be proud of their race. The power of drama to effectively communicate stories to both actors and audiences means that educators must be careful with what stories are being shared.

'Exposing poison' aptly describes the embodied nature of engaging with stories through drama. Whether the participants "sort of knew" (JAZ) the history or were "realising and dealing with this for the first time" (KISAL), their responses were felt and known through the body as much as through the mind.[59] Participants' reflections post-performance were visceral. They described feeling "hurt…in the heart" (STAN), "a kick in the guts" (ELLA), "a conflict [in the heart]" (LALI), "stuck and confronted" (JAZ), "mind[blown]" (NITA), and that "we're dragging our heels even now" (JONAH). As awkward and uncomfortable as it was for the participants,[60] their first step towards healing was acknowledging, naming, and embodying their responses as they "peel[ed] off the final scab of thinking that everything's fine" (ELLA).

Aiming to evoke transformative learning through engaging so deeply with emotions and bodily responses opens possibilities of enduring rather than temporary discomfort. It is risky, in the supercomplex sense of the word. Facilitators and learners are all likely to be shifting their frames of reference, making it challenging to assess and prepare for all possibilities.[61] While some may experience joy and empowerment, others may be troubled, confused, or deeply uncomfortable. Experiences may spark innovation and transformation—or they may not. Embracing risk, uncertainty, and messiness is a core part of supercomplexity.[62] Non-Indigenous participants cannot experience the pride and joy of recognising their ancestors' strength and spirit, nor of reconnecting with and experiencing their cultures.[63] Instead, they may struggle with guilt and want to apologise for what their ancestors have done.[64] Teachers may question their place in this system that is "so broken" (LALI) and feel overwhelmed by fear, frustration, and shame. There is a danger in this kind of learning that learners will become "numb with anger and disgust" (JONAH). Encouraging learners to disclose traumatic, personal, and emotional information requires the facilitator to support their learners in making sense of and affirming their stories and responses.[65] Yet, guiding learners to feel empathy and engage in self-reflection may also be unproductive if they become focused only on themselves rather than feeling responsibility towards others.[66] It is this tricky tightrope that Kisal and I attempted to walk, exemplified in KISAL's "Catch up!" speech.

KISAL's speech represents the facilitator's delicate role in this kind of professional learning and the embodied value of having First Nations Peoples involved in such projects. Both Kisal and I supported and guided the participants through their learning journeys; ultimately, it was my responsibility as researcher and main facilitator. However, this specific moment of being told to "catch up!" was named by several participants as one of their most powerful learning experiences. As a First Nations person with lived experience of the education system, Kisal's counter-narratives carried power that my words could not, to "unmoor people from received truths so that they might consider alternatives."[67] Often, my role was to create space and support for Kisal to share her perspective, as well as to share other First Nations perspectives through different texts. The process of creating this supportive space together, as well as the transformative moments we experienced as facilitators, will be explored elsewhere (Stewart & Hradsky, forthcoming).

Verbatim theatre as a pedagogy creates opportunities for learners to engage deeply with people and texts from historico-spatial contexts different to their own. *Connections* itself is a form of verbatim theatre, albeit one with composite characters rather than direct representations of real people.[68] Verbatim theatre is a complex ethical space with no currently agreed guidelines for creating and performing verbatim texts.[69] I suggest that educators carefully consider what the aim of the exercise is, as well as whose stories are being explored, why those stories are chosen, and how permission to explore these stories is being granted.[70] For example, the quotes selected for this exercise all came from published texts. I recommend collaboratively considering these questions with students, as well as ways to sensitively and respectfully represent individuals and stories from marginalised or vulnerable communities.

Ideas and strategies for de/colonising Australian history education through drama and theatre

There is an established tradition of using drama in learning with transformative and de/colonising aims. Past studies have mainly documented drama educators engaging their learners with history,[71] although there are some examples of history educators engaging their students through drama.[72] For educators interested in exploring this space, I offer the following starting points:

- Establish expectations of
  - using embodied pedagogies (see Figure 3.1) to explore, question, and comment on the world;
  - intending to produce change; and
  - refusing the possibility of certainty or completion.[73]
- Familiarise yourself with and follow approved advice around embodying First Nations roles and stories.[74]
- Drama can both expose and conceal poisons of colonisation. Ensure that First Nations voices and perspectives are centred and heard. For First Nations educators, be cautious of sharing personal stories. For non-Indigenous educators, do not ask First Nations People to do so. Many published narratives are already available. Seek permission to use them before doing so, particularly for public performances.
- Exposing poison is a visceral, frequently discomforting process that will affect everyone differently. Allow time for reflection and sharing. Remember that reflecting can also be an embodied process. Support your learners to make sense of and affirm their stories and responses. Encourage learners to understand their responses within the context of First Nations trauma. Create space for your own unwinding processes as well.
- It is challenging to assess and prepare for all possibilities and risks when learning and teaching through embodiment. Reflection is essential to make

sense of what has occurred. Embrace strangeness and respond to learners' experiences with flexibility, creativity, and openness.
- Drama offers particular possibilities for exploring spaces between realities. Verbatim theatre is not the only option. Theatre of the Oppressed[75] and process drama[76] are both valuable entry points to these spaces, as is engaging with scripts written by First Nations playwrights. For a non-exclusive list of scripts exploring a wide range of topics, including history, I suggest reading the "Narragunnawali Resource Guide for the Arts—Drama."[77]
- Give it a go! You may 'get it wrong' and that is scary. But you may also find yourself "coming alive, connecting to…others' hope."[78] Listen. Hear. Let stories be told. Teach the truth. Let excitement overcome your fear. If we don't do this, it won't happen.

Conclusion

In this chapter, I have shared the story of one particular study using drama-based learning to engage with Australian education's colonising history. In sharing this story, I do not offer a rulebook that can be meticulously followed to produce exactly the same results. Drama-based learning is inherently unpredictable. Since finishing this study, I have taught this programme multiple times with different educator groups and had each group produce different verbatim theatre performances, share different reflections, and have different discussions. Nonetheless, each time, participants have reported that they found this exercise challenging, discomforting, and ultimately empowering. If we are to move beyond the 'history wars' into a more healing future, the poison of colonising histories must be exposed. Embodied and drama-based learning offer powerful possibilities for experiencing, sharing, and reflecting upon new truths.

Notes

1 Hradsky, D. (2023). "I've got no connection": Engaging teachers through embodied, drama-based professional learning with the supercomplexities of teaching for reconciliation. [Doctoral thesis, Monash University]. Figshare. pp. 188–189. https://doi.org/10.26180/22114988.v1
2 Burridge, N., & Chodkiewicz, A. (2012). An historical overview of Aboriginal education policies in the Australian context. In N. Burridge, F. Whalan, & K. Vaughan (Eds.), *Indigenous education: A learning journey for teachers, schools and communities* (pp. 11–21). Sense Publishers. https://doi.org/10.1007/978-94-6091-888-9; Moodie, N., Maxwell, J., & Rudolph, S. (2019). The impact of racism on the schooling experiences of Aboriginal and Torres Strait Islander students: A systematic review. *The Australian Educational Researcher, 46*, 273–295. https://doi.org/10.1007/s13384-019-00312-8; Hradsky, D. (2022). Education for reconciliation? Understanding and acknowledging the history of teaching First Nations content in Victoria, Australia. *History of Education, 51*(1), 135–155. https://doi.org/10.1080/0046760X.2021.1942238
3 Australian Institute for Teaching and School Leadership. (2011). *Australian professional standards for teachers*. https://www.aitsl.edu.au/teach/standards

4 Australian Curriculum Assessment and Reporting Authority. (2018). *Australian curriculum version 8.4.* https://www.australiancurriculum.edu.au/
5 Ma Rhea, Z., Anderson, P., & Atkinson, B. (2012). *Final report: Improving teaching in Aboriginal and Torres Strait Islander education: National professional standards for teachers: Standards focus areas 1.4 and 2.4.* Australian Institute for Teaching and School Leadership. https://www.aitsl.edu.au/docs/default-source/default-document-library/improving-teaching-in-aboriginal-and-torres-strait-islander-education-professional-development-and-the-australian-professional-standards-for-teachers-monash-university.pdf?sfvrsn=55e7ec3c_0; Baynes, R. (2016). Teachers' attitudes to including Indigenous knowledges in the Australian science curriculum. *The Australian Journal of Indigenous Education, 45*(1), 80–90. https://doi.org/10.1017/jie.2015.29; Booth, S. R., & Allen, W. J. (2017). More than the curriculum: Teaching for reconciliation in Western Australia. *International Journal for Cross-Disciplinary Subjects in Education, 8*(2), 3123–3130. https://doi.org/10.20533/ijcdse.2042.6364.2017.0420
6 Ma Rhea et al. *Final report.*
7 Dénommé-Welch, S., & Montero, M. K. (2014). De/colonizing preservice teacher education: Theatre of the academic absurd. *Journal of Language and Literacy Education, 10*(1), 136–165.
8 Hradsky. *"I've got no connection."*
9 Barnett, R. (2017). Researching supercomplexity: Planes, possibilities, poetry. In L. Ling & P. Ling (Eds.), *Methods and paradigms in education research* (pp. 291–308). IGI Global.
10 McMillan, M., & Rigney, S. (2018). Race, reconciliation, and justice in Australia: From denial to acknowledgment. *Ethnic and Racial Studies: Special Issue: Rethinking Reconciliation and Transitional Justice after Conflict, 41*(4), 759–777. https://doi.org/10.1080/01419870.2017.1340653; Elder, C. (2017). Unfinished business in (post)reconciliation Australia. *Australian Humanities Review, 61*, 74–93.
11 Reconciliation Australia. (2020). *What is reconciliation?* https://www.reconciliation.org.au/what-is-reconciliation/
12 Hradsky, D., & Forgasz, R. (2022). Possibilities and problems of using drama to engage with First Nations content and concepts in education: A systematic review. *The Australian Educational Researcher, 50*(3), 965–989. https://doi.org/10.1007/s13384-022-00536-1
13 Summerskill, C. (2021). *Creating verbatim theatre from oral histories.* Routledge.
14 All names in this chapter are pseudonyms.
15 Koorie is a postcolonising term used in self-reference by some First Nations Peoples in Australia's south-east (the state of Victoria).
16 Ling, L. (2017). The power of the paradigm: Methods and paradigms in education research. In Ling & Ling (Eds.), *Methods and paradigms in education research* (pp. 19–41). IGI Global; Barnett, R. (2017). Researching supercomplexity: Planes, possibilities, poetry. In L. Ling & P. Ling (Eds.), *Methods and paradigms in education research* (pp. 291–308). IGI Global.
17 I drew particularly upon the work of Professor Aileen Moreton-Robinson (Goenpul, Quandamooka); for example, Moreton-Robinson, A. (2015). *The white possessive: Property, power, and Indigenous sovereignty.* University of Minnesota Press.
18 Mezirow, J. (2018). Transformative learning theory. In K. Illeris (Ed.), *Contemporary theories of learning: Learning theorists…in their own words* (2nd ed., pp. 114–128). Routledge; Taylor & Francis Group (2009).
19 Further detail on this methodological process can be found in Hradsky, D. (2023). Composing cultural connections: Exploring tensions of creating composite ethnodramatic characters. *Qualitative Inquiry, 0*(0). https://doi.org/10.1177/10778004231196182

20 Bell-Wykes, K., Forgasz, R., & Hradsky, D. (2019). *Teaching First Nations content and concepts in the drama classroom: Advice for teachers in Victorian schools*. ILBIJERRI Theatre Company; Drama Victoria; Monash University. https://www.dramavictoria.vic.edu.au/public/51/files/Teaching%20First%20Nations%20Content%20and%20Concepts_VAEAI%20endorsed.pdf
21 Hradsky. *"I've got no connection"*, pp. 189–190.
22 Anderson, M. J., & Freebody, K. (2012). Developing communities of praxis: Bridging the theory practice divide in teacher education. *McGill Journal of Education, 47*(3), 359–377. https://doi.org/10.7202/1014864ar
23 Shay, M. (2021). Extending the yarning yarn: Collaborative yarning methodology for ethical Indigenist education research. *The Australian Journal of Indigenous Education, 50*(1), 62–70. https://doi.org/10.1017/jie.2018.25
24 Tuck, E., & Yang, K. W. (2012). Decolonization is not a metaphor. *Decolonization: Indigeneity, Education & Society, 1*(1), 1–40.
25 Elder. *Unfinished business in (post)reconciliation Australia*.
26 McMillan & Rigney. *Race, reconciliation, and justice*.
27 Zembylas, M., & Papamichael, E. (2017). Pedagogies of discomfort and empathy in multicultural teacher education. *Intercultural Education, 28*(1), 1–19. https://doi.org/10.1080/14675986.2017.1288448
28 Singleton, J. (2015). Head, heart and hands model for transformative learning: Place as context for changing sustainability values. *Journal of Sustainability Education, 9*(3), 171–187; Sipos, Y., Battisti, B., & Grimm, K. (2008). Achieving transformative sustainability learning: Engaging head, hands and heart. *International Journal of Sustainability in Higher Education, 9*(1), 68–86. https://doi.org/10.1108/14676370810842193; Law, J. (2004). *After method: Mess in social science research*. Routledge.
29 Lowe, K., & Yunkaporta, T. (2013). The inclusion of Aboriginal and Torres Strait Islander content in the Australian national curriculum: A cultural, cognitive and socio-political evaluation. *Curriculum Perspectives, 33*(1), 1–14; Moreton-Robinson, A. (2013). Towards an Australian Indigenous women's standpoint theory: A methodological tool. *Australian Feminist Studies, 28*(78), 331–347. https://doi.org/10.1080/08164649.2013.876664
30 Singleton. *Head, heart and hands model*.
31 Law. *After method*.
32 Singleton. *Head, heart and hands model*.
33 Reconciliation Australia. *What is Reconciliation?*
34 Hradsky. *Education for reconciliation?*
35 Summerskill. *Creating verbatim theatre*.
36 Bell-Wykes et al. *Teaching First Nations content and concepts*.
37 For clarity, the TEACHERS play roles in all of the eras (rather than just one era, as occurred in real life). However, the script as presented here accurately represents the participants' words and actions.
38 The expedition of Burke and Wills. In *The Royal Readers: No. IV*. (1896). Thomas Nelson and Sons. pp. 333–334.
39 The Australian Aborigines. In *The School Papers: Classes V and VI* (June 1900).
40 The story of Flinders—Part 1. In *The Royal Readers: No. IV*, pp. 293–294.
41 The Fisheries, Brewarinna. In *The School Papers: Classes V and VI* (September 1918).
42 Preface. In Education Department Victoria (Ed.). (1928). *Eighth book* (1st ed.). Government Printer.
43 Patten, J. T., & Ferguson, W. (1938). *Aborigines claim citizen rights! A statement of the case for the Aborigines Progressive Association* [Pamphlet]. The Publicist.

44 Yunupingu, M. (1994). Yothu Yindi: Finding balance. *Race & Class, 35*(4), 113–120, pp. 116–119. https://doi.org/10.1177/030639689403500412
45 Howard, J. (1996). *Prime Minister interview (John Howard)* [Interview]. Australian Government, Department of the Prime Minister and Cabinet. https://pmtranscripts.pmc.gov.au/sites/default/files/original/00010149.pdf
46 Ibid.
47 Hradsky. *"I've got no connection"*, pp. 190–194.
48 Saldaña, J. (2011). *Ethnotheatre: Research from page to stage*. Left Coast Press.
49 Hradsky. *"I've got no connection"*, pp. 194–198.
50 Big Head, R. (2012). "Strike them hard!" The Baker massacre play: Staging historical trauma with Blackfoot children. *Canadian Journal of Native Education, 35*(1), 117–130. p. 124.
51 Dupuis, J. K., & Ferguson, K. (2016). Fostering remembrance and reconciliation through an arts-based response. *In Education, 22*(1), 127–147. https://doi.org/10.37119/ojs2016.v22i1.235; Big Head. *"Strike them hard!"*
52 *The Royal Readers: No. IV.*
53 Howard. *Prime Minister interview.*
54 Patten & Ferguson. *Aborigines claim citizen rights!*
55 Neelands, J. (2004). Miracles are happening: Beyond the rhetoric of transformation in the Western traditions of drama education. *Research in Drama Education: The Journal of Applied Theatre and Performance, 9*(1), 47–56. https://doi.org/10.1080/1356978042000185902
56 Dupuis & Ferguson. Fostering remembrance and reconciliation through an arts-based response, p. 138.
57 Big Head. *"Strike them hard!"*
58 Education Department Victoria. *Eighth book.*
59 Romano, A. (2019). New scenario for transformation: How to support critical reflection on assumptions through theatre of the oppressed. In T. Fleming, A. Kokkos, & F. Finnegan (Eds.), *European perspectives on transformation theory* (1st ed., pp. 161–176). Palgrave Macmillan.
60 Big Head. *"Strike them hard!"*
61 Ling. *The power of the paradigm.*
62 Ibid.
63 Big Head. *"Strike them hard!"*
64 Dupuis & Ferguson. Fostering remembrance and reconciliation through an arts-based response.
65 Bessarab, D., & Ng'andu, B. (2010). Yarning about yarning as a legitimate method in Indigenous research. *International Journal of Critical Indigenous Studies, 3*(1), 37–50. https://doi.org/10.5204/ijcis.v3i1.57
66 Boler, M. (1999). *Feeling power: Emotions and education*. Routledge.
67 Ladson-Billings, G. (2021). Critical race theory - What it is not! In M. Lynn & A. D. Dixson (Eds.), *Handbook of critical race theory in education* (pp. 34–47). Routledge. p. 42.
68 Salvatore, J. (2014). Scripting the ethnodrama. In P. Leavy (Ed.), *The Oxford handbook of qualitative research* (2nd ed., pp. 1045–1083). Oxford University Press.
69 Summerskill. *Creating verbatim theatre.*
70 Ibid.
71 Hradsky, D. (2017). A personal reflection on using embodied drama to explore Indigenous perspectives in the classroom. *NJ: Drama Australia Journal, 41*(2), 106–116. https://doi.org/10.1080/14452294.2017.1400397; Dupuis & Ferguson. Fostering remembrance and reconciliation through an arts-based response; Fitzpatrick, E. (2011). How to get along with others: Children exploring

issues of racial-ethnic identity in multicultural and multiethnic communities through drama. *NJ: Drama Australia Journal, 35*(1), 90–104. https://doi.org/10.1080/14452294.2011.11649544; Big Head. *"Strike them hard!"*; Doerksen, R. (2016). Looking inward to 21st century pedagogy. *McGill Journal of Education, 51*(3), 1197–1203. https://doi.org/10.7202/1039636ar
72 Wang, V. C., & King, K. P. (2010). Transformative learning and ancient Asian educational perspectives. In V. C. Wang (Ed.), *Assessing and evaluating adult learning in career and technical education* (pp. 11–22). IGI Global. https://doi.org/10.4018/978-1-61520-745-9.ch002
73 Neelands. *Miracles are happening*.
74 For example, Bell-Wykes, et al. *Teaching First Nations content and concepts*.
75 Boal, A. (1974/2008). *Theatre of the oppressed* (McBride, McBride & Fryer, Trans.). Pluto Press.
76 Bowell, P., & Heap, B. S. (2001/2013). *Planning process drama: Enriching teaching and learning* (2nd ed.). Routledge.
77 https://www.narragunnawali.org.au/storage/media/page/drama-resource-guide-final-2020_c3wkV.pdf
78 Hradsky. *"I've got no connection"*, p. 198.

Chapter 4

Challenging the *Great Australian Silence*

Aleryk Fricker

Author positioning

I have been working in the education sector for over ten years. During that time, I have been a primary and a secondary teacher, as well as an academic, and even spent some time coordinating programmes designed to support university engagement for secondary First Nations students in Victoria as well. I have done all of these roles as a sovereign and a proud *Dja Dja Wurrung* man. My research focuses on decolonising education and First Nations education contexts, with a view to incorporating as much as possible with the confines of Australia's neo-colonial education structures. I recognise that what is good for First Nations students is good for all students, regardless of their own cultural contexts. This chapter details my efforts to move beyond the abstract and theorising of my research into the applied to have a real-world impact on teachers and classrooms across Victoria.

Introduction

In 1968, W.E.H. Stanner conducted a landmark survey of Australian history books available between 1935 and 1955. In this survey, he explored and described the phenomenon within the books which largely ignored First Nations history in favour of a colonial narrative that supported setter futurity in Australia. He described this as a "cult of forgetfulness practiced on a national scale."[1] In the decades since, and in the context of the ongoing culture wars that have raged through political, academic, and social contexts, Australian history textbook publishers have been slow to adjust their offerings to include accurate, authentic, and appropriate engagement with First Nations histories. This chapter explores a case study of a publication of an Australian education textbook where the creation of First Nations content has been created as part of a wider decolonial process. This case study illustrates the process and the outcome of the production of a market-leading text focused on the Australian Curriculum's Year 10 History Rights and Freedoms depth study that has included accurate, authentic, and insightful information for teachers and students to begin to challenge the *Great Australian Silence*.

DOI: 10.4324/9781003435617-4

The education system in Australia is a colonial construct that has been established to support settler-colonial futurity.[2] Australia established its education system based on models from Industrial Revolution Europe, where national governments made elementary education accessible, universal, and free for their citizens.[3] To pay for this new government subsidised service, taxation was levied upon the emerging capitalist class, which in return wanted to have a controlling stake in how the education system would be structured and defining the aims and outcomes for young people.[4] Previously, the only education systems that existed in Europe anywhere near this kind of scale were controlled by the Church, where the focus and aims were on religious doctrine and ethics.[5] With the removal of religious doctrine and the inclusion of capitalistic ideologies, the new education system was focused on the ability to create governable and productive citizens, who, once graduated, would be prepared to sell their labour for the profit of others.[6] With this overarching ideology of citizenship, education systems were created globally that championed a capitalist system heavily influenced by economic and social forces and entrenched inequalities within and beyond the classroom. The outcome was the creation of students who were educated just enough to be effective in a workplace but not educated enough to recognise the inherent inequitable distribution of wealth across society.

The challenge faced by the education system in Australia today is that it has been shaped by colonisation and capitalism as closely related phenomena[7] and foundational ideologies.[8] It has been a common experience of places that have been colonised to have their Indigenous[9] education systems usurped and replaced by those that were designed to directly benefit the children of colonists along well-defined intersections including whiteness, able-bodiedness, heteronormativity, masculinity, and class, among many others. The current education system in Australia reflects a capitalist mentality through the inequitable funding between and within the private[10] and public school sectors,[11] the devaluing of teachers and teaching as a profession,[12] the application of carceral logics in the classroom,[13] the reduction of funding to higher education,[14] and cutting government fee contributions towards specific disciplines and research that is not a national priority or can be easily commercialised.[15] The impact for teachers is an education system that is increasingly complex, and for students who are attracted to Humanities qualifications for the critical thinking skills these degrees advance, they will have to pay more to access this higher-order learning.

Given the complexities of teaching in the Australian system, there has been a secondary industry established to support teacher practice. There are many aspects of this adjacent industry that include teaching manuals, student workbooks, professional development programmes, and, importantly, textbooks. These textbooks have been produced to fulfil a need for 'time-poor' teachers who are seeking a text that has compiled structure, information, and activities for students that allow teachers more time to teach rather than having to 're-invent the wheel' to create content for students. Like the neo-colonial education system in Australia, these textbooks have also traditionally reinforced the same colonial and capitalistic values mentioned earlier.

Decolonising publishing

The international publishing industry has been a clear influence on the ongoing success and impact of colonisation globally. A 2018 press release published by the UK Publishers Association stated that, in the context of the then looming Brexit negotiations, British publishing had established England as a "global research and development powerhouse and as the creative centre of the world."[16] This press release also quoted the chief executive of the Publishers Association as describing Britain as "the world's publisher for more than 300 years" and quoted the British minister of state for trade and export promotion that the UK publishing industry had "promoted British people, culture, landscape, and commerce across the world for generations."[17] These statements, although provided in the context of a perceived threat to the publishing industry that Brexit would create, are indicative of the imperialist global colonising project operationalised by British authorities around the world. In conjunction with the territorial seizures and genocides of settler colonialism, the 'sharing' of British culture has shaped the publishing and authoring experiences of readers around the world and thus has resulted in British colonial descriptions, ideas, and culture being normalised as part of the normal human existence.[18]

In a contemporary context, educational publishing perpetuates the dominance of the global North through the systems and processes that influence and inform publishing practices globally. Primarily, this manifests in a phenomenon where publishers control the flow of information from the global North to South and West to East via the core and subsidiary publishing offices.[19] That is, it is far more likely for a book published in the United Kingdom to be distributed worldwide, where they have distribution rights, than one published from a subsidiary office in China for example.[20] For the books that are able to buck this trend, they are often perpetuating racial tropes and colonial domination, the reasons why these books achieve publishing success.[21]

Beyond the flow of publications, there are other systemic and structural limitations—namely, a homogenised demographic that controls the selection and advertisement of published works. A recent survey of the UK publishing industry found that only 17% of respondents identified as being people of colour.[22] This lack of diversity can shape many publishing decisions and determine whether a book will be released. Often, this is skewed to appeal to readers who are also white middle-class men, regardless of the actual demographics of readers accessing the texts. Furthermore, decisions about stocking are shaped by recommendations of reviewers who usually align with a similar demographic of authors (white, middle-class, male).[23] The outcome of such homogenous publishing processes is a centring of white, middle-class, and patriarchally orientated stories; any texts from *other* contexts are often positioned as being less valuable or less important.

The process of decolonisation in publishing can be considered to be occurring at two specific levels. The first is at a publishing level, where the systems and structures that have maintained over two centuries of hegemonic neo-colonial publishing need to be dismantled in order to create a sector that is capable of publishing content that gives visibility to First Nations stories and contexts. The second level is then reflected in the classroom where teachers are better equipped to engage with First Nations content in the classroom via the student textbooks and teacher resources that are then available to them.

Australian context

The first major study undertaken of Australian History books used in teaching in Australia was conducted by Bill Stanner in 1968.[24] In this study, he highlighted the absence of First Nations content in texts and dubbed this phenomenon the *Great Australian Silence*. Stanner described this as a "structural matter, a view from a window which has been carefully placed to exclude a whole quadrant of the landscape" and "what may well have begun as a simple forgetting of other possible views turned under habit and over time into something like a cult of forgetfulness practiced on a national scale."[25] The implication was that, for decades, the prevailing view of history through textbooks in Australia had little to no content that related to First Nations content.

In more recent scholarship, where additional texts have been explored, including from the same period of Stanner's survey, they have been found to have more First Nations–focused content. However, this content was found to have been constructed to distort the history and First Nations content to outright deny, lessen, and avoid content that was perceived to be too controversial or uncomfortable for non-Indigenous teachers and students.[26] The outcome of avoiding this 'challenging' content was that the textbook publishers directly contributed to the continued distortion of Australian history by denying the violence, genocide, and dispossession of First Nations People from Country, and, in turn, the continuation of the neo-colonial construction of contemporary Australia through the curriculum, teacher, and student resources.

The uncertainty with the curriculum discourse and the teaching of Australian history has also been compounded by other factors placed on teachers that have resulted in excessive workloads.[27] This has been further impacted by having the inclusion of First Nations contexts in the classroom being embedded within the professional standards for teachers[28] and as a cross-curriculum priority in the Australian Curriculum.[29] The outcome has been a professional requirement to engage with First Nations content, but not enough support being given to teachers to do this confidently.[30]

It is exactly this issue of a lack of confidence, skills, and knowledge possessed by teachers as they attempt to undertake curriculum work relating to First Nations perspectives where textbook publishing companies can have an impact. In the case study presented in this chapter, this has required the textbook publisher to recognise that their publications are as much for the students who will learn directly from them as it is for the teachers who will be, in the case of out-of-discipline or inexperienced teachers, doing the same.

Furthermore, from my own experience as a *Dja Dja Wurrung* History teacher, I gain confidence that through the process of decolonising History textbooks to embed more and better quality First Nations content, this can become an industry standard in Australia. This will support the teaching sector to move beyond the isolated individual classroom or school practices focusing on embedding First Nations content well, and instead, it can be embedded throughout all the tools that teachers can use to support their practice.

Australian publishing

The diversity surveys discussed earlier have provided inspiration to conduct similar surveys in the Australian publishing industry. In the recent Australian publishing industry workforce survey on diversity and inclusion it was found that, like the United Kingdom, the staffing in the publishing sector in Australia was limited in diversity and was mostly white and middle-class.[31] Across the publishing sector, less than 1% of the respondents identified as First Nations, 10.5% of the respondents identified as being European but not British, and 8.5% of the sector identified as being part of an Asian culture. This contrasted with the broader community in Australia where people identifying as European but not British made up 18%, and those identifying as part of an Asian culture are 17%.[32] The overarching context is that publishing as a sector, globally and in Australia, and in all spheres including academic, trade, and education, has limited diversity, and this shapes the publishing decisions that are made and, in turn, in the case of education publishing impacts the content available to students and teachers in the textbooks.

The decolonial process undertaken as part of the following case study to produce the content in the Australian history textbook was influenced by the scholarship of Frantz Fanon.[33] In his book, *The Wretched of the Earth*, Fanon argued for two significant aspects of the decolonial process. The first was that all decolonial struggles would require the application of violence. He created a compelling argument that the colonisation of Algeria was perpetrated through acts of violence and that any successful decolonial resistance would have to apply violence, as this was the only language that the colonisers would understand.[34] Additionally, Fanon argued that the nature of the unique context of each decolonial struggle would require an entirely unique response. As such, he argued that decolonial processes that would work in Algeria would not necessarily translate into other decolonial contexts.[35] This is especially relevant given Australia's context of occupation over the sovereign lands of many hundreds of First Nations Peoples but with no treaty to negotiate and set legal protections for First Nations and non-Indigenous contexts.

In the application of a decolonial process in the Australian publishing context, the scholarship of Tuck and Yang[36] is influential. Their scholarship argues that the end stage of decolonisation needs to be a redistribution of land and wealth back to First Nations Peoples, and that this process should also work to *unsettle* the neo-colonial contexts. The concept of *unsettling* has also informed the process of beginning to decolonise education publishing in Australia as part of this case study. The concept of unsettling is based on the application of the opposite concept, settlement. Settlement, as it has been applied in an Australian context, refers to the occupation of a previously uninhabited place. The lack of habitation that underpins this term provides for an implication that settlement, by its very nature, is peaceful. This was established as part of a legal fiction with the misapplication of *terra nullius* over the Australian continent and adjacent islands by the British. What is known, however, is that the colonisation of Australia was anything but peaceful, with the Frontier Wars lasting for over 140 years.[37] In the unique Australian context, the application of violence as part of a decolonial process can manifest as an 'unsettling' of the neo-colonial status quo. In this case, the violence does not manifest through a physical means but rather is manifested through a non-physical unsettling of the content published within the relevant textbooks, and in turn, the unsettlement that occurs within the History classroom when teachers and students learn about content that otherwise might have been ignored.

The second aspect of the decolonial process that influenced the actions taken when producing the History textbook chapter was the recognition that in contemporary Australia, the ways that discrimination is applied to various minoritised groups is also a colonial construct. This is evidenced via the discrimination relating to queerphobia,[38] misogyny,[39] classism,[40] ableism,[41] and ageism,[42] as examples. Such discrimination is an inheritance from the 'British values' that were imposed as part of colonisation. This means that in addition to the application of non-physical violence as part of the decolonial process, there needs to be an awareness of the intersectional nature of colonisation and an engagement with this process beyond the context of race and First Nations sovereignty alone.

The case study

The textbook chapter produced was part of the *Matilda Education Good Humanities* series of textbooks for the Victorian Curriculum. This was located within the Year 10 *Good Humanities* textbook and focused on the in-depth study at Year 10 on Rights and Freedoms.[43] This book chapter covered the in-depth study of the early First Nations resistance leaders through the formation of early First Nations political organisations and continued into the height of the Civil Rights Movement in Australia during the 1960s and 1970s and finished with contemporary history exploring the Reconciliation Movement, the destruction of the Juukan Gorge in Western Australia, and the destruction of the Directions Tree in Victoria. This chapter of the textbook differed from what had previously been produced by using the Victorian Curriculum as a foundation to include additional content beyond the minimum mandated. As such, the content in this chapter began focusing on an earlier period than just the Civil Rights Movement of the twentieth century and was able to provide a narrative of history that identified the connections between the early First Nations resistance, the Civil Rights Movement, and into the contemporary context of the Reconciliation Movement.

Another area of focus of the textbook chapter was to challenge the prevailing focus on the American Civil Rights Movement in relation to the Australian context. Previous iterations of the textbook and others in the market focused on the US Civil Rights Movement as an influence on the Australian equivalent. This chapter identified the instances when this was the case and was able to provide the context of the US Civil Rights Movement in such a way that it did not dominate the content of the chapter. It also identified how the information exchange between the US and Australian movements had been occurring for several decades prior to the Civil Rights period and that rather than being a one-way influence from the United States to Australia, there was more two-way exchange between the two movements. The textbook chapter used the curriculum as a stepping-off point but was able to provide additional detail and nuance to this in-depth study, and this culminated in the creation of a market-leading resource that provided a well-researched, accurate, and authentic resource for students and teachers.

When considering the applied aspect of this decolonial process, I engaged the principles and process outlined in Hughes and Fricker,[44] which articulated a model for decolonisation in an initial teacher education context. As part of this model, there is a distinction made between *indigenising* and *decolonising* processes. As such, the authors argue that indigenising can only be facilitated by Indigenous stakeholders, and decolonising should be engaged by all. Furthermore, the decolonising process has been articulated through a three-stage process. These involve an initial critical self-reflection of the non-Indigenous stakeholder to understand whiteness and how this exercises power and privilege in contemporary Australia.

The second stage relates to the capacity of the non-Indigenous stakeholder to recognise the existence of First Nations sovereignty. This reflects the power that non-Indigenous people have in contemporary Australia and that First Nations sovereignty cannot manifest unless the prevailing power systems and structures recognise that it exists. Once this is the case, First Nations sovereignty manifests as self-determination. This allows First Nations stakeholders to tell First Nations stories.

The third stage relates to a potential partnership between First Nations and non-Indigenous stakeholders. In this context, this stage recognises that it is inappropriate to expect the First Nations stakeholders to take on the burden of all of the decolonial labour, especially considering the power imbalance that needs to be overcome also. As such, this stage of the process recognises that it is the non-Indigenous stakeholders who must take on the burden of labour under the leadership of the First Nations stakeholders. This means that the process is assisted by non-Indigenous stakeholders leveraging their power and privilege to challenge the neo-colonial power structures and is still controlled through First Nations leadership. This also reflects that First Nations people may not have the capacity to take on the entire burden of decolonial labour due to the cultural load that this would entail.

The three-stage process was modified to match the context of education publishing rather than initial teacher education and reflected that the co-construction of the textbook was applied as part of the wider textbook publishing, revision, and editing process more broadly. In this case, as well, I was able to combine the decolonising and indigenising[45] processes together as I was completing these simultaneously through the creation of the content that I was authoring in the chapter. I did not require critical self-reflection, as this is something that I am already acutely aware of through my experiences of navigating race and racism as a fair-skinned sovereign *Dja Dja Wurrung* man.

The second stage of a recognition of First Nations sovereignty and the manifestation of self-determination[46] discussed earlier was also something that I was enabled to embed throughout the process of creating the textbook chapter. This was achieved by engaging directly with First Nations primary sources and using those sources to tell First Nations histories. Throughout the textbook chapter, I used documents produced by various First Nations community-controlled organisations from the time period, as well as engaging secondary sources produced by First Nations historians. This meant that I was able to prioritise First Nations accounts and First Nations scholarship as part of my research for the textbook chapter.

The co-construction stage was also adjusted as part of the production of the textbook chapter.[47] This, too, was slightly different as I was able to construct the chapter with little input from the non-Indigenous stakeholders and was able to complete this task myself. In this case, I had the capacity to both decolonise the textbook chapter and indigenise it at the same time. I had the capacity to take on the cultural load, and this also meant that I was able to lead and control the content in the chapter to ensure its suitability. In terms of the leadership, rather than being applied on an individual context with separate non-Indigenous stakeholder teachers in separate classrooms, I was able to create the resource that would be in hundreds of classrooms with teachers who could teach directly with the chapter with the confidence that it was appropriate and had already been cleared by an expert from the community. This significantly increased the scale that my impact could have. The differences in this stage also reflected the trust and willingness that the publishers had in giving me the autonomy to create the chapter with minimal editorial control.

Matilda Education was established in 2019 in the wake of the closure of the Australian operations of an international education publisher. Many of the staff who were retrenched from the other publisher connected with this newly formed organisation, and I was invited to continue working as a cultural consultant and reviewer. From these negotiations, I was able to request an expansion of my role from one of reviewing and editing to authorship. From the outset of my engagement, the organisation was conscious of a lack of First Nations content in their books and had a keen enthusiasm to improve their offerings in this area in line with the shifts of focus of the curriculum and community and teacher expectations. The team was also acutely aware that they did not have adequate First Nations representation within the organisation and that this was also indicative of the sector more broadly, and they felt that having adequate First Nations representation within the organisation would be an important factor in the creation of quality texts with First Nations content included.

As part of the negotiations to author a chapter in this textbook, we discussed what the expectations were from the viewpoint of each stakeholder, and I was able to articulate my responsibilities and expectations in terms of decolonisation and how I wanted to work. I was clear that in addition to the legal responsibilities that would be established through the contract with Matilda Education, I had important responsibilities to my community as cultural protocols relating to the research conducted as part of the textbook chapter and that anything that I was going to put my name to had to be appropriate and working towards supporting First Nations community outcomes.[48] As such, I requested as little editorial control over my content as possible and the freedom to go beyond the Victorian Curriculum, as I felt it was necessary to embed First Nations content and voices within the chapter as part of the process to decolonise and indigenise the textbook chapter. To their credit, they were incredibly supportive and embraced this opportunity to 'shake up the sector' with this content and demonstrate a commitment to begin their own process of decolonising publishing and provide an example for other organisations in the sector.

Beyond the content of my textbook chapter, I advocated for my revision of cross-over content and other historical topics within the textbook to ensure a decolonial process was being operationalised. This meant I was able to influence other topics that otherwise could have been problematic in how they described and positioned First Nations Peoples within the historical narrative. Another important outcome of the negotiation was the opportunity to provide professional development sessions with the publishing, sales, administrative, and executive staff within the organisation. This allowed me to go beyond the confines of the specific textbook chapter and have a broader impact on the rest of the organisation. Importantly, this enabled me to provide a greater contextualisation of the book with the sales team to allow them to better discuss the content with Victorian teachers and facilitate culturally safer and more appropriate ways of working with First Nations stakeholders to improve the potential future engagement with other First Nations authors.

At this point, I began an in-depth engagement with the Levels 9–10 History Rights and Freedoms topic in the Victorian Curriculum. I isolated problematic language and discourses, historical inaccuracies, and structural limitations.[49] From this point, I began constructing the structure of the chapter within the style and structures of the textbook series. This included the creation of the framing question for each two- or four-page spread, the incorporation of many images, and the specific *learning ladder* questions for student activities.[50] The adjustments to the structure were related to the limited chronological study of the curriculum. In the curriculum, it structured the Civil Rights Movement to have only been in existence during the decades across the mid-twentieth century.[51] The adjustments that I made to this structure were to include some two-page and four-page spreads detailing the creation of important First Nations political organisations that had their origins several decades prior to the Civil Rights period, as well as establishing links between these early political organisations. These topics were beyond the scope of the curriculum, but including them provided much-needed context to the civil rights focus. To contextualise concepts that many teachers and/or students may not be familiar with due to processes of colonisation, I also included a spread specifically to cover the topic of *Critical Race Theory*.[52] This was included to ensure that the students studying this period would have a useful theoretical lens to better understand the questions focused on 'why' the fight for civil rights occurred in the first place.

Beyond the chronological and theoretical adjustments, and additions to the curriculum content, I also examined and adjusted the civil rights content to focus on the Australian Civil Rights Movement rather than the equivalent occurring in the United States during the same time, as is often prioritised in Australian History textbooks on the assumption that Australia did not experience civil rights movements. There is no doubt that there were several key events in the Australian context that were influenced by US protests, but there was also much more happening in parallel or even separately from the US context.[53] As the curriculum was written, it distorted the historical context to imply that the Australian Civil Rights Movement was almost wholly influenced by the US Civil Rights Movement. This also reflected my own experiences whilst on one of my teaching placements where I witnessed an entire Year 10 History Civil Rights unit focused on the US context with only a cursory engagement with the Australian content. The justification for this was to follow the curriculum as well as having textbooks that had little Australian history content. As such, I sought to prioritise the Australian context and limit the US content in the textbook chapter to only what was necessary to understand the Australian events. This was an outcome of the decolonial process of the textbook chapter, where the focus was strongly placed on First Nations content to provide detail, accuracy, and an authentic engagement with Australian history. The outcome was that whilst there were some spreads about the US context related to the end of slavery and the *Freedom Rides*, as well as the birth of the *Black Power Movement*, beyond these events, the content was specifically focused on Australia, and as such, the decolonial process had enabled the indigenising process to begin, and the outcome was a greater engagement with First Nations content in accurate and authentic ways.

The decolonial process allowed me to work authentically without having to compromise my cultural context. As such, I made sure to use resources authored by First Nations people, specifically by authors who were present and active during the Civil Rights period. One of the first resources that I engaged with was a website that was introduced to me many years ago when I was studying for my undergraduate degree. At that time, I had the privilege to be taught by Professor Uncle Gary Foley, and during the semester of transformative lectures, he mentioned that he had created a website and compiled an extensive archive of important documents and resources from that time.[54] This website provided me with the foundation for finding crucial primary source documents from the Civil Rights period. This reflected the decolonial process of not only privileging First Nations sources but also allowing me, as a First Nations stakeholder, to have the space and the voice to share First Nations histories. As such, the content was not being informed by non-Indigenous voices that traditionally have included a certain level of implied editorialising in texts focused on First Nations content, but rather, I was able to prioritise First Nations voices to tell our own stories about our own selves, and even more specifically, engage with a powerful voice from a person who was there and making the civil rights history that was being explored in the textbook.

Beyond the exceptional archival scholarship of Professor Uncle Gary Foley, I was also focused on including other marginalised viewpoints that have also been traditionally ignored and incorporating other decolonial intersections like feminism, gender, class, and others who have traditionally been marginalised through colonisation. Wherever possible, I included stories and histories from important First Nations women to challenge the intersectional nature of the marginalisation of First Nations women's voices that can be further marginalised, as discussed earlier. These important women included Louisa Briggs and Pearl Gibbs,[55] who were both influential First Nations women who fiercely advocated for First Nations children and communities, and both had a significant impact on the fight for equality at different times in the struggle. Louisa Briggs advocated for the improvement of living conditions within the missions and reserves in their initial establishment, and Pearl Gibbs was an important figure in their eventual abolishment after the 1967 referendum. This ensured that the Year 10 Civil Rights chapter I was writing celebrated the importance and legacy of their impact on the Australian Civil Rights Movement and the First Nations communities that have benefited from them since.

In addition to the focus detailed earlier, the textbook chapter critically engaged with the curriculum by including content that predated and postdated the Civil Rights period. This improved the quality of the chapter in two important ways. The first was providing historical context to the chapter relating to the historical context of the Civil Rights Movement to argue that it was not just a specific phenomenon related to a specific period. The textbook chapter demonstrated how the Civil Rights Movement in Australia was a continuation of the resistance to colonisation that has been present in Australia since the arrival of the British. Additionally, the textbook chapter also included content related to more contemporary contexts. This reflected the consistent thread that despite the Civil Rights Movement being positioned as a discrete period of time, it is an ongoing process that is still occurring in Australia today. In highlighting this, the textbook chapter has also been able to challenge the implication that the Civil Rights period was successful and that all the rights were achieved. This is an inaccurate characterisation of the time, and extending the topics into contemporary Australia meant that the chapter was able to engage with ongoing issues relating to First Nations civil rights and the ongoing issues with racism in Australia.[56]

The outcome was a textbook chapter that used the Victorian Curriculum content descriptors and the elaborations within as a foundation for the stories, topics, and content that was included in the chapter. This meant that unlike older textbooks, where the content was often dominated and driven by the US Civil Rights Movement, this one was distinctly Australian in its focus. Furthermore, by virtue of the source material, it meant that non-Indigenous history teachers and out-of-discipline teachers using this textbook can engage with the content confidently, knowing that it has been constructed by a First Nations author using many First Nations sources. This is something that has been unheard of in education publishing in Australia until recently, and this is a direct outcome of beginning the decolonial process in textbook publishing.

Finally, another important outcome has been the production of a teaching resource that can be used with confidence given that it conforms to the Year, Author, Representations, Nouns, and Sensitivity (YARNS) First Nations evaluation tool.[57] The YARNS tool evaluates content resources by helping to shape questions to ascertain if the resource is appropriate to use.[58] As such, when teachers apply this evaluation tool, they will find that this chapter was published recently, the author does identify as First Nations, the representations are appropriate, the nouns used to name First Nations Peoples are appropriate, and the correct language conventions have been used, and appropriate sensitivity has been observed where First Nations Peoples have been identified through their specific cultural affiliations, and there have been no instances of restricted knowledge being shared inappropriately. This reflects the importance of the decolonising process to help shape the production of high-quality resources measured in Indigenous and non-Indigenous terms.

Conclusion

Australian History curriculum is still heavily impacted by the *Great Australian Silence*,[59] and education publishers have a role to play in addressing these limitations. In addition, the impact of conservative and moderate constructions of Australian History curriculum and the associated aims of these ideological contexts has further complicated what is already a highly contested space. This, combined with a growing number of inexperienced teachers and out-of-discipline teachers, has necessitated the investment in, and creation of, resources that can adequately support education in these contexts.

Beyond the specific need to create accessible teaching resources, decolonising education publishing in Australia creates opportunities to go beyond the limitations of the Australian History curriculum and directly challenge the prevailing neo-colonial systems and structures inherent across the education context. The textbook chapter represents a co-constructed high-quality resource to support the teaching of First Nations History in Australia that passes the YARNS test and that non-Indigenous teachers can use with confidence.

Decolonisation allows non-Indigenous authors, editors, and publishers to have insight into appropriate ways of working, authoring, and publishing potentially problematic materials rather than always relying on the workload capacities of First Nations authors. There is a growing awareness within the publishing sector that more needs to be done to support the engagement and outcomes of including First Nations content within education textbooks, and a growing role that education publishers have in facilitating these outcomes is something that decolonisation can enable. This is a project that has only just begun, but it has the potential to irrevocably change the sector to embrace post-history wars Australian history education.

Overall, understanding that despite the changes in policy and curriculum, there are still many teachers who have experienced an education system as students heavily influenced by the *Great Australian Silence* and textbook publishing has a role to play in challenging this silence. By engaging with First Nations authors, photographers, editors, and publishing agents, the sector as a whole will enable First Nations stakeholders to finally have the authority and, importantly, the ability to tell our own stories, histories, cultures, and knowledges.

Ideas and strategies for sourcing and evaluating textbooks with sovereign First Nations voices:

- A way to begin this process is to conduct an audit of your current textbook resources used in the History classroom.
- Apply the YARNS measure to your resources and consider both the content and the characterisations of both First Nations and non-Indigenous contexts within the resource.

- If producing resources for a local First Nations context, ensure that you have First Nations stakeholders leading the project and that they are being remunerated for their time and expertise.
- When sourcing new resources, begin by exercising your due diligence to determine how much authentic engagement there has been with First Nations stakeholders.

Notes

1. Stanner, W. (1968). *After the dreaming: The 1968 Boyer lectures*. Australian Broadcasting Corporation. pp. 24–25.
2. See, Hickling-Hudson, A., & Ahlquist, R. (2003). Whose culture? The colonising school and the miseducation of Indigenous children. *Journal of Postcolonial Education, 2*(2), 15–35; Guenther, J., et al. (2017). Decolonising colonial education researchers in 'near remote' parts of Australia. In G. Vass, J. Maxwell, S. Rudolph, & K. Gulson (Eds.), *The relationality of race in education research* (pp. 108–120). Routledge; O'Donoghue, T. (2009). Colonialism, education and social change in the British Empire: The cases of Australia, Papua New Guinea, and Ireland. *Paedagogica Historica, 45*(6), 787–800; Brown, L. (2019). Indigenous young people, disadvantage and the violence of settler colonial education policy and curriculum. *Journal of Sociology, 55*(1), 54–71.
3. Barry, A. (2016). 'Equal to children of European origin': Educability and the civilising mission in early colonial Australia. *History Australia, 5*(2), 41.1–41.16.
4. Bowels, S. (1978). Capitalist development and education structure. *World Development, 6*, 783–796.
5. Soysal, Y., & Strang, D. (1989). Construction of the first mass education systems in nineteenth-century Europe. *Sociology of Education, 62*(4), 277–288.
6. Ibid.
7. Blaut, J. (1989). Colonialism and the rise of capitalism. *Science & Society, 53*(3), 260–296.
8. Welch, A. (2006). Aboriginal education as internal colonialism: The schooling of an indigenous minority in Australia. *Comparative Education, 2*, 203–215.
9. In this chapter when referring to First Nations contexts in the Australian continent and adjacent islands a capital 'I' is used. When referring to First Nations contexts globally, a lowercase 'i' has been used.
10. Cahill, R., & Gray, J. (2010). Funding and secondary school choice in Australia: A historical consideration. *Australian Journal of Teacher Education, 35*(1), 121–138; Hagland, T. (2023). *Think tanks in Australia: Policy contributions influence*. Springer.
11. Rowe, E., & Perry, L. (2022). Voluntary school fees in segregated public schools: How selective public schools turbo-charge inequity and funding gaps. *Comparative Education, 58*, 106–123; Thompson, G., Hogan, A., & Rahimi, M. (2019). Private funding in Australian public schools: A problem of equity. *The Australian Education Researcher, 46*, 893–910.
12. Rubin, D., & Kazanjian, C. (2011). "Just another brick in the wall": Standardization and the devaluing of education. *Journal of Curriculum and Instruction, 5*(2), 94–108.
13. Sriprakash, A., Rudolph, S., & Gerrard, J. (2022). *Learning whiteness: Education and the settler colonial state*. Pluto Press.
14. Howard, J. (2021). *Rethinking higher education: Towards a diversified system for the 21st century*. Howard Partners.

15 Duffy, C. (2020). *University fees to be overhauled, some course costs to be doubled as domestic student places boosted*. Australian Broadcasting Corporation. https://www.abc.net.au/news/2020-06-19/university-fees-tertiary-education-overhaul-course-costs/12367742
16 Publishers Association. (2018). *The Publishers Association launches a blueprint for UK publishing*. https://www.publishers.org.uk/the-pa-launches-a-blueprint-for-uk-publishing/
17 Ibid.
18 Moreton-Robinson, A. (2004). Whiteness, epistemology and Indigenous representation. In A. Moreton-Robinson (Ed.), *Whitening race: Essays in social and cultural criticism* (pp. 75–88). Aboriginal Studies Press.
19 Mohamed, L. (2021). Publishing must decolonise. *The Conduit*. https://www.theconduit.com/insights/arts-culture/publishing-must-decolonise/#:~:text=Decolonising%20the%20industry%20requires%20more,our%E2%80%9D%20audience%20where%20they%20live
20 Gani, J. & Marshall, J. (2022). The impact of colonialism on policy and knowledge production in International Relations. *International Affairs, 98*(1), 5–22. https://doi.org/10.1093/ia/iiab226
21 Mohamed, Publishing must decolonise.
22 Publishers Association. (2023). *The UK publishing workforce: Diversity, inclusion and belonging in 2022*. https://www.publishers.org.uk/publications/the-uk-publishing-workforce-diversity-inclusion-and-belonging-in-2022/
23 Mohamed, Publishing must decolonise.
24 Stanner, *After the dreaming*.
25 Ibid., pp. 24–25.
26 Stastny, A. (2019). The fabrication of settler legitimacy: Managing colonal violence and wars in Australian school textbooks from the 1870s to present. *Postcolonial Studies, 22*(3), 262–283. https://doi.org/10.1080/13688790.2019.1655184
27 Heffernan, A., Bright, D., Kim, M., & Maygar, B. (2022). 'I cannot sustain the workload and the emotional toll': Reasons behind Australian teachers' intentions to leave the profession. *Australian Journal of Education, 66*(2), 196–209.
28 Australian Institute for Teaching and School Leadership [AITSL]. (2017). *Professional standards for teachers*. https://www.aitsl.edu.au/standards
29 Australian Curriculum, Assessment, and Reporting Authority [ACARA]. (2023). *Understand this cross-curriculum priority*. https://v9.australiancurriculum.edu.au/teacher-resources/understand-this-cross-curriculum-priority/aboriginal-and-torres-strait-islander-histories-and-cultures
30 Harrison, N., & Greenfield, M. (2010). Relationship to place: Positioning Aboriginal knowledge and perspectives in classroom pedagogies. *Critical Studies in Education, 52*(1), 50–68.
31 Bowen, S., & Driscoll, B. (2022). *Australian publishing industry workforce survey on diversity and inclusion*. Australian Publishers Association and The University of Melbourne.
32 Ibid.
33 Fanon, F. (1963). *The wretched of the earth*. C. Farrington (Trans.). Grove Press.
34 Ibid.
35 Ibid.
36 Tuck, E., & Yang, K. (2012). Decolonization is not a metaphor. *Decolonization: Indigeniety, Education & Society, 1*(1), 1–40.
37 Connor, J. (2005). *The Australian Frontier Wars 1788–1838*. University of New South Wales Press.

38 Ali, M. (2017). Un-mapping gay imperialism: A postcolonial approach to sexual orientation-based development. *Reconsidering Development, 5*(1), 1–20.
39 Spencer-Wood, S. (2016). Feminist theorizing of patriarchal colonialism, power dynamics, and social agency materialised in colonial institutions. *International Journal of Historical Archaeology, 20*(3), 477–491.
40 Lynch, K., & O'Neill, C. (1994). The colonisation of social class in education. *The British Journal of Sociology of Education, 15*(3), 307–324.
41 Ineese-Nash, N. (2020). Disability as a colonial construct: The missing discourse of culture in conceptualizations of disabled Indigenous children. *Canadian Journal of Disability Studies, 9*(3), 25–51.
42 Blume, A. (2022). Colonial-isms and COVID-19. In A. Blume (Ed.), *Colonialism and the COVID-19 pandemic: Perspectives from indigenous psychology* (pp. 57–86). Springer.
43 Lawless, B., Fricker, A., Green, D., O'Brien, P., Shephard, N., Elliott, S., & Van Weringh, I. (2021). *Good humanities: History 10*. Matilda Publishing.
44 Hughes, R. & Fricker, A. (2024). Decolonising practice in teacher education in Australia: Reflections of shared leadership. *Australian Educational Researcher.* https://doi.org/10.1007/s13384-023-00670-4
45 Ibid.
46 Ibid.
47 Ibid.
48 Smith, L. (2012). *Decolonising methodologies: Research and indigenous peoples* (2nd ed.). Zed Books.
49 Fricker, A. (2017). Indigenous perspectives: Controversy in the history classroom? *Agora, 52*(4), 4–12.
50 Lawless, et al., *Good humanities: History 10*.
51 ACARA. (2017). *History (Version 8.4)*. 08/08/23. https://www.australiancurriculum.edu.au/f-10-curriculum/humanities-and-social-sciences/history/?year=12321&strand=Historical+Knowledge+and+Understanding&strand=Historical+Skills&capability=ignore&capability=Literacy&capability=Numeracy&capability=Information+and+Communication+Technology+%28ICT%29+Capability&capability=Critical+and+Creative+Thinking&capability=Personal+and+Social+Capability&capability=Ethical+Understanding&capability=Intercultural+Understanding&priority=ignore&priority=Aboriginal+and+Torres+Strait+Islander+Histories+and+Cultures&priority=Asia+and+Australia%E2%80%99s+Engagement+with+Asia&priority=Sustainability&elaborations=true&elaborations=false&scotterms=false&isFirstPageLoad=false
52 Delgado, R. & Stefancic, J. (2023). *Critical race theory: An introduction* (4th ed.). New York University Press.
53 Foley, G. (2022). *The Koorie history website*. http://www.kooriweb.org/foley/indexb.html
54 Ibid.
55 Lawless, et al., *Good humanities: History 10*.
56 Fricker., Indigenous perspectives.
57 Madsen, B., Perkins, R., & Shay, M. (2021). Critical selection of curriculum materials: Tools for educators. In M. Shay & R. Oliver (Eds.), *Indigenous education in Australia: Learning and teaching for deadly futures* (pp. 133–147). Routledge.
58 Ibid.
59 Fricker, Indigenous perspectives.

Chapter 5

Positionality

The foundational threshold concept for decolonising practices

Sara Weuffen

Author positioning and prelude

As a non-Indigenous woman of German, Scottish, and Welsh descent, I write on this topic as a comrade with a lived experience of working through the almost invisible conditioning of settler-colonialism on my learning and teaching practices. Growing up on Gundijtmara Country, I never learnt during my education, or from the Warrnambool community, the strong and present cultural heritage of Gundijtmara Peoples, particularly in sports and military endeavours. Only since living on Wadawurrung Country in Ballarat have I come to learn more about First Nations Peoples and cultures on the Australian continent through university education, Traditional Custodians/Owners teachings, and employment as a teacher-researcher in this field.

The information presented in this chapter is an accumulation of learnings, experiences, observations, and interactions of study and work in First Nations studies. Since first being exposed to the veracity of First Nations presence and activism documented in European records since contact in my undergraduate education studies (2010), I have sought to unpack the reasons why I didn't learn much—if anything at all—about First Nations Peoples on the Australian continent beyond tokenistic representations. I have also sought to unpack why non-Indigenous people in the system (students and teachers) have scarily had the same experiences for decades, despite a plethora of reports, interventions, policies, regulations, and curriculum changes.[1]

In my work over the past 13 years, I have observed an almost disabling reluctance and hesitation by non-Indigenous teachers to step into their unknowingness around First Nations studies. This is not to say that non-white and/or First Nations Peoples have not had similar experiences. However, as a non-Indigenous woman, I have written this chapter from a situated standpoint to focus on the challenges faced by, opportunities offered, and essential need for non-Indigenous teachers to unpack their positionality and interrogate settler-colonial ideologies that challenge an operationalised status quo in Australian education discourses. This is because First Nations voices and perspectives continue to remain largely ignored, relegated to the margins, or outright silenced in Australian education.² While this chapter is concerned with the discipline of History, such limited pedagogical practices are reported to permeate across all disciplines.³ It is plausible, then, to postulate that such fear-based practices are an extension of contestation around Australian History, which has been a consistent theme for the 'history wars' and *hyper nationalism* debates across the States and Territories for decades.⁴

To combat fear-based limiting pedagogies, I proposed the notion of critical self-reflection of non-Indigenous positionality.⁵ In recent years, scholars⁶ have agreed that critical positionality is a foundational skill beneficial for non-Indigenous teachers to undertake because it constantly "challenges deep exploration and understanding of the underlying assumptions, values, and beliefs that shape"⁷ engagement with First Nations Peoples and perspectives. I argue that attempts to decolonise pedagogy without self-awareness is one of the main reasons why epistemic inertia and tokenistic practices persist in Australian schooling. Therefore, I offer my theorising of positionality as the first stepping stone for non-Indigenous teachers in identifying, naming, addressing, and developing more nuanced decolonising teaching practices.

The persistence of tokenistic teaching

As a means of replacing various state- and territory-based curricula, in 2011, the national History curriculum marked a distinctive moment in the federal government's desire to establish an officially sanctioned version of Australia's nation-making story. The curriculum was conceptualised originally because there were strong concerns that the next generation of Australian citizens was not receiving an equitable understanding of the key moments and people in history that underpinned the *fair go for all* and *pioneering spirit* of *early* Australian culture.⁸ Yet, in this curriculum, and in many previous state-and-territory versions, First Nations perspectives were largely *othered*, relegated to the margins, or silenced.⁹ It is perhaps no surprise then that Moodie and colleagues¹⁰ reported that more than half the Australian population in 2019 had low to nil level of knowledge about First Nations histories. This is interesting given that 80% of that same population believe that First Nations perspectives ought to be a compulsory part of schooling.¹¹ While it is beyond the scope of this chapter to delve into the genealogy of the national curriculum and consistent debates surrounding it, this point is raised to highlight the contentious socio-political nature of Australia's History curriculum even when compared to other discipline areas.

As there are no mandated reporting requirements detailing the degree to which First Nations perspectives and content are included in curricula and student learning activities, such pedagogies depend entirely on the willingness, confidence, and commitment of individual teachers.¹² Furthermore, despite the authoritative nature of the national curriculum, it is ultimately schools and teachers who are held accountable for deciding what content is delivered to students.[13] Such precarious responsibility is one of the root problems reported to be associated with tokenistic, stereotypical, or absent representations of First Nations Peoples and cultures.[14] Several factors have been argued to play a role, including the reality that over 95% of teachers employed in Australian secondary schools identify as non-Indigenous and the lack of critical unpacking of First Nations perspectives presented across education journeys (early childhood through to initial teacher education), in resources, and within professional development.[15] This was exemplified in a systematic review of 27 years of education literature, where Moodie and colleagues[16] highlighted that racist and whitewashed pedagogies have been inextricably interwoven throughout historical nation-making narratives which underpin the pervasive western-centric and settler-colonial educational discourses.

As First Nations perspectives have increasingly been integrated across schooling via the cross-curriculum priority area, research has indicated strongly that non-Indigenous teachers are frequently caught up in a professional unknowingness of how to do this effectively and responsively.[17] Critically conceptualised in conjunction with colleagues as *epistemic inertia*,[18] there seems to be fear associated with misrepresenting cultural information, saying the wrong thing, offending someone, or being overwhelmed paradoxically by the lack of/conflicting information/plethora of content available. This leads to a perception that it is much easier and more comfortable to simply do nothing, stick with what has been taught historically, or employ ready-to-use resources that have been developed without context to the First Nations Country upon which learning is taking place.[19] This is particularly the case with history teaching because historical discourses have been used consistently as socio-political weapons for mobilising dominance and difference along the lines of nationality, social class, and race. In Australia, while there has been an official political apology for the substantial negative impacts on First Nations Peoples and cultures as a result of the western imperialistic governing structures, and a strategy of reconciliation touted to address some wrongs, many non-Indigenous teachers continue to experience epistemic inertia in their everyday practice.

Where First Nations perspectives are integrated into curricula, pedagogy, and student learning, it is often predicated on a logical association to the knowledge, skills, and/or assessments associated with specific disciplines.[20] A plethora of recommendations have been proposed about ways in which history teaching may pivot towards more culturally inclusive, responsive, and nourishing representations, including increased frequency of professional development opportunities, more inclusive and trustworthy resources, and revised curriculum to make First Nations perspectives more present.[21] Yet, the ongoing prevalence of tokenism and/or pedagogical avoidance highlights that current recommendations and processes are not adequate for developing sustained intercultural intelligence or implementing truth-telling approaches.[22] The lack of such practices reinforces the status quo of uncritical pedagogy, which "negates commitment to developing knowledge, [and] avoiding any collective action by non-Indigenous organisations, governments, and policies to take responsibility and/or lead action on more culturally inclusive education for redirection towards Indigenous-led pedagogy."[23] As Lowe and colleagues[24] argue, this only maintains "the smoke and mirrors of reconciliation." The argument is put forth that current failures to transform teaching practice reside in the reality that the complex socio-cultural challenges underpinning cross-cultural studies in Australia are not examined, critiqued, or embodied on a personal level.[25]

In the remainder of this chapter, I unpack the notion of threshold concepts and their value in expanding how decolonial teaching practices in Australian history may be operationalised. From there, I propose why critical self-reflection of positionality should be considered the foundational threshold concept for non-Indigenous teachers seeking to decolonise their practice. Underpinning this concept are two meta-questions that I consider essential to reflective positionality. This is because they assist in illuminating the core messages about non-Indigeneity and First Nationhood that have been developed and (re)enforced since contact under a settler-colonial ideological regime. As this book aims to move beyond academic posturing, I then propose a series of sub-questions that seek to explore the ontological (ways of being), axiological (values and beliefs), and epistemological (views of knowledge) roots of positionality contained in these two meta-questions. The aim in doing so is to identify teaching processes that strive to move beyond inertia or tokenism to develop relationally responsive spaces for conceding deficits in knowledge of First Nations Peoples and perspectives and welcoming new learning to fill this void.

Threshold concepts and decolonial teaching practices

It has become evident in recent years that once forms of knowledge are learnt, they cannot be unlearnt, but they can be ignored. The transformation and evolution occurring from this process is known as threshold concepts.[26] Threshold concepts are akin to conceptual gateways of knowledge. They are transformative, irreversible, integrative, bounded, discursive, reconstructive, troublesome, and liminal; once learnt, they elevate a person to new ways of thinking and being.[27] In the process of gaining new knowledge, individuals are considered to have grasped a threshold concept when learning troubles and transforms their current understanding of the world to a point where thinking and acting according to former comprehension has been altered. For example, when the pedagogical skill of scaffolding[28] is learnt in initial teacher education, this practice may come to underpin ways of thinking about, supporting, and assessing student learning. But, as agentic individuals, while teachers may understand this pedagogical practice exists and its value to education, they can choose not to adopt it based on their perceived value to student learning. However, once a threshold concept is grasped, it does not mean the work is done. Rather, they should be considered as avenues that may "lead to transformed thought [and ongoing] transfiguration of identity and extended discourse[s]."[29]

Threshold concepts in decolonial teaching require identifying and unpacking racist discourses that have been cemented in the core values and beliefs of the dominant society over time.[30] As will be explained in the next section, to grasp the threshold concept of positionality in relation to teaching First Nations presence in History, it is valuable to understand better the construct of race as influencing ways of thinking and relating to others—namely, the perception that culture is something possessed by *others* of a different race, a perception which "inadvertently reinforces status differences."[31] Decolonial theory is a process of active epistemic critique of subject positioning and subjectivity construction that exposes power-knowledge relations which have been couched with settler-colonial ideologies.[32] In other words, it is a critical process where individuals unpack how they have been categorised (socially, economically, relationally, etc.) in ways that have been informed by a settler-colonialist mindset. Decolonial theory is actively focused on tackling the perceived and unquestioned superiority of western ways of being, thinking, and doing. As Wilson and Yellow Bird[33] state, it is the "intelligent, calculated, and active resistance to the forces of colonialism that perpetuate the subjugation and/or exploitation of our [First Nations] minds, bodies, and lands." Both First Nations and non-Indigenous people may take up decolonial theory to liberate their agency, "militantly confront, and [challenge] the devastating consequences of internalised racism"[34] in order to comprehend that "knowledge is represented and reproduced through methodological structures that continue to colonise other knowledges, and subvert the voice of Indigenous peoples."[35]

As decolonial theory gained momentum during the late 2000s, the role of non-Indigenous people in First Nations spaces began to emerge more prominently. At this time, a strong argument was presented that decolonial work cannot happen from within the framework in which colonisation has/continues to occur.[36] In the case of positionality, this is because the understanding of non-Indigenous identity and perspectives is informed largely by settler-colonial onto-epistemologies and normalised by hegemonic structures which are devoid of any cultural/racial positioning in a detached and scientific manner.[37] In other words, non-Indigeneity is framed heavily by western ways of being, knowing, and doing so that westernisation becomes the hidden norm to which others are viewed, judged, and validated. Hughes and Fricker[38] argue that to engage in decoloniality, individuals need to adopt a "consciousness that considers the process, seeks to transform reality, and provoke social change." Because decolonial work seeks to challenge the primacy of settler-coloniality, responsibility for undertaking this work should fall "primarily [to] non-Indigenous people in this space"[39] because there is a need to "emancipate colonised peoples and reinstate Indigenous world views"[40] so that truth-telling in Australian education can happen.

In the recent *Closing the Gap* report,[41] the Australian government stated that well-trained, skilled, and knowledgeable teachers are essential to contemporary education endeavours and that further research is needed to examine critically how these may be developed for impactful success-orientated outcomes. Yet, the question remains as to how such skills may be developed if never learnt throughout the typical education journey and if professional pedagogies that reflect and reinforce western schooling practices are normalised. This is why I argue that threshold concepts may function as gateways by which non-Indigenous teachers may begin to decolonise practice, acknowledge fears associated with epistemic inertia, explore the conditions which may be impacting inaction, and begin developing ways of working with First Nations Peoples and perspectives in a more culturally nourishing and responsive manner.[42]

Positionality: Critical self-reflective work

Arguably, a critical underpinning of any reflexive work involving others starts with the self.[43] This is because an informed understanding of the factors that influence one's onto-epistemological stance is laid open for investigation.[44] The relational nature of personal characterisation means that comprehension the self is communicatively and discursively constructed with others and the "broader social and cultural contexts with its changing institutional norms, practices, beliefs, and discourses."[45] That is, by understanding how we have been influenced by our experiences, the values and beliefs we hold, and the views we have about particular knowledge, we become more perceptive to how others may be influenced by their own experiences, values and beliefs, and education. Armed with this knowledge, relational interactions lean towards being more sympathetic of different viewpoints and better attuned to working with differences rather than resisting them.

For non-Indigenous teachers who have been raised within the Australian education system, they are caught up in an indoctrination process that has been operationalised to a point where pedagogical practices become inextricably aligned to a particular settler-colonial ideology without them even knowing it.[46] Or, in other words, due to their own education journeys and training, there is a conditioning process to thinking and doing education according to western ideologies. The outcome of such conditioning is observed in the seemingly harmless expressions of support for First Nations Peoples and cultures in statements such as "I don't see colour," or "we should all be treated equal," or in declarations of cultural identity that are moves towards innocence such as "I was born here, so I am Indigenous too," or "I'm Australian, I have no culture." Such statements possess an assumptive working order, whether acknowledged or not, that Eurocentricity (or ancestry thereof) comes with it an assumed authority and superiority in cultural relations.[47] Under this regime, the settler-colonial order of things validates and legitimates failure to include First Nations perspectives in curriculum, pedagogy, and learning, on the basis that (a) this work is too complex or sensitive, and/or (b) the power of the privileged position afforded to non-Indigeneity is a legitimate excuse for inaction.[48]

Since the 2000s, discussions around non-Indigenous positioning and associated notions of resistance began to be addressed in the literature.[49] Speaking from the tertiary space, Mackinlay and Barney[50] discussed unpacking resistance to their non-Indigenous positioning in ways that were vigilant to not "re-centre whiteness, resettle theories, or extend innocence to the pre-existing discourses." Similarly, Castejon's[51] work sought to question "whether those of us who are non-Indigenous academics looking at Indigenous issues are using our research as part of our unconscious quest for identity?" Smith[52] proposed that while non-Indigenous people are "capable of being anti-identity or post identity, [they] understand identity only in relation to brown subjects." Nakata argued that because of "the complexities [that] revolve around the positioning effects of knowledges,"[53] there has been an inextricably tying of non-Indigenous identity to hierarchical superiority in the Australian socio-political landscape. Furthermore, Nakata[54] argued that the historical and ongoing effects of settler-colonialism have constituted a racial dichotomy where First Nations Peoples and customs are always in contrast to the non-Indigenous position space. Yet, Thornley[55] suggested that by "turning the gaze onto the interior space of [her] own colonised-colonising mind, the invisibility of whiteness [that was] laid down so deep in unconscious [was exposed]." Such scholarship highlights that there continues to be an ongoing theorisation and questioning of what it means to be a non-Indigenous person engaging with First Nations Peoples and matters in ways that identify and speak back to the apparent and assumed superiority of whiteness.

As non-Indigenous teachers attempt to decolonise settler-colonial principles embedded within their positionality, they become caught up in a "centripetal force of dominant ideology [where] existing oppressive colonial structures"[56] condition [re]perpetuation. For decolonial work to be more successful, a "humbling of the self"[57] must occur so that the "proliferation of theories, knowledge, ideas, and analyses that speak to a 'beyond settler colonialism' [which can seem] unknowable"[58] is laid open for investigation. As Yunkaporta and Shillingsworth[59] argue, decolonial positionality work requires recognition of the "destructive impact that colonisation and globalisation [has had] on human existence,"[60] and they suggest a way forward lies in a relationally responsive standpoint which explores the ontologies, axiologies, epistemologies, and methodologies held by individuals. Fundamentally, for decolonial work by non-Indigenous people to be most effective, it requires a willingness to be vulnerable, an understanding that the process may feel uncomfortable, and courage to tackle some unassumed norms and taken-for-granted privileges associated with the dominance of non-Indigeneity within Australian society.

Who am I, and where do I come from?

The first step for non-Indigenous teachers seeking to move towards deeper and more meaningful understanding and engagement of First Nations Peoples and perspectives in curriculum and pedagogy begins with a critical self-reflexive decolonising of positioning.⁶¹ It should not be a performative act to be done once and considered complete. Rather, it is most effective as an ongoing understanding of oneself in relation to others that deepens over time as the complexity of knowledge-making and relationality in settler-colonial systems is consistently interrogated.⁶² At the core of this work is a necessity for rethinking historical socio-cultural relations between the non-Indigenous position and others.⁶³ Based on my work and collegial interactions in the field, along with a critical review of the literature, the place to being starts with questioning *Who am I?* and *Where do I come from?* This is because these two questions tackle the ontological, axiological, and epistemological underpinnings of identity.⁶⁴ In other words, these questions 'invoke' a critical self-review of how we introduce, describe, and understand ourselves based on our views of the world, the values and beliefs we hold, and the ways in which we understand and value knowledge.

It is vital to comprehend that critical self-reflection of non-Indigeneity in the Australian history space cannot happen without interrogating the socio-colonial-political conditioning effects of imperialism. Many non-Indigenous teachers of European descent have been caught up in processes of indoctrination to settler-colonial ideologies and western ways of thinking and being throughout their lives.⁶⁵ This process begins at birth and becomes more embedded throughout one's lifespan with consistent exposure to ancestral histories, media stories, and formal education, as well as participation in cultural activities, processes of teaching and learning, and social norms, to name a few.⁶⁶ While not a completely passive process, non-Indigenous teachers continue to be "the product of the process of colonization"⁶⁷ until such a time as the development of self-reflective critical consciousness emerges.⁶⁸ Scholars suggest that any attempts by non-Indigenous people to identify and/or position themselves without interrogating western knowledge systems only continue to reconstitute the assumed authority of a white settler-colonial narrative.⁶⁹

Beyond an arbitrary and performative cognitive undertaking, the questions of *Who am I?* and *Where do I come from?* have a cultural basis, yet different connotations, for both First Nations and non-Indigenous people. First Nations Peoples' positioning is dependent on cultural relationality first, whereas non-Indigenous positioning tends to be predicated on Marxist principles.⁷⁰,⁷¹ Developing a relationally responsive standpoint and reflexive understanding of who we are and where we come from enables non-Indigenous History teachers to start comprehending how their perception of the world, and thus interpretation of curriculum, is influenced by "what we know, how we know it, and what we do with that knowledge."⁷²

Questioning *Who am I?* delves into the onto-axiological underpinnings of positionality. That is, how we see the world, operate within it, and the values and beliefs we consider important. It encourages a journey of seeking connection with others and forms the foundation for respectful interaction.⁷³ This is particularly important for non-Indigenous History teachers as a westernised view of the world, couched within Christian beliefs, has been privileged in Australian society and historical investigations of the past. For example, government-sanctioned public holidays revolve around religiously significant moments for Christianity—Easter and Christmas[74]—and socio-cultural moments that define non-Indigenous notions of *Australianness*–Australia Day,[75] ANZAC Day,[76] and Labour Day.[77] In addition, socially acceptable behaviours revolve around Christian values[78]–hope, integrity, respect, morality, sacrifice, freedom, justice—and are considered the unequivocable norms of how citizens should/not behave in modern Australian society; any transgressions against these are seen as distasteful and/or legislated as illegal. In mainstream society, First Nations beliefs and values, while seemingly respected and acknowledged, for example, Acknowledgement of Country ceremonies,[79] are generally not taken up, and thus positioned as other. For example, only recently have some organisations understood and respected *Sorry Business*[80] as a legitimate form of leave. Generally, the notion of an open-ended time frame for grieving is an alien concept to a westernised society where it is assumed that once a funeral is conducted, citizens should return to work and resume normal duties. As another example, *Dreaming Stories*[81] are often mythologised or infantilised for mass consumption in the non-Indigenous society. Yet, stories associated with Christianity are used as the moral compass for social relations. By questioning the onto-axiological roots of positionality, non-Indigenous teachers can begin to decolonise their practice to examine how a settler-colonial regime manifests throughout society and historical discourses to maintain dichotomies of difference.[82]

The question of *Where do I come from?* requires onto-epistemological interrogations. That is, uncovering how an individual's view of the world may be informed by their beliefs about knowledge and validity. Investigations in this realm of positionality broaden relational respect for others' ways of being, doing, and knowing by reflecting on how knowledge has been constructed and situated within society.[83] This is important because a public-facing desktop review of the Years 7–10 *Australian Curriculum: History* (Version 8.0) highlights a linear timeline inextricably tied to notions of imperialism.[84] Interestingly, while the curriculum presents an account of Australian history, the main narrative focuses on a European way of life with First Nations presence "tolerated so long as it does not disrupt the foundation of the settler-colonialism and advancement narrative in curriculum."[85] The presentation of such knowledge is based on western historical roots of empirical scientific knowledge and categorised according to disciplines.[86] Known as disciplinarity, it is a process that determines to what extent content can be included and excluded, what thoughts and skills are considered normal practice within the discipline, and what type of knowledge is, and should be, given precedence over others.[87] In conjunction with critical self-review, by questioning the onto-epistemological roots of knowledge, and *othering* of First Nations knowledges, gateways for finding and celebrating interpersonal connections beyond a simplistic duality of "the ships of England [compared to] the shores [and waters] of Australia"[88] are opened.

Ideas and strategies for critiquing positionality

In line with the innovative aim of this book to provide teachers with real-world recommendations and strategies for enhancing pedagogies and learning practices to foreground applied decolonising approaches, the following is an initial list of questions for framing a critical pursuit of non-Indigenous positionality. It is not an exhaustive list and remains a work in progress. The questions have been proposed based on my own lived experience as a cis-gendered, able-bodied, regionally raised and located, survivor of family violence, first in family to receive a tertiary degree, now middle socio-economic status, and precariously contracted non-Indigenous woman with European ancestry, collegial interactions, and review of the literature[89] over the past 13 years.

Given the intersectional and evolving nature of identity linked to knowledges and experiences,[90] this list should be considered a starting point for interrogating the ontological, axiological, and epistemological underpinnings of non-Indigenous positionality. As Hughes and Fricker[91] argue, "[d]ecolonising work and practice[s] for teachers is not only essential from policy perspectives but likely, requires a personal project," aka critical self-reflection. Therefore, it is recommended that these questions be undertaken as an iterative professional learning exercise of a private reflective nature so that teachers of Australian History remain aware of the ideologies being delivered in the curriculum while maintaining a constant awareness of one's "role within the [profession] but also within society."[92] The list is offered as a means of better understanding "what we know, how we know it, and what we do with that knowledge"[93] in service of facilitating relationally responsive standpoints and uncovering how settler-colonial ideologies position First Nations Peoples and perspectives in contrast and deficit in historical studies of societies on the Australian continent.

Who am I?—ontology, axiology

- What are the historical origins and meanings of my name?
- Who do I consider family (biological and/or social)?
- How do I identify myself in relation to race, gender, sexuality, and language?
- How would I describe my cultural identity?
- How would a significant person in my life introduce me to someone I didn't know?
- What are my hobbies and interests, and how did they emerge?
- What are my religious/spiritual beliefs, and how have they been informed?
- What are my political views and core values underpinning this alignment?
- What are my views about what makes a good person and society?
- What am I good at and why?

Where do I come from?—ontology, epistemology

- Where was I born (First Nations Country and Australian geographical location)?
- What is the cultural heritage of my ancestors and their stories of migration?
- What are my family's hospitality practices (i.e., shoes off at the door), and where have they emerged from?
- What language was spoken (a) at home growing up, (b) in the community, and (c) learnt as a language other than English at school (if any)?
- Who was visible in the community in which I grew up? What roles did my family/I play in the community?
- What type of schooling did I receive growing up (private and/or public), and what was my favourite subject at school and why?
- How would I describe my socio-economic upbringing, and what are the things I had/did not have that other people around me appeared to have/not have?
- How would I define success academically, socially, relationally, and economically?

Using positionality to address epistemic inertia

Self-reflection as a process to articulating positionality about *Who am I?* and *Where do I come from?* requires critical exploration and analysis of one's "location in the geopolitics of knowledge production [but also] its implications."[94] While knowledge underpins threshold concepts, positionality work should be considered an ongoing practice where oscillation and regression may occur but where further knowledge deepens transformative understandings.[95] Given that this book aims to shift current discussions beyond the *us versus them* binary dichotomy of the 'history wars,' when non-Indigenous History teachers come to understand better *Who am I?* and *Where do I come from?*, they make a move towards a relationally responsive space for conceding deficits in knowledge about First Nations Peoples and perspectives, and welcoming new learnings to fill this void.[96] While the task of exploring and understanding positionality may be viewed as a trivial and politically correct exploit that is reflective of gross cultural sensitives in the contemporary Australian socio-political landscape, it is critical to unpacking how westernised ways of being and thinking have influenced non-Indigenous history teachers alignment with a prescribed racially superior settler-colonial mindset, as presented in the curriculum, whether they are aware of it or not.[97] Without a systematic tackling of epistemic inertia and better understanding of positionality, First Nations Peoples will continue to do a disproportionate amount of heavy lifting in the Australian education space and in efforts to decolonise the Eurocentric (re)telling of history on the Australian continent, thus leaving the largely non-Indigenous teaching workforce as functionally racially illiterate.[98] Furthermore, without a pushing back against racial privileging elicited in pedagogical and curriculum work, First Nations presence will continue to be presented in deficit and/or used to prop up the superiority of European civilisation on the Australian continent. While decolonising positionality is not isolated to History teachers solely—there exist opportunities for considering how western ways of being, knowing, and doing within other discipline areas are constructed and influence the degree to which integration of First Nations perspectives is seen as valid, logical, or aligned—the investigative foundational knowledge and skills associated with history studies positions History teachers as potential leaders of decolonising pedagogies in their schools. Having said this, there exist opportunities for future studies to examine the reality of executing decolonial positionality work with students. The ultimate provocation of this chapter is that when non-Indigenous History teachers are willing to be vulnerable and interrogate the roots of epistemic inertia, the foundation for integrating First Nations perspectives in curricula in relational and authentic ways begins to be poured.[99]

Notes

1 Guenther, J., Harrison, N., & Burgess, C. (2019). Special issue. Aboriginal voices: Systematic reviews of Indigenous education. *Australian Educational Researcher*, 46(1), 207–21. https://doi.org/10.1007/s13384-019-00316-4; Weuffen, S., Lowe, K., & Burgess, K. (2023). Identity matters: Aboriginal educational sovereignty and futurity pushing back against the logic of elimination. *Australian Educational Researcher*, 50(1), 1–10. https://doi.org/10.1007/s13384-023-00608-w
2 Hughes, R., & Fricker, A. (2024). Decolonising practice in teacher education in Australia. Australian Educational Researcher. Published online 02 Jan 2024 pp. 1-19. https://doi.org/10.1007/s13384-023-00670-4; Lowe, K., & Weuffen, S. (2023). "You get to 'feel' your culture": Aboriginal students speaking back to deficit discourses in Australian schooling. *Australian Educational Researcher*, 50(1), 33–53. https://doi.org/10.1007/s13384-022-00598-1
3 Guenther, et al., Special issue; Moodie, N., Lowe, K., Dixon, R., & Trimmer, K. (2023). *Assessing the evidence in Indigenous education research: Implications for policy and practice*. Palgrave MacMillian. https://doi.org/10.1007/978-3-031-14306-9
4 Clark, A. (2009). Teaching the nation's story: Comparing public debates and classroom perspectives on history education in Australia and Canada. *Journal of Curriculum Studies*, 41(6), 745–762. https://doi.org/10.1080/00220270903139635; Weuffen, S. (2018). Surveying the landscape five years on: An examination of how teachers, and the teaching of Australia's shared-history is constructed within Australian Academic literature. *Teaching and Teacher Education*, 78(1), 117–124. https://doi.org/10.1016/j.tate.2018.11.010
5 Weuffen, S. (2017). *Your stories, my stories, our stories: Power/knowledge relations and Koorie perspectives in discourses of Australian History education*. [Unpublished dissertation]. Federation University Australia. http://researchonline.federation.edu.au/vital/access/HandleResolver/1959.17/160409
6 Brookfield, S. (2014). Teaching our own racism: Incorporating personal narratives of whiteness into anti-racist practice. *Adult Learning*, 25(3), 89–95. https://doi.org/10.1177/1045159514534189; Broughton, A. (2019). *Evidence-based approaches to becoming a culturally responsive educator: Emerging research and*

opportunities. Hershey USA: Information Science Reference; Castell, E., Bullen, J., Garvey, D., & Jones, N. (2018). Critical reflexivity in Indigenous and cross-cultural psychology: A decolonial approach to curriculum? *Community Psychology, 62*(3–4), 361–271. https://doi.org/10.1002/ajcp.12291; Hughes & Fricker (2024). Decolonising practice; Proud, A. D., & Morgan, A. (2021). Critical self-reflection: A foundational skill. In S. Oliver & R. Oliver (Eds.), *Indigenous education in Australia* (pp. 38–50). Routledge; Moghli, A., & Kadiwal, L. (2021). Decolonising the curriculum beyond the surge: Conceptualisation, positionality and conduct. *London Review of Education, 19*(1), 1–6. http://doi.org/10.14324/LRE.19.1.23; Thorpe, K. R. (2017). *Narratives of learning at the cultural interface: The influence of Indigenous studies on becoming a teacher*. [Unpublished dissertation]. http://hdl.handle.net/2123/17641; Yunkaporta, T., & Shillingsworth, D. (2020). Relationally responsive standpoint. *Journal of Indigenous Research, 8*(2020), 4. https://doi.org/10.26077/ky71-qt27
7 Proud & Morgan (2021). Critical self-reflection, p. 39.
8 Burgess, C. (2009). What good a national curriculum for Indigenous students. In *Australian Association for Research in Education annual conference: Creating global networks: A capital idea!* Nov 30, 2009, Canberra, ACT; Gilbert, R. (2011). Can history succeed at school? Problems of knowledge in the Australian history curriculum. *Australian Journal of Education, 55*(3), 245–258. https://doi.org/10.1177/000494411105500306; Kennedy, K. (2009). An idea of a national curriculum in Australia: What do Susan Ryan, John Dawkins and Julia Gillard have in common? *Curriculum Perspectives, 29*(1), 1–9. https://doi.org/10.1007/s41297-019-00081-5
9 Ditchburn, G. (2012). A national Australian curriculum: In whose interests? *Asia Pacific Journal of Education, 32*(3), 259–269. https://doi.org/10.1080/02188791.2012.711243; Lowe, K., Moodie, N., & Weuffen, S. (2021). Refusing reconciliation in Indigenous curriculum. In B. Green, P. Roberts, & M. Brennan (Eds.), *Curriculum challenges and opportunities in a changing world: Transnational perspectives in curriculum inquiry* (pp. 71–86). Palgrave Macmillan. https://doi.org/10.1007/978-3-030-61667-0_5
10 Moodie, N. (2019). Learning about knowledge: Threshold concepts for Indigenous studies in education. *The Australian Educational Researcher, 46*(1), 235–749. http://doi.org/10.1007/s13384-019-00309-3
11 Ibid.
12 Anderson, C. (2012). Teacher education, Aboriginal studies and the new national curriculum. *The Australian Journal of Indigenous Education, 41*(1), 40–46. https://doi.org/10.1017/jie.2012.7; Booth, S. (2014). *Teaching Aboriginal curriculum content in Australian high school* [Unpublished dissertation]. Edith Cowan University, Western Australia; Hart, V., Whatman, S., McLaughlin, J., & Sharma-Brymer, V. (2012). Pre-service teachers' pedagogical relationships and experiences of embedding Indigenous Australian knowledge in teaching practicum. *Compare, 42*(5), 703–723. https://doi.org/10.1080/03057925.2012.706480; Maxwell, J. (2013). Teachers, time, staff and money: Committing to community consultation in high schools. *The Australian Journal of Indigenous Education, 41*(2), 120–130. https://doi.org/10.1017/jie.2012.31
13 Lowe et al. (2021). Refusing reconciliation.
14 Burgess, C., Tennent, C., Vass, G., Guenther, J., Lowe, K., & Moodie, K. (2019). A systematic review of pedagogies that support, engage and improve the educational outcomes of Aboriginal students. *Australian Educational Researcher, 46*(1), 297–318. https://doi.org/10.1007/s13384-019-00315-5; Weuffen, S. (2022). 'You'd be surprised how some people probably feel uncomfortable': The

compliance–resistance continuum of planning integrated Australian History curricula. *Teacher Development, 26*(2), 221–239. https://doi.org/10.1080/1366453 0.2022.2027266; Weuffen, S., Maxwell, J., & Lowe, K. (2023). Inclusive, colour-blind, and deficit: Understanding teachers' contradictory views of Aboriginal students' participation in education. *The Australian Educational Researcher, 50*(1), 89–110. https://doi.org/10.1007/s13384-022-00517-4
15 Hughes & Fricker (2024). Decolonising practice; Lowe, K., & Galstaun, V. (2020). Ethical challenges: The possibility of authentic teaching encounters with Indigenous cross-curriculum content? *Curriculum Perspectives, 40*(1), 93–98. https://doi.org/10.1007/s41297-019-00093-1; Lowe, K., & Yunkaporta, T. (2013). The inclusion of Aboriginal and Torres Strait Islander content in the Australian curriculum: A cultural, cognitive and socio-political evaluation. *Curriculum Perspectives, 33*(1), 1–15. http://acsa.edu.au/pages/images/KLowe_article%20(2).pdf; Weuffen (2018). Surveying the landscape.
16 Moodie, N., Maxwell, J., & Salter, P. (2019). The impact of racism on the schooling experiences of Aboriginal and Torres Strait Islander students: A systematic review. *Australian Educational Researcher, 46*(1), 273–295. https://doi.org/10.1007/s13384-019-00312-8
17 Hart et al. (2012). Pre-service teachers' pedagogical; Maxwell (2013). Teachers, time, staff; Weuffen et al. (2023). Inclusive, colour-blind, and deficit.
18 Epistemic relates to knowledge and ways of knowing, with inertia being a directional force that is resistant to change. Thus, epistemic inertia is a static way of thinking about a topic that invalidates contradictory views which challenge the foundational knowledge that informs thinking about the topic.
19 Weuffen (2022). 'You'd be surprised'; Weuffen, S., Lowe, K., Burgess, C., & Thompson, K. (2023). Sovereign and pseudo-hosts: The politics of hospitality for negotiating culturally nourishing schools. *Australian Educational Researcher, 50*(1), 131–146. https://doi.org/10.1007/s13384-022-00599-0; Weuffen, S., Maxwell, J., & Lowe, K. (2022). Inclusive, colour-blind, and deficit; Weuffen, S., & Willis, K. (2023). The fallacy of cultural inclusion in mainstream education discourses. In S. Weuffen, J. Burke, S. Emmett, M. Plunkett, & A. Groiss-Hunter (Eds.), *Inclusion, equity, diversity, and social justice in education: A critical exploration of the sustainable development goals* (pp. 91–108). Springer. https://doi.org/10.1007/978-981-19-5008-7_7
20 Lowe et al. (2021). Refusing reconciliation; Weuffen, S., Lowe, K., Amazan, R., & Thompson, K. (2024). The need for First Nations narratives: Epistemic inertia and complicating in (re)creating the settler-colonial education state. *Journal of Curriculum Studies. 56*(1), 58–72. https://doi.org/10.1080/00220272.2023.2294723; Weuffen & Willis (2023). The fallacy.
21 Weuffen et al. (2023). Inclusive, colour-blind, and deficit.
22 Lowe et al. (2021). Refusing reconciliation.
23 Ibid., p. 81
24 Ibid.
25 Hughes & Fricker (2024). Decolonising practice; Weuffen & Willis (2023). The fallacy.
26 Moodie, N. (2019). Learning about knowledge; Meyer, J. H. F., & Land, R. (2005). Threshold concepts and troublesome knowledge (2): Epistemological considerations and a conceptual framework for teaching and learning. *Higher Education, 49*(1), 373–388. https://doi.org/10.1007/s10734-004-6779-5; Nahavandi, A. (2016). Threshold concepts and culture-as-meta-context. *Journal of Management Education, 40*(6), 794–816. https://doi.org/10.1177/1052562916655185
27 Moodie (2019). Learning about knowledge.

28 The process of breaking up learning into smaller and sequential chunks of knowledge that are supported with skills to inform students' overall comprehension of concepts.
29 Meyer & Land (2005). Threshold concepts and troublesome, p. 375.
30 Kinefuchi, E., & Orbie, M. P. (2008). Situating oneself in a racialised world: Understanding student reactions to crash through standpoint theory and context-positionality frames. *Journal of International and Intercultural Communication, 1*(1), 70–90. https://doi.org/10.1080/17513050701742909; Moreton-Robinson, A. (2013). Towards an Australian Indigenous women's standpoint theory. *Australian Feminist Studies, 28*(78), 331–347. https://doi.org/10.1080/08164649.2013.876664; Weuffen et al. (2023). The need for First Nations narratives.
31 Nahavandi (2016). Threshold concepts and culture, p. 800.
32 Mackinlay, E., & Barney, K., (2014). Unknown and unknowing possibilities: Transformative learning, social justice, and decolonising pedagogy in Indigenous Australian studies. *Journal of Transformative Education, 12*(1), 54–73. https://doi.org/10.1177/1541344614541170; Tuck, E., & Yang, K. (2012). Decolonisation is not a metaphor. *Decolonization: Indigeneity, Education & Society, 1*(1): 1–40.
33 Wilson, A., & Yellow Bird, M. (2005). Beginning decolonization. In A. Wilson & M. Yellow Bird (Eds.), *For Indigenous eyes only: A decolonization handbook* (pp. 1–8). School of American Research Press. p. 2.
34 hooks, b. (1994). *Outlaw culture: Resisting representations*. Routledge. p. 205.
35 Harrison, N., & Clarke, I. (2022). Decolonising curriculum practice: Developing the Indigenous cultural capability of university graduates. *Higher Education, 83*, 183–197. p. 184. https://doi.org/10.1007/s10734-020-00648-6
36 Hughes & Fricker (2024). Decolonising practice.
37 Aldama, A. J., & Quifionez, N. H. (Eds.). (2002). *Decolonial voices: Chicana and Chicano cultural studies in the 21st century* (1st ed.). Indiana University Press; De Lissovoy, N. (2010). Decolonial pedagogy and the ethics of the global. *Discourse: Studies in the Cultural Politics of Education, 31*(3), 279–293. https://doi.org/10.1080/01596301003786886; Schiwy, F. (2007). Decolonization and the question of subjectivity. *Cultural Studies, 21*(2–3), 271–294. https://doi.org/10.1080/09502380601162555
38 Hughes & Fricker (2024). Decolonising practice, p. 5.
39 Ibid, p. 14.
40 Nakata, M., Nakata, V., Keech, S., & Bolt, R. (2012). Decolonial goals and pedagogies for Indigenous studies. *Decolonization: Indigeneity, Education, and Society, 1*(1), 120–140. p. 132.
41 Australian Government. (2018). *Closing the gap: Prime Minister's report*. Australian Government. https://www.pmc.gov.au/sites/default/files/reports/closing-the-gap-2018/sites/default/files/ctg-report-20183872.pdf?a=1
42 Moodie (2019). Learning about knowledge; Meyer & Land (2005). Threshold concepts and troublesome; Nahavandi (2016). Threshold concepts and culture.
43 Proud & Morgan (2021). Critical self-reflection.
44 Meyer & Land (2005). Threshold concepts and troublesome.
45 Arvaja, M. (2016). Building teacher identity through the process of positioning. *Teaching and Teacher Education, 59*(1), 392–402. p. 393. https://doi.org/10.1016/j.tate.2016.07.024
46 Burgess, C., Bishop, M., & Lowe, K. (2022). Decolonising Indigenous education: The case for cultural mentoring in supporting Indigenous knowledge reproduction. *Discourse: Studies in the Cultural Politics of Education, 43*(1), 1–14. https://doi.org/10.1080/01596306.2020.1774513; Phillips, J., & Lampert, J. (2012).

Introduction: Constituting the space for embedding Indigenous perspectives. In J. Phillips & J. Lampert (Eds.), *Introductory Indigenous studies in education: Reflection and the importance of knowing* (pp. 1–6). Pearson Education Australia; Weuffen et al. (2023). The need for First Nations narratives.
47 Broughton (2019). *Evidence-based approaches.*
48 Weuffen & Willis (2023). The fallacy.
49 Bird-Rose, D. (2001). Aboriginal life and death in Australian settler nationhood. *Aboriginal History, 25*(1), 148–162. https://www.jstor.org/stable/45135476; Mackinlay, E. (2001). Performative pedagogy in teaching and learning Indigenous women's music and dance. *The Australian Journal of Indigenous Education, 29*(1), 12–21. https://doi.org/10.3316/informit.249030642479863; Mackinlay & Barney (2014). Unknown and unknowing possibilities; Somerville, M., Power, K., & De Carteret, P. (2009). *Landscapes and learning: Place studies for a global world* (Transgressions - Cultural Studies and Education). Sense.
50 Mackinlay & Barney (2014). Unknown and unknowing possibilities, p. 58.
51 Castejon, V. (2010). Identity and identification: Aboriginality from the Spanish civil war to the French ghettos. In F. Peters-Little, A. Curthoys, & J. Docker (Eds.), *Passionate histories: Myth, memory and Indigenous Australia* (pp. 219–228). National Library of Australia: ANU E Press and Aboriginal History Incorporated. p. 219.
52 Smith, A. (2014). Native studies at the horizon of death: Theorising ethnographic entrapment and settler self-reflexivity. In A. Smith (Ed.), *Theorising native studies* (pp. 207–234). Duke University Press. p. 218.
53 Nakata, M. (1997). *The cultural interface: An exploration of the intersection of western knowledge systems and Torres Strait Islander positions and experiences.* [Unpublished dissertation'. James Cook University. p. 32.
54 Ibid., p. 288.
55 Thornley, J. (2010). Island home country: Working with Aboriginal protocols in a documentary film about colonisation and growing up white in Tasmania. In F. Peters-Little, A. Curthoys & J. Docker (Eds.), *Passionate histories: Myth, memory and Indigenous Australia* (pp. 247–280). National Library of Australia: ANU E Press and Aboriginal History Incorporated. p. 262.
56 Mackinlay (2001). Performative pedagogy in teaching, pp. 13–15.
57 Meyer & Land (2005). Threshold concepts and troublesome, p. 376.
58 Smith (2014). Native studies, p. 231.
59 Yunkaporta & Shillingsworth (2020). Relationally responsive standpoint.
60 Ibid., p. 9.
61 Weuffen & Willis (2023). The fallacy.
62 Yunkaporta & Shillingsworth (2020). Relationally responsive standpoint.
63 Weuffen et al. (2023). Sovereign and pseudo-hosts.
64 Broughton (2019). Evidence-based approaches; Proud & Morgan (2021). Critical self-reflection; Yunkaporta & Shillingsworth (2020). Relationally responsive standpoint.
65 Weuffen et al. (2023). The need for First Nations narratives.
66 Brookfield (2014). Teaching our own racism; Weuffen et al. (2023). The need for First Nations narratives.
67 De Lissovoy (2010). Decolonial pedagogy, p. 287.
68 Thorpe (2017). *Narratives of learning.*
69 Castell et al. (2018). Critical reflexivity; Smith (2014). Native studies, p. 218.
70 Positioning in relation to class systems (economic, social, occupation, education, etc.).

71 Proud & Morgan (2021). Critical self-reflection; Weuffen (2017). *Your stories*; Yunkaporta & Shillingsworth (2020). Relationally responsive standpoint.
72 Ibid, p. 1.
73 Ibid.
74 From a Christian perspective, the death and resurrection of Jesus (https://www.history.com/topics/holidays/history-of-easter), and the birth of Jesus (respectively) (https://www.history.com/topics/christmas/history-of-christmas).
75 From the perspective of Australian History, the arrival of Captain Cook. However in recent years, Australia Day celebrations have been diluted or cancelled in recognition that this seemingly nationally-significant day does not reflect the reality of events for First Nations peoples, that, it was the beginning of a very long and somewhat successful invasion of sovereign lands (https://www.australiaday.org.au/about).
76 Memorialisation for the courage and bravery of Australian and New Zealand comrades during World War I (https://austria.embassy.gov.au/vien/AnzacDay_background.html).
77 Celebration of the adoption of an eight-hour working day resulting for union socio-economic campaigning (https://www.anmfnt.org.au/resources/may-day-australia#:~:text=Labour%20Day%2C%20also%20known%20as,contributions%20towards%20the%20nation's%20economy)
78 Australian Christians. (2013). *Core Values.* https://australianchristians.org.au/core-values/
79 Acknowledgement of Country is a millennial old cultural practice of First Nations Peoples that has been adopted by non-Indigenous people in Australia as an enactment of reconciliation and recognition of one's guest role on unceded Country (https://www.commonground.org.au/article/acknowledgement-of-country).
80 Sorry business is a mourning period in First Nations communities upon the passing of a family and/or community member (https://www.courts.qld.gov.au/__data/assets/pdf_file/0017/723203/ccq-cultural-competency-guide.pdf)
81 The onto-axiological underpinning of First Nations cultural beliefs and practices (https://www.aboriginal-art-australia.com/aboriginal-art-library/understanding-aboriginal-dreaming-and-the-dreamtime/).
82 De Lissovoy (2010). Decolonial pedagogy; Mackinlay (2001). Performative pedagogy in teaching; Smith (2014). Native studies.
83 Yunkaporta & Shillingsworth (2020). Relationally responsive standpoint.
84 Weuffen, S., & Lowe, K. (2022). Monkey see, Monkey do: Unpacking the practice of pedagogical narratives construction. In *First Nations education symposium: The state of research in First Nations education and the potential to impact national, state/territory and jurisdictional education policy and practice.* University of South Australia. November 25–26.
85 Weuffen et al. (2024). The need for First Nations narratives.
86 Foucault, M. (2004). *Abnormal: Lectures at the college de France 1974–1975* [Les anormaux. Cours au Collège de France 1974–1975. Paris: Seuil, 1999.] (G. Bell Trans.). Picador; Nakata (1997). *The cultural interface*; Weuffen & Willis (2023). The fallacy.
87 Lowe et al. (2021). Refusing reconciliation; Shay, M., Sarra, G., & Lampert, J. (2022). Indigenous education policy, practice and research: Unravelling the tangled web. *The Australian Educational Researcher, 50*(1), 73–88. https://doi.org/10.1007/s13384-022-00581-w; Weuffen et al. (2023). Inclusive, colour-blind, and deficit.
88 Craven, K., & Price, K. (2011). Misconceptions, stereotypes and racism: Let's face the facts. In R. Craven (Ed.), *Teaching Aboriginal studies: A practice resource for primary and secondary teaching* (pp. 42–67). Allen and Unwin. p. 59.

89 Broughton (2019). *Evidence-based approaches*; Proud & Morgan (2021). Critical self-reflection; Weuffen (2017). *Your stories*.
90 Wijeyesinghe, C. L., & Jones, S. R. (2019). Intersectionality, identity, and systems of power and inequality. In D. Mitchell, C. Y. Simmons, & L. A. Greyerbiehl (Eds.), *Intersectionality and higher education: Theory, research, and praxis*. Peter Lang. pp. 9–19.
91 Hughes & Fricker (2024). Decolonising practice.
92 Chambers, D., & Buzinde, C. (2015). Tourism and decolonisation: Locating research and the self. *Annals of Tourism Research*, 51(1), 1–16. http://dx.doi.org/10.1016/j.annals.2014.12.002. p. 13.
93 Yunkaporta & Shillingsworth. (2020). Relationally responsive standpoint, p. 1.
94 Moghli & Kadiwal (2021). Decolonising the curriculum, p. 4.
95 Meyer & Land (2005). Threshold concepts and troublesome.
96 Ibid.
97 Moodie et al. (2023). *Assessing the evidence*; Weuffen (2022). 'You'd be surprised'.
98 Hughes & Fricker (2024). Decolonising practice; Weuffen (2022). 'You'd be surprised'.
99 Weuffen et al. (2023). Sovereign and pseudo-hosts.

Chapter 6

Learning, unlearning, and relearning history in early childhood education

Carolyn Briggs, Karen Anderson, and Ann Slater

Authors' positioning statements

Boon Wurrung Elder N'arwee't Dr. Carolyn Briggs, Karen Anderson, and Ann Slater (non-Indigenous teachers at Balnarring Preschool, Victoria) began their relationship in 2013. During this time, N'arwee't has shared her knowledge with the Balnarring Preschool teaching team including the importance of connecting with nature, which has led to us creating this chapter together. In this chapter, we position N'arwee't as our teacher. It is N'arwee't's wisdom, teaching, and knowledges that provide the context for each section of this chapter.

Dr Carolyn Briggs

I am a descendant of the First Peoples of Melbourne, the Yulukit Weelum clan of the Boon Wurrung. Yalukit Weelum is my home of the river; we are the people of river. I am the great-granddaughter of Louisa Briggs, a Boon Wurrung woman born near Melbourne in the 1830s. I am of First People who inhabited the scared Lands of the people who lived and died before we were here. I have been involved in developing and supporting opportunities for Indigenous youth and strategies for the promotion and maintenance of Boon Wurrung culture and heritage for over 40 years. I am committed to sharing the values and heritage of Melbourne's First Peoples—the Boon Wurrung—and believe that a sense of a shared history of Melbourne is important in uniting the whole community. I completed a bachelor's degree in language and linguistics in the hope of recording my Boon Wurrung language in oral and written form. Later, I taught design anthropology at Swinburne University whilst doing my master's, which then became a PhD in the roles and responsibilities of an Elder. I completed my PhD at RMIT University in 2020, titled "Defining an Elder: Roles and Responsibility of an Elder and How Does an Elder Transmit Knowledge to Urban Youth, Exploring the Different Ways to Transmit Knowledge through Song, Dance, Art, Technology." I was appointed Elder in Residence at RMIT in 2019, In 2021,I was appointed a Professor in research in Design in social context my role also is to teach in Architecture studios and landscape architects and in 2022, I took on the role of Elder in Research at the College of Design & Social Context.

Karen Anderson

I am a non-Indigenous person, and I have been teaching at Balnarring Preschool on Boon Wurrung Country since 1984. Ngarnga Biik (Country learning) is the philosophy that runs through the programme in which I teach. That involves teaching with the beach and bush one day a week all year round. I strongly believe that all children have the right to learn with First Nations Peoples stories of the past and the present.

Ann Slater

I currently live, learn, and teach as an early childhood teacher on the unceded Lands of Boon Wurrung Country. Ten years ago, after many years of teaching I joined the teaching team at Balnarring Preschool with Karen. I have now committed to taking responsibility for reconciliation both personally and with my pedagogical practices.

Introduction

> *Womin djeka Birrangang-ga, Mar-ran biik biik.*
> *Boon Wurrung Nairm derp bordupren uther weelam.*
> N'arwee't Dr Carolyn Briggs, *The Time of Chaos*[1]

This chapter will acknowledge First Nations Peoples stories beyond history to knowing relationality and ways of showing respect within all relationships through learning, unlearning, relearning, and connecting with Country. At Balnarring Preschool, learning with First Nations Peoples teachings is supporting pedagogical understandings beyond tokenistic references to First Peoples history, knowledges, cultures, and languages.

It will articulate our reflections as non-Indigenous teachers who teach with and seek ways to challenge the realities of ongoing colonisation. Karen and Ann are not writing as academics but as practitioners with over 40 years of experience, each in the early childhood profession. In this chapter, we will provide our insights into the pedagogy of learning, relearning, and unlearning through learning with Elders and First Nations Peoples.

This chapter will share stories from the teaching cultural perspectives of Boon Wurrung Elder N'arwee't, who is teaching and sharing her knowledge with Karen and Ann as non-Indigenous early childhood teachers within a community preschool. The stories we share reflect our relationships that are built on deep respect, trust, and care in honouring of Boon Wurrung Law and positioning N'arwee't as the teacher. Together, we share our stories, reflections and realities, learning, unlearning, and relearning through the history and cultures of First Nations Peoples.

We share with you how storytelling for us became a pedagogical tool to teach adults and children of all ages the true history of First Nations Peoples and connected us with their cultures. This practice recognises and acknowledges oral storytelling as both a traditional and contemporary way to learn, unlearn, and relearn as First Nations Peoples have for thousands of years.

As an act of decolonisation, we acknowledge this Land remains unceded and that we teach and live with the reality that the colonisers have never left. We have committed to teaching that this is not a young country and challenge the colonised history of *terra nullius* taught to us when we were children.

Experience has taught us that young children/students are able to learn, unlearn, relearn, and connect with the stories of this Land. In practice, this includes the story of invasion and all that has come from that, learning the cultural stories before invasion, and respectfully connecting with these stories in a contemporary context. Examples of how First Nations Peoples teachings are shared with children will be described in this chapter, including the importance of respectfully Acknowledging Country, connecting with and taking responsibility for caring for the Land, understanding the importance of all relationships, and practising, with truth-telling, the colonised history of this Land.

You will hear the voices of N'arwee't, Karen, Ann, the children, and Country throughout this chapter. This quote by N'arwee't demonstrates the importance of listening to Country as a strong decolonising practice:

> Trees hold the knowledge of the past, the present and tomorrow. They are related to my people, the Yullukit Willum of the Boon Wurrung.
> I invite you to learn from the tree with djil bruk (respect).[2]

Part one

The past: Learning/unlearning

In this section, Karen and Ann describe how at Balnarring Preschool, the teaching team and children are learning with Boon Wurrung Country every day. Teachings, relationships, and stories once silent to us due to the dominance of colonial ways meant we positioned Country as a resource and ourselves as part of a new country. However, we now know differently. Listening with First Nations Elders and Peoples, we are learning the true history of this Land. Together, we have come to understand our roles as non-Indigenous teachers in this space of learning, unlearning, and relearning. This learning has supported us to respectfully teach young children the truths, histories, and stories of First Nations Peoples, Country, and Cultures. Before we could do that, we had to go on our own journeys of learning to unlearn and relearn what we had been taught as knowledge. Recognising we had been teaching only with the stories of colonisation, the reality that this one perspective had dominated our time both as teachers and learners in education systems led us to commit to transforming our pedagogical practices.

We acknowledge the realities for First Nations Peoples of colonial policies, violence, and the horrific injustices endured. Learning the truths of this Land became the unlearning. This involved learning about First Nations Peoples cultures past and present, and gaining knowledge about their continual connection with the Land.

At Balnarring Preschool, participating in critical reflection around the team's knowledge or lack of knowledge raised challenges and more questions. The team felt uncomfortable about their lack of knowledge and understanding and began to reflect on their own stories.

Karen's story

For the first 25 years of my career, my knowledge of the First Peoples cultures and histories was minimal. I recall attending a conference and hearing Karen Martin, a Noonuccal woman, tell us her story. I could not believe what I was hearing. I couldn't believe that the story she was telling me about her life was occurring in my lifetime. It was then that I made a commitment to find out what I had not been told and start to learn about Australia's First Peoples. In 2015, I began developing a nature programme at the beach and bush. As this programme evolved, it became clear that the voices of First Peoples were missing from the programme and from my pedagogical knowledge and practice. My commitment to learning and developing practice continues today. As my knowledge and understanding have grown, I find myself using different terminology. When I first began exploring how to include First Nations teachings into practice, I was not using words such as learning, unlearning and relearning, reconciliation, colonisation, unceded and decolonisation. My commitment continues to be strong as I ensure all children hear the stories I was never told.

Ann's story

My ancestry connects me to Ireland, England, and Denmark; my relatives were settlers who travelled across the sea and claimed this Land as their own. As a child, I was taught to know this Country as 'young', as *terra nullius*, nobody's Land when Captain Cook claimed this Land for England. I now recognise that I have, for many years, lived and taught with the limits, blindness, and bias of colonised ways to know and do. During these times, I remember feeling unsure how to respectfully position First Nations Peoples teachings into pedagogical practice, so "not wanting to get it wrong," I chose to do very little, believing this was the respectful way to be a teacher. I now know these actions continued the silences, ignorance, and untruths of the history of this Land we know as Australia.

Children's story

As teachers, we wondered what thoughts were going through children's minds. What stories had they heard, and who had they heard them from? We learnt that the children were only learning the colonial history of this Land. A few years ago, we invited a First Nations person to visit the children. The children were provided with information about a woman who was visiting us, who was from lutruwita Country (Tasmania). One child then commented, "I thought all Aboriginal people from Tasmania were dead, and did you know the children were taken away?" More recently, a child was looking at the poster of Aboriginal and Torres Strait Islander Children's Day, where the child is painted with ochre and wearing adornments. They asked, "Was that person still alive?" We reflected that as part of our role, we needed to support the children to go on their own journeys of learning, unlearning, and relearning the stories of First Nations Peoples history and cultures and how important it was for teaching teams to provide this in the curriculum.

The team's story

The more we came to understand and relearn the stories of this Land with First Nations Peoples teachings, the more questions we had. Supporting our learning to progress further, an opportunity came for us to connect with Gamilori/Yularoi woman and early childhood consultant, Priscilla Reid-Loynes, who began working with the teaching team. Relearning and learning with Priscilla offered many opportunities to listen, ask questions, challenge current practices, and for her to join the children, families, and teachers in their everyday programmes.

There were many questions asked by the team, and we share some of them here to support your ongoing reflection:

- How could we, as non-Indigenous teachers and educators, teach young children/students First Nations Peoples knowledges?
- Was the history of First Peoples appropriate for young children/students to learn?
- What would truth-telling in pedagogical practice look like? What knowledge do you need before you can engage with truth-telling practices?
- What if the truth frightened the children/students?
- How do we construct the learning for children/students that supports their actions to be proactive?
- How do we assist children/students to unlearn and understand the stories of the Land they have grown up with?

Priscilla guided our learning, became a role model for us, taught us that not all knowledge is ours to share and suggested where to go for more information. This commitment to relearn and learn as a teaching team with Priscilla enabled everyone's understandings to deepen and their confidence to develop to position First Nations Peoples teachings within pedagogical practices.

As teachers, we believe it is important to engage in professional learning, to think about and find your own ways to address these questions. By committing yourself both personally and professionally to processes of relearning and learning, you will learn to respect and take responsibility for what you teach and the approach you use. We have become acutely aware of not appropriating First Nations Peoples knowledges or positioning ourselves as the experts. It may not always be appropriate for teachers to share stories they have heard or told. Learning what can be shared and what is just yours to know is all part of learning to be respectful; it is important to seek permission to share stories and respect what you are told.

A moment to pause...

The realisation that the knowledge you have been taught is biased can lead to feelings of discomfort and of not knowing what to do. When teachers speak about embedding First Nations Peoples teaching into their curriculum, they often comment, "What if I do it wrong?" Self-reflection can be confronting, and you may not know what to do with such feelings. Sitting with the discomfort can lead to deeper learning, a stronger commitment, and changes to pedagogy and practice. Not acting on these feelings keeps the current learning environment in the status quo.

We invite you to reflect as individuals and/or a team before reading further into this chapter. At Balnarring Preschool, many questions arose both as individuals and as a team. We wondered how we were going to change our pedagogy and practice to reflect our commitment to decolonising history. What responses would you or your teams give to these questions?

- What would be your starting point?
- What is your story?
- What stories did you hear as a child? Which stories and information were reputable? Who were the experts?
- How would you write your own position statement?
- How do you unlearn and relearn?
- How do you connect with and listen to First Nations Peoples voices so that you can learn from them?
- How will you access books, music, performances, conferences, exhibitions, and professional development to learn, unlearn, and relearn?

- Which learning opportunities are available that support the individual learning styles of each team member: literature, conversations, performances, art galleries, exhibitions, museums, First Nations Peoples organisations, being with Country, or sitting with First Nations Peoples?

Now let's continue....

Part two

The present: Unlearning/relearning

We believe that teaching teams will only feel confident including decolonised history in their pedagogy when they themselves have experienced learning, unlearning, and relearning. This requires a commitment from the teaching teams to unlearn the colonial world views and relearn the truth. When teaching teams commit to immersing themselves and listening to First Nations Peoples teachings and stories there are many ways to increase their knowledge and understanding. This learning has great potential to inform and guide the teaching teams on the appropriate and respectful knowledge to share with children and which teaching approach to use.

Learning, unlearning, and relearning with stories

As we became aware of a mismatch between the stories our parents and ourselves had grown up with and those that we now knew, we questioned what we had been taught as students and teachers within a colonised education system. When we explored old texts and children's books, we discovered that First Nations Peoples were positioned as an inferior race. These publications were not written by First Nations Peoples, didn't acknowledge the sources of their knowledge, and prioritised the colonial voice. We drew these conclusions after looking through old texts. What is your conclusion from the following examples?

Example 1   Poem published in a children's book in 1944

Captain James Cook
While from the beach, some black-men
Threw spears in wild dismay
With rank and file he landed
Unfurled a flag from a tree
And claimed this land, Australia,
For England, you and me.
(James, 1944, p. 9)[3]

Example 2 offers this historical perspective, which was viewed as best practice in regard to what children should know and learn about First Australians in 1943 and is a story about an emu.

> Now blacks were among the natural enemies [of emus]. For long months they would go away to other parts, fishing and hunting and holding their strange ceremonies, telling their stories or gathering grubs in dilly bags; then, once every two or three years they would revisit the emu flocks.
> The stringy lithe black men with mops of dusty hair and smoky eyes had many tricks catching and destroying emus.[4]

Teaching in a contemporary space, after reading these extracts, what feelings and thoughts arise? These were the teaching resources that, at the time, were viewed as best practice. We wonder what messages children took away from their education that influenced their adult views of First Nations Peoples.

Whose stories have you been listening to?

As teachers, we intentionally decide which stories to tell and share with children, students, and families. Reflecting on conversations between teachers, it became clear that previous knowledge and colonised ways had influenced pedagogy and practice—they were only teaching with and sharing the colonial story. We believe it becomes the teacher's responsibility to learn the stories of the Land before invasion, as well as the contemporary story, as we position Country and First Nations Peoples as the teachers.

Children, students, and adults are surrounded by stories. Storytelling is a teaching approach that bridges all age groups. Through learning with First Nations Peoples, we have come to know there are many stories and perspectives. Stories are told in a multitude of ways, most commonly orally through conversation and looking for the stories within in the landscape, art, music, and books, both picture books and adult fiction. There are many storybooks available that provide teachers with resources to build their knowledge and confidence. This allows them to teach through different perspectives and provide learning opportunities that reflect the history of this Land.

In recent times, many books have been written by First Nations Peoples that contain stories from which the children and students can learn, unlearn, and relearn. These stories have been passed on through generations but have also been written for contemporary times. For example, the book *Somebody's Land*[5] by Adam Goodes, an Andyamathanha and Norungga man and Australian Football League (AFL) star, challenges the concept of terra nullius by starting a conversation about acknowledging Country and the peoples who have lived here for many years and their cultural practices. This story also brings First Nations Peoples into the present, as the final image is of a city which is still Aboriginal Land. These stories assist to inform us and make connections between the past, present, and future.

When presenting these stories to the children, we have found it valuable to display the books for the families to look at so they are informed about what their children have been learning. They are then prepared for any further questions their children may have. Often, families comment that they don't know the story and ask where they can purchase the books. The learning and messages of these stories become stronger when the texts are visited multiple times. As the children's knowledge grows and they have experiences with the Land, they hear the stories at deeper levels. They gain greater empathy and understanding of the injustices, which leads them to want to take action. At the end of the book *Finding Our Heart* by Torres Strait Islander man Thomas Mayo,[6] there is a list of suggested actions on how to find your heart, to which the children at Balnarring loudly and proudly express, "We are doing that!"

Teaching with stories written by First Nations Peoples supports their voices to be strong and present within the curriculum and demonstrates actions of reconciliation and decolonising pedagogical practices. As a teacher, it is important to explore and learn the stories of the Land you teach on whenever possible. Some stories written by Elders and illustrated by First Nations Peoples are teaching the truth-telling of the history of Australia, whereas other books will support learning about individual First Nation Peoples, their Country, and their stories about their culture. It is always important to acknowledge which Country the story has come from and who is telling the story. The following are examples of some local Kulin Nation stories that are shared at Balnarring Preschool in everyday practice.

- Boon Wurrung story books written by Boon Wurrung Elder N'arwee't Dr Carolyn Briggs: *Bundjil Creation Story*,[7] *Barraeemal*,[8] and *The Time of Chaos*.[9] These stories and the children's strong connections with the Land led to the children at Balnarring Preschool becoming the illustrators.
- Boon Wurrung Elder Aunty Fay Stewart-Muir and Sue Lawson have produced three books, all of which share culture and relate to the importance of children developing relationships with each other, families, and Country: *Respect*,[10] *Sharing*,[11] and *Family*.[12]
- Wurundjeri Elder Aunty Joy Murphy has shared cultural knowledge and language through *Welcome to Country*[13] and *Wilam: A Birrarung Story*.[14]

We invite you to reflect further on the importance of stories through the words of Dr Karen Martin from *Voices and Visions: Aboriginal Early Childhood Education in Australia*:

> Stories are important for various reasons, matched only by the number of ways in which they are shared. This can be verbally, physically or visually. Stories can be grounding, defining, comforting and embracing. There are stories that also admonish, tease, celebrate, irritate and challenge. A good story might do one or all of these things. A good story grabs your attention. Stories are about identity. They connect us and confirm our sense of belonging. We know we belong when we are ready to hear the strength of the messages a story contains. That's why our old people often tell a story many many times and, we often don't get the deeper messages until we are ready and able to really listen.[15]

There are many resources and stories available to support teaching, but we caution you to ensure they are appropriate and ethical. We also emphasise, where possible, the importance of starting local first. Advice can be gained on evaluating resources and localising approaches from organisations such as the Australian Institute of Aboriginal and Torres Strait Island Studies (AIATIS) *Guide to Evaluating and Selecting Education Resources*,[16] the YARNS First Nations resource evaluation tool,[17] and the Victorian Aboriginal Education Association (VAEAI) *Aboriginal Early Childhood Cultural Protocols*.[18]

Part three

The future: Relearning/Learning

In Parts One and Two, we introduced the concepts of learning and unlearning, which can lead to further learning and relearning as part of a cyclic process. In Part Three, the learning continues as we listen and learn with N'arwee't Dr Carolyn Briggs.

> More than Tarrang Biik (Tree Country)
> Kummargi Gadhaba Yulendj Tarrang
> (Rough translation: The knowledge of trees is rising up)

These statements were shared by N'arwee't with Karen when she was speaking about the *More than a Terrang* exhibition at the Melbourne Museum. They express how First Nations Peoples position trees as having a vital role in creating harmony with Mother Earth. N'arwee't concludes this conversation by posing reflective comments (Figure 6.1):

> Tree Literacy (decolonise in the words)
> Colonisation deconstructs the way we understand the tree.
> A tree is more than an object, it is a living breathing entity (the lungs, the energies) that reminds us of the past and the future.
> Important to understand the connection to the living breathing entity.

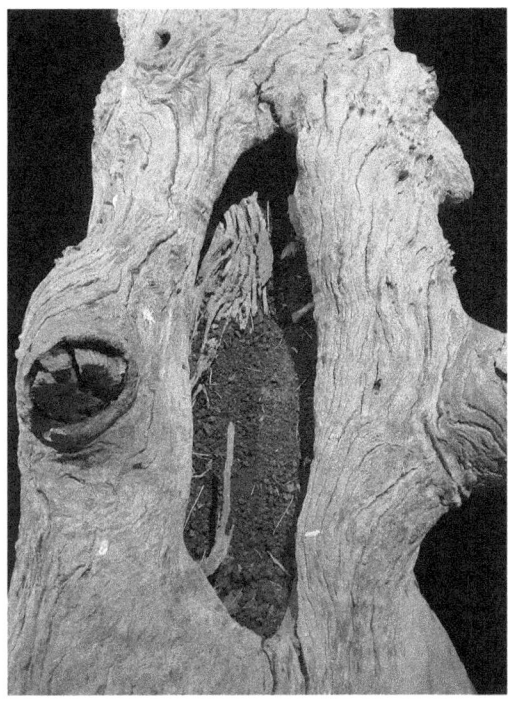

Figure 6.1 Tree from ***More than a Terrang*** exhibition at the Melbourne Museum. Photograph by Karen Anderson, 2023

They are living entities which articulate our relationship to Country, to each other, and to the Ancestors
Trees talk to each other, tree has families, they look after the nutrients of the next tree.
Tree is part of an element of Mother Earth.
Weegabeel Tarrang (old tree) continues to live after it falls, providing homes to many beings and giving living matter back to Parbinata (Mother Earth).
Trees are never part of the negotiation about what happens to them.
Tree has memory.
Old trees have thousands of generations of memories, it's a collective memory of many people who went before us.
Old tree is a tool for reading, understanding, and reconnecting.
Nature has many stories to tell you just need to listen to be witness.
Tree gives witness to the many different times of change. How do we hear it?
The tree is in your presence and you are in the presence of the tree.
Do you remember what it is like to lay under a tree?
How do we learn to respect?
How do we value tree?

98 Carolyn Briggs et al.

More than a tree: Boon Wurrung Tarrang story board and tree knowledge

This was not the first time we had been asked to think about the significance of trees. The knowledge represented in the Boon Wurrung Tarrang Story Board in Figure 6.2 came about when we told N'arwee't the children were

Figure 6.2 Boon Wurrung Tarrang story board by Jane Reiseger[19]

going to make clap sticks. N'arwee't asked us, "What context did the children have?" To which we had no answer. Then N'arwee't asked, "Where do sticks come from?" We responded, "From a tree." N'arwee't continued, "Trees have stories, so the sticks have a story." N'arwee't then began describing all the things she wanted the children to reflect about where the sticks came from and what they could learn from the sticks. We worked with Jane Reiseger, the artist of Figure 6.2, to create a visual representation of N'arwee't's words. We hoped this drawing would be a more accessible format for both children and adults to learn from and listen to N'arwee't's words.

We draw the reader's attention to the four key teachings on the trunk of the tree:

1 Knowledge is part of the law of the Land.
2 Self-reflection: How do you look after nature?
3 This knowledge is the beginning of the journey of understanding the musical process.
4 Self-reflection: What did you learn today while working with the clicking sticks? Trees care for us. How will you care for them?

N'arwee't is asking us to listen deeply and reflect on how to learn and be with the tree. Use the words in Figure 6.3 for your own reflections and actions.

Learning with the tree
Are the trees of the Country native to the area?
Why do we need trees, and why are they important?
Trees give us oxygen
Trees clean the air of carbon dioxide
Everything connects us to something from the past
When to clear the undergrowth for regeneration?
What do trees tell us? All trees tell a story
What is happening in the tree? Is there sap? Are there hollows?
Gaining understanding and valuing the assets of Mother Earth
Chanting for a new way of knowing when there is a full moon
Ceremonies are held with the sticks
Understand the sounds of nature
Sticks create the sounds of nature, mimic animal sounds
Energising memories
Nature informs design
The trees talk to each other
The sticks are part of the tree; that tree has knowledge
Importance of acknowledging the makers of the sticks
Home to birds and other animals

Figure 6.3 N'arwee't's words from the Boon Wurrung Tarrang Story Board

Tree as teacher

Connecting the children with the Land, developing relationships with nature, and listening to the stories nature tells us, honours both Country and nature as a learning environment. At the 2023 Early Childhood Australia symposium, Alison Overeem, a palawa woman from Southeast lutruwita[20] (Tasmania), described Country as a classroom that is 65,000 years old. Early childhood pedagogy values play and a hands-on approach, and through this approach learning with nature pedagogy can be used as a form of decolonising practice.

Reflecting on N'arwee'ts teachings about "more than a tree" and how we once knew trees changed our pedagogy and the ways we now know trees. We come to show respect to tree and teach history beyond colonisation. With permission from Elders, we sing in language as we acknowledge Country. Tree becomes a co-teacher with us; it supports us in teaching the colonial realities for First Nations Peoples: the settlement, land acquisition, and exploitation of Boon Wurrung Country.

Tree stands old, branches cut, trunk so wide you cannot reach around even with arms stretched. Positioned in the middle of a camping space at Balnarring Beach in Victoria, a contemporary gathering place, we wonder Tree's history. Estimated at being over 300 years old, its life began before colonisation; 235 years later, we sit in front of Tree, and we wonder who else has gathered here before. Did Tree hear the languages of the Boon Wurrung Peoples as it grew? Did the Boon Wurrung Peoples gather here too? Did Tree listen to the stories of the Boon Wurrung Peoples as they sat around their fires, danced, sang, and slept under its branches just as many do today?

When Tree was 70 years of age, the stories it heard changed with the arrival of the invaders to this area; it was now hearing another voice–that of the invaders. First Nations Peoples stories, around the tree, spoke of the disposition of its Peoples. We wonder how Tree knew about the removal of Boon Wurrung Peoples and experienced their death from diseases introduced by the settlers, and did Tree provide shelter for those being hunted? For many years, Tree grew with the silence of the Boon Wurrung Peoples and their language. Tree waited for the Boon Wurrung Peoples and their language to return, for First Nations Peoples to return.

This tree is now known to us at Balnarring Preschool as the Storytelling Tree. Leafless, its branches shortened, it may appear dead. We gather to listen to Tree; all children are encouraged to listen to Tree, to hear its stories and begin their relationship with Tree. What are the stories of this Land that tree can tell, what has Tree seen, known? Can you hear? Do we need to listen harder? More deeply? (Figure 6.4).

Learning, unlearning, and relearning history in early childhood 101

Figure 6.4 Storytelling Tree, Balnarring Beach. Photograph by Karen Anderson

Storytelling with Tree: Karen's story from practice

At Balnarring Beach camping reserve in Victoria, the children gather around the base of the very old tree known as the Storytelling Tree. Karen begins to introduce the Storytelling Tree and tells the story it tells her.

A long time ago, a tiny seed was dropped in this space. The seed began to grow. I wonder what it has seen? I listen to the tree. ... The Tree told me that when it started to grow, there were no roads, cars, houses, shops.

Question from child: Were there any people here?

Yes, there were Boon Wurrung People here. They lived in harmony with the Land; they made houses, took care of the Land, took only what they needed, hunted for food on the Land and in the sea; they knew what all the plants could be used for. When they made canoes, they took part of the tree, but made sure the tree would still live. Many animals lived here: kangaroos, koalas, reptiles, echidna, wombats, emus, possums.

Child says: And there were cows and pigs and sheep.

No, those animals didn't live here then. Then one day, people came across the sea and started cutting down the trees and not caring for the plants. They thought this was nobody's Land, but it was…somebody's Land (children chorus).

They killed the animals, they poisoned the creeks, so there was no drinking water, and the creatures who lived in the creeks died, and they were unkind to the Boon Wurrung People. They hurt them.

Child asks: Did they kill them?

Yes, they did, and many Boon Wurrung People went away. The people are called invaders. They bought cows, pigs, chickens.

Child calls out: And sheep?

And foxes. These animals destroyed the ground and killed the animals that belonged here. The invaders bought trees that didn't belong, which killed the trees and undergrowth that did belong. The invaders didn't think the Boon Wurrung knew anything and that they weren't clever.

After many years, the Boon Wurrung People and other First Nations Peoples have come back to the Land.

Child states: Yes, and they care for the trees and animals.

The children were then invited to listen to the tree and share the stories they heard with the team. Some of the stories they heard were as follows:

> "The invaders cut the Storytelling Tree's branches off, the Tree told me."
> "Boon Wurrung People are looking after the trees and animals now."

At the base of this tree, the ranger has placed a sign explaining the significance of the tree to Balnarring Preschool, inviting the community to listen. The children proudly lead their families to the Storytelling Tree, sharing what they have heard and encouraging everyone to listen for more stories.

We have given an example of storytelling being the vehicle to teach children about invasion. These teachings about the invaders continue as the children connect with the Land each week, revisit the trees, listen for more stories, and learn about the plants and their importance to Boon Wurrung Peoples. Each week, the children are reminded that the invaders didn't know anything about the bush or how to care for it; instead, they brought many things that didn't belong.

Where will you find your storytelling trees? What truths will they share with you?

We learnt from Gamilaroi/Yularoi woman Priscilla Reid-Loynes that it is not only trees that tell stories. She asked us to be observant and look for the stories within the whole landscape:

> If they don't know the stories of these lands, what will they do when they grow up, who will then know the stories? When we share stories, we need to walk and learn about Country, so it is carried onto future generations.[21]

These are some examples of the practices we developed after learning with Priscilla and many other First Nations Peoples:

1 **Stories of the landscape**
 As you walk with Country, wonder at the stories the landscape is sharing of the present and the past. For example, there may be lots of leaves on the ground; the children are asked to wonder what happened here last night, or the sea might be extremely rough. Why? There may be invasive species. How did they get here? The rangers might be baiting foxes. Why?
2 **Gratitude exercises**
 The children are asked to find a piece of nature and bring it back to the circle. In the centre of the circle are some sticks, maybe a small log and some clap sticks. Each person is invited to place the piece they collected into the centre. As they place their item down, they express what they are grateful for or thankful for. This can be said out loud or in their heads.
3 **Stories with natural materials**
 After several weeks of modelling how to create stories with items from nature, the children become the storytellers. A child is invited to be the storyteller. They collect items to create a story scene. Several of their peers sit around the story scene and listen to the story. Story topics often involve creatures they see and hear in the bush space, their families, and they use Boon Wurrung words.
4 **Resources that support storytelling**
 - Games: *Spin A Yarn*[22] is a storytelling game available at Yarn Strong Sista that was developed by Taungurung artist Annette Sax and Priscilla Reid-Loynes. Each tile contains a symbol that can be used to develop a story in many ways.
 - Music: Many First Nations musicians and songwriters use music to tell the stories of truth-telling, family, relationships with Country, strength, resilience, celebration, and culture. Have you really listened to the lyrics and heard the sounds?
 - Artwork: The art on National Aborigines' and Islanders' Day Observance Committee (NAIDOC) posters[23] ask the observer to look deeply and wonder what story the art on the poster communicates and provide diverse examples of First Nations Peoples artistic styles. Placing the posters for children to discuss and wonder about celebrates First Nations Peoples cultures and stories.

5 **An example of decolonising practice with a gratitude story**
   We begin by touching the ground, connecting with the Land, and acknowledging Boon Wurrung Country; then the children and other teaching team members continue.

We express our gratitude to the sun…the waves…the shells…the sand…the clouds…the birds by acknowledging their presence and connectedness. Our gratitude reflects the children's discoveries and deepening relationships with the Country they live on and learn with. Today, we express our gratitude to the crabs, the fish we have watched swim in the rock pools, and the creatures we have wondered about. We do not know all their names; we may not have seen them before; we have photographed these creatures and will investigate them further back at our preschool. Through the Laws of Bundjil, the wedge-tailed eagle ancestral being, we have come to know that it is our responsibility to treat all creatures with care and respect.

Guided by the Law of Bundjil, we take responsibility for caring for Boon Wurrung Country; we walk on the tracks, show care for the trees we climb; we identify and safely remove the rubbish we find. When we find lots of rubbish left, the children have been heard to say, "Bundjil will not be happy!"

They take responsibility for and show pride in making the Land safer for the animals, birds, and sea creatures that they watch and hear each week. They have come to understand the impact that their actions and the actions of others can have on the environments we live in and learn with. We express our deepening gratitude for Elders and First Nations Peoples whom we now position as our teachers and for the knowledge they are sharing with all of us.

Before we leave the beach, we listen again; we hear the waves; feet move in the sand, and then we hear Waang the black raven. The children know the sound of Waang; they call out, greet Waang, interpret the stories, and view Waang as a friend and teacher. We are grateful to know the story of Waang. Respecting the Laws of Bundjil that have been taught to us by the Boon Wurrung Elders, we have all come to know the message Waang tells as a protector. Waang teaches us to care for the waterways, that we are all responsible for caring for the creatures and Country that we have explored and walked on today.

Walking back along a bush track, one child yells out, "Thanks Bundjil for creating nature!"

Conclusion

In this chapter, we have shared knowledges, relationships, and stories through many voices. As this chapter was developed, our relationship with each other continued to grow. Together, we reflected on what we knew and were learning as 'truths' of the history of this Land we know as Australia. As non-Indigenous teachers, we believe continual reflection is required as we navigate through the knowledges we had been told within colonised education systems and as we now listen to First Nations Peoples voices and stories. We feel truth-telling through pedagogy, practice, and thinking with decoloniality requires commitment to listening, reflecting, and being constantly challenged as our knowledge and practices evolve.

As teachers writing this chapter, we were reminded that the journey of learning, unlearning, relearning, and learning is continuous. We now celebrate First Nations Peoples achievements and strengths as our pedagogy and practice become voices for change. Learning with First Nations Peoples knowledges, cultures, and stories connects us all with our responsibilities to all relationships and the importance of caring for Country. With N'arwee't Dr Carolyn Briggs positioned as the teacher, we encourage you to revisit her Tree teachings, listen deeply and reflect on this wisdom. How can these learnings transform pedagogical practices, and what do they mean for sustainable futures? We end this chapter here but hope that by sharing these stories, you will be encouraged and inspired to continue listening with First Nations Peoples voices towards learning, unlearning, relearning, and learning.

Ideas and strategies for the classroom

Throughout this chapter, we have identified a range of reflection prompts, pedagogical strategies, story books (see publication details in the references section), and resources that early childhood educators can explore with their teams. Here are some other general resources:

AIATIS (2022) *Australian Institute of Aboriginal and Torres Strait Islander Studies (AIATIS) Guide to Evaluating and Selecting Education Resources*. https://aiatsis.gov.au/education/guide-evaluating-and-selecting-education-resources

Briggs, C. (2014). *The Journey Cycles of the Boon Wurrung: Stories with Boon Wurrung*. Victorian Aboriginal Corporation for Languages.

Narragunnawali supports schools and early learning services to foster knowledge and pride in Aboriginal and Torres Strait Islander histories, cultures and contributions: https://www.reconciliation.org.au/our-work/Narragunnawali/

Hughes, F., Elliott. S., Anderson, K., & Chancellor, B. (2022). *Early Years Learning in Australian Natural Environments: Immersive Nature Play Programs*. Oxford University Press.

VAIAI. (2016). *Protocols for Koorie Education in Victorian Primary and Secondary Schools*. http://www.vaeai.org.au/wp-content/uploads/delightful-downloads/2020/01/Protocols-for-Koorie-Education-in-Victorian-Primary-and-Secondary-Schools-2019.pd

Yarn Strong Sista: https://yarnstrongsista.com

YARNS First Nations resource evaluation tool helps teachers evaluate resources to make they are culturally appropriate. Find it in Madsen, B., Perkins, R., & Shay, M. (2021). Critical selection of curriculum materials: Tools for educators. In *Indigenous Education in Australia* (pp. 133–147). Routledge.

Notes

1. Briggs, C. (2023). *The time of chaos.* Self-published (Available from Balnarring Preschool, publicationsbw@gmail.com).
2. Briggs, C. (2023). *More than a Terrang.* Exhibition, Bunjilaka Aboriginal Cultural Centre, Melbourne Museum.
3. James, M. (1944). *Yabba Yabba, stories and verses of Australia: Birds-Bush-Blackfellows.* St Vincents Boy Home. Please note this is not a recommended resource; it demonstrates the colonial teachings, the untruths that were taught to generations of the 1950s and 1960s.
4. Rees, L. (1946). *The story of Karrawingi the Emu.* John Sands Pty Ltd. p. 12. Please note this is not a recommended resource, it demonstrates the colonial teachings, the untruths that were taught to generations of the 1950s and 1960s. It was the winner of the best children's book in 1946.
5. Goodes, A., & Laing, E. (2021). *Somebody's land.* Allen & Unwin.
6. Mayo, T. (2020). *Finding our heart.* Hardy Grant Publishing.
7. Briggs, C. (2019) *Bundjil creation story.* Self-published (Available from Balnarring Preschool, publicationsbw@gmail.com)
8. Briggs, C. (2020). *Barraeemal.* Self-published (Available from Balnarring Preschool, publicationsbw@gmail.com)
9. Briggs, C. (2023). *The time of chaos.* Self-published (Available from Balnarring Preschool, publicationsbw@gmail.com)
10. Muir, F., & Lawson, S. (2020). *Respect.* Magabala Books.
11. Muir, F., & Lawson, S. (2021). *Sharing.* Magabala Books.
12. Muir, F., & Lawson, S. (2021). *Family.* Magabala Books.
13. Murphy, J. (2016). *Welcome to country.* Black Dog Books.
14. Murphy, J., & Kelly, A. (2019). *Wilam: A Birrarung story.* Black Dog Books.
15. Martin, K. L. (2011). *Voices and visions: Aboriginal early childhood education in Australia.* Pademelon Press. p. 24.
16. Australian Institute of Aboriginal and Torres Strait Island Studies (AIATIS). (2022). *Guide to evaluating and selecting education resources.* https://aiatsis.gov.au/education/guide-evaluating-and-selecting-education-resources
17. Marsden, B., Perkins, R., & Shay, M. (2021). Critical selection of curriculum materials: Tools for educators. In Eds. M. Shay & R. Oliver, *Indigenous education in Australia* (pp. 133–147). Routledge.
18. Victorian Aboriginal Education Association (VAEAI). (2016). *Protocols for Koorie education in Victorian primary and secondary schools.* http://www.vaeai.org.au/wp-content/uploads/delightful-downloads/2020/01/Protocols-for-Koorie-Education-in-Victorian-Primary-and-Secondary-Schools-2019.pd
19. Jane Reiseger studied art at the Victorian College of Arts, Melbourne completing a BA in fine arts majoring in painting and now works as an illustrator.
20. As per the palawa language conventions, place names are not capitalised.
21. Reid-Loynes, P. (2014). Extract from Balnarring Preschool video.
22. Yarn Strong Sista. (n.d.). *Spin a yarn.* https://www.yarnstrongsista.com/product/spin-a-yarn-game/
23. NAIDOC. (n.d.). *NAIDOC poster gallery.* https://www.naidoc.org.au/posters/poster-gallery

Chapter 7

"Mummy, what did YOU do in the history wars?" White teachers decolonising Australian curriculum...and themselves

Lucinda McKnight

Author positioning statement

Dr Lucinda McKnight is a White Australian former secondary History teacher, now senior lecturer in pedagogy and curriculum, living on Wurundjeri land and interested in inclusive education and curriculum design. She wrote, chaired, and taught in Deakin University's *Culture, Diversity and Participation in Education* unit, providing an introduction to principles of decolonisation for students across the university.

Introduction: Inspiration and concepts

This chapter is written at my home on Wurundjeri land, never ceded. As a White Australian with British ancestry, I acknowledge the traditional custodians and pay my respects to Elders past, present, and emerging. This place where I live, in the eastern suburbs of Naarm (Melbourne), is steep, and my house is at the top of a hill. Daily, when I walk the colonists' street grids, overlaid on land traversed by Wurundjeri People for millennia, I can see the distant Dandenongs, a horizon of low mountain ranges. These beautiful blue hills belong to both the Wurundjeri and Bunurong/Boon Wurrung Peoples; they are the same hills I looked out onto from my secondary school classrooms as a student in the nearby suburb of Burwood, also on Wurundjeri land. These hills I gazed at dreamily from History classes had been inhabited for over 65,000 years. Yet this was a history I did not learn at school.

In this chapter, I consider the colonising impacts of education on White teachers and the value of invoking memory work to identify and reflect on these impacts as a decolonising move and a contribution to truth-telling in the 'history wars.' I begin by proposing why this is critical work for White, Anglo-Celtic Australian teachers. I then provide a definition of memory work to support teachers in better understanding its potentials. To support my claims, I offer examples from my own storied memories to give a concrete sense of 'historical' racist curricular addresses potentially internalised by even those who consider themselves to be allies. This is not to excuse enduring racism but

DOI: 10.4324/9781003435617-7

to better articulate its workings and avoid its continuation. The chapter concludes with a framework to support teachers running their own Memory Work Workshop as a professional learning activity informing professional reflection and curriculum design for racial justice.

The history wars

The title of this chapter, "Mummy, What Did **YOU** Do in the History Wars?" is a play on the text of a poster[1] produced by the British Parliamentary Recruitment Committee in 1915 to encourage volunteers to fight in World War I (WWI). The poster is held in the collections of both the British Library and the Australian War Memorial; it shows a pensive White man in a business suit, seated in an armchair with his daughter on his lap and his son at his feet, playing with a set of toy British soldiers. The little girl has a history book open on her lap, and she looks at her father as she asks the question that runs across the bottom of the picture in cursive script: "Daddy, what did **YOU** do in the Great War?" The "you" is in bold capitals and underlined.

The aim of the poster was to impel men to volunteer to fight. Its message was that "in the future, children would hold their fathers to account on the service that they performed for their country."[2] The title of the chapter shifts this call from masculinised warfare to feminised teaching; teachers who are in the majority, White, female, and speakers of English. It shifts from the perceived responsibility to support a nation battling a foreign enemy to the responsibility to decolonise history education, again in the service of nation. The 'history wars,' said to be enacted from the 1980s to the present, is an Australian term that even has its own Wikipedia page. It is related to the broader notion of 'culture wars' and debates about what can be said where, when, and by whom.

In this instance, however, the 'history wars' are about both what has actually happened in Australian history and what can be taught about it. These 'history wars' are not merely discursive but grounded in the material realities of the violent land-based battles fought between colonisers and the First Australian peoples. These wars are grounded in the loss of country and of life. For example, near the place where I grew up, again on Wurundjeri land, the Battle of Yering was fought on 14 January 1830 between Wurundjeri People and colonial troops. This was local history I was never taught at school.

There is a central irony in my reference to the poster: Britain was the colonial aggressor in these Australian land wars, not the courageous defender of the nation that 'Daddy' is expected to be. Yet the notion of obligation to nation is resonant across both calls. 'Daddy,' if he is brave enough, defends his country. 'Mummy,' as a notional White female History teacher, if she is brave enough, seeks to teach an Australian history that supports the human rights of First Nations Australians. This is potentially an increasingly decolonised history that pursues truth even while problematising this concept. This is the history that can contribute to Reconciliation and ultimately to Australia's maturity as a nation.

I note here that I do not mean to elide First Nations Australian History teachers but to position the work of decolonising largely with White teachers, just as the labours and costs of working towards Reconciliation reside with White Australians. As Genine Hook says, "[A] decolonising project depends on non-Indigenous people considering the conferred benefits they have inherited as a result of European invasion."[3]

The choices implied in the obligatory calls of the poster and chapter title are complex. In hindsight, the WWI poster is both poignant and ironic: soldiers' families often became destitute, and the survival of his children may have been the reason 'Daddy' did not enlist. For 'Mummy,' the White History teacher, the choice appears to be whether to take a moral and pedagogical stance in the 'history wars' that is inevitably politicised and risky or to stay silent. At the time of writing, History teachers in parts of the United States are facing extraordinary pressures to conscribe what the History curriculum says about enslaved African Americans and conceal facts about the nation's past. Yet the larger global momentum to decolonise curriculum continues, and White History teachers will need to answer to future generations to justify the stances and actions they chose in this process; the project and content of subject History are closely tied to truth-telling. This chapter aims to support White teachers in considering their own positionalities and the pedagogies they have experienced as students themselves as they undertake this work. This may mean considering the "truths" told in their own educations.

Decolonising: What is it, and whose job is it?

Decolonising curriculum in settler-colonial nations is an enormous task, including but not limited to excising Eurocentrism, locating and removing Western universalism, critiquing colonial dominance and workings of power, correcting distortions, and providing authentic and diverse representation of events and of First Nations Peoples and cultures, and placing the researcher (or teacher) reflexively and consciously "in the colonial context."[4] Decolonising the curriculum may be tackled at the most basic of levels through Brown Band-aid approaches such as attending to representation and voice; these are presented as remedies for racism and the enduring legacies of the colonial theft of country (see Sapto et al.,[5] for a mapping of global curriculum decolonising initiatives). 'De- colonising' potentially sounds like something potentially easy to achieve, with the prefix 'de' meaning to 'do the opposite of,' 'reverse,' or 'remove.'[6] Can the 'colonial' within an individual subject simply be removed or 'fixed' inside the masters' houses[7] of national curriculum and the Australian education system? Yet decolonisation, in this form, is always already the work of recolonising, as Simone Bignall[8] explores, as opposed to a bolder project of 'ex-colonising' that does not simply adjust settler-colonial norms, for example, via insertion of a unit on 'Indigenous History' within a programme that otherwise ignores Indigenous history.

This focus on representation can mean a simplistic, binarised checkbox list denoting the presence or absence of First Nations content. Attending to representation has a kind of productive insufficiency; it is something, but never enough. In recognising this, the real work can start. Instead of locating racism in exteriorities (curriculum, textbooks, school rules, media, students), there have been calls for White teachers to start decolonisation with the self through critically reflective professional learning.[9] Instead of assumptions about 'knowing' students and understanding 'Blackness' (processes in which Whiteness is normalised), White teachers are exhorted to start with understanding their own colour and the biases and assumptions that may go with it. It is through this process that they can potentially move beyond the superficial in their contribution to creating and sustaining change, and to making an honest and worthwhile contribution to the 'history wars.'

Is critical cultural competence enough?

This process is understood to be part of the development of 'critical cultural competence,' defined as being beyond just knowing facts about diversity.[10] While teaching a unit on cultural diversity in education, however, I have found that preservice teachers struggle to understand what this might mean. 'Cultural competence' also carries implications of bare functionality. It is more important to seek epistemological honesty about the specific knowledge projects framing White teachers' own educations; this is a process parallel to truth-seeking projects in Australia more broadly. But how to go about this? What knowledges and approaches could support this kind of work?

Tyson Yunkaporta,[11] for example, has emphasised that people need support not to become experts in Aboriginal knowledges but to connect with their own. Natalie Harkin,[12] similarly, suggests that non-Indigenous researchers look to their own histories and cultures for methodologies and methods rather than borrowing from Indigenous approaches. Yunkaporta and Harkin provide ways here to think about decolonising without merely appropriating and applying Indigenous knowledges to reflective professional practice and thereby merely inscribing settler-colonialism.

Memory work

What can White teachers do in these 'history wars'? Building on Yunkaporta and Harkin's advice, and on the findings of my own doctoral studies, professional learning could involve memory work in which teachers use writing to connect with an educational archive of the self. This writing operates somewhere in the borderlands[13] between autobiography, autoethnography, narrative inquiry, fictocriticism and fiction as educational research.[14] It draws on both actual personal, lived, embodied experience, and yet also recognises memory as, inevitably, an act of imagination.[15] It takes the form of a "dialogue with the self about the other" and also about the notion of truth;[16] this kind of writing aspires to truth based on whether there is integrity in the ways the writing displays "the universal in the particular."[17] To decolonise history education means to understand how societal racism plays out in the everyday practices of remembered and recreated classrooms.

Writing fictionalised accounts of personal experience may be understood to be "a valid mode of inquiry into professional practice"[18] that can serve to raise awareness, to produce knowledge differently to link pasts, presents, and futures, creating spaces in which readers might recognise versions of themselves.[19] bell hooks has said that the purpose of such memory work is "to make the past useable."[20] White teachers' own history educations, as revisited through narrative, can function as a *"memory space"*[21] (italics in original) to explore the workings of colonial power. Writing to explore this space can then be understood not in a deterministic way (this led to that) but to relocate the personal in cultural frames.[22]

Writing into history education as a memory space is not about establishing an essentialised, remembered true self but is rather "a way of working with experience"[23] to find out what emerges as powerful in the storied past in relation to the present. Such writing provides a direct challenge to one of the multiple forms of "systematically supported amnesia"[24]: the ways First Nations Peoples have been, or have not been, woven into history education. Identifying the workings of power also assists with finding and addressing barriers to the broader project of decolonisation.

Vignettes as memory space writing

The following vignettes, refined for this chapter, emerge from writing completed for my arts-based thesis on curriculum design; at that time, I sought

> eclectic practices of writing, collection and assemblage, of both "real" and fictive elements, to alchemise the connection between practice and life that hooks (1994) also advocates. This might be realised as a kind of critical curriculum writing for teacher reflection…linking personal history to the design process.
>
> [unpublished doctoral thesis]

I sought to identify (1) the subject positions negotiated by teachers in curriculum design work, (2) the struggles from which curriculum emerges, (3) how research can offer more nuanced and reflexive ways to think about curriculum, and (4) how the study could create a space for an absent subject (the teacher/designer marginalised in discourses of the mandated curriculum in Australia). All these questions have resonances with the goal of decolonising curriculum through attention to the White History teacher self, but without essentialising this notional self.

The following vignettes blend my own experiences as a student and teacher, anecdote and fiction, as a way of getting closer to a past that can never actually be relived but can be reimagined to better understand the present. My story here, told as an adult former History teacher remembering/imagining being a Year Nine History student in a Victorian school, is a generational story that may ring true for other White teachers in their 40s, 50s, and 60s; these are teachers who are now in positions of authority in schools and systems, creating policy and materials, and leading practice.

In respecting cultural safety for First Nations readers, I would like to point out that there are words used in this account that are direct quotations from the past when cultural norms allowed the routine debasement of First Nations Peoples through language. I argue that it is important not to ignore or forget this language and its echoes, and the fight for dignity and respect that was necessary to shift attitudes, along with the work still to be done. Confronting this language requires both acknowledging its truthfulness to the attitudes and discourses of the time but also that it potentially reinscribes these attitudes through repetition in any form. This is the kind of tension memory work can present for teachers in professional learning, where they could debate and critique the use of this language not only in their own writing but in the classroom.

For readers of this chapter, the following vignettes can serve as examples of memory work to give a concrete sense of how it might be enacted (though without serving as any kind of template). The vignettes can be the basis of discussion and critique, giving rise to debate as described earlier. They can be used to identify historical and enduring racism and to suggest where echoes of this may exist in readers' own histories. After the vignettes, I offer more specific suggestions for how they may be used.

In writing this series of three vignettes, I revisit a single curriculum document from my history education and teaching career: the paper handout of instructions I gave a Year Nine Australian History class for an assignment in my first year of teaching (just four years after having finished school myself). This vividly remembered artefact functions to anchor the story in history while I try to reconstruct its context and what made it possible. Almost four decades later, I try to remain true to the essence of the experiences described here. I adopt the standard layout of literary narrative fiction writing, and all 'people' here are fictional, non-identifiable amalgams, not actual people, as an ethical move. I take these fictional liberties to protect all those involved, including feints such as writing this from the perspective of a student in the class, not the teacher; I blend experiences from my own school education and my teaching here to create the first-person protagonist persona of student 'Imogen.'

Vignette one: Welcome to our tribe

Year Nine Australian History. 1990. Period Six. I am sitting by the window, and Mrs Hall is at her desk at the front of the room.

"Girls, you may have realised this year we have a new textbook." I know this: my mother was cursing because we couldn't buy it second-hand.

"However, before we start it, I want to announce that for the first time, we will be commencing our year with the Aborigines, the native people of our continent, prior to the discovery of Australia. We will study their tribes, how they lived and their fascinating customs." She sighs. Mrs Hall writes historical romance novels, and she sometimes reads out sections of her manuscripts to us. *Eileen Hall* is the name on her book covers, with their paintings of dukes and pirates. She'd rather be in a gown and cloak, on the castle ramparts, watching for a knight on the horizon, than teaching us.

"Our first assignment is the *Welcome to Our Tribe Handbook*, an opportunity to research and understand how the natives really lived. It's a group task. Imogen, hand out the sheet." I shuffle between the rows of desks, putting a piece of paper on each one, and then return to my own. My assignment sheet says,

> Imagine you are a member of an Aboriginal tribe who is welcoming a new member and write a guide to fitting in. Include:
>
> - family structure
> - religion
> - food
> - shelter
> - social rules/etiquette

Below the text, a man in a loincloth has been sketched, crouching in the dirt and rubbing two sticks together, and another man in the background, silhouetted on a cliff, with a spear, one leg bent, and his foot resting inside the other knee.

"Oh God," says the girl next to me. "Bor-ing." A mutinous hum fills the room. We wish we had Mr Randwick, who would surely skip this new stuff and be playing tragic convict songs on his guitar. He's in a band that plays all the traditional instruments, tin whistles and Jew's harps, and the songs from Van Diemen's Land, the saddest ones, because the cruellest things happened there. He even performed in assembly at the start of term. A plaintive minor chord sounds from Mr Randwick's class down the corridor, and we give a collective sigh. Mrs Hall stands up.

"Anyone who is reluctant to get to work might remember my method of managing group work. Any group problems, including delays, will be taken directly to the principal."

We get to work. A box full of library books sits out on the front desk, many of them in torn plastic bindings with chewed edges. History doesn't change. These books are never out of date. Their covers show bare Black people wearing nothing but white paint stripes, dancing or squatting, rubbing fire sticks. Each group of students sends a person up the front to collect a few books.

When word simmers around that you can see penises in many of the photos, girls start showing much more interest in the library books. Constant traffic between desks. Consultation between groups. Books borrowed from the front desk, passed around and returned. Mrs Hall is delighted with how the group work is going. Then we start reading some of the text aloud:

> "Can you believe this? They knocked the boys' front teeth out when they turned fifteen!"
> "They ate grubs. Look at the dirt on them!"
> "They speared each other for pretty much anything."
> "They thought pointing a bone could kill."
> "Oh, how cruel. They left their elderly people up in trees to die."
> "They had no shoes."

Then, "This is the worst of all! Wait until you hear this! They actually ate their enemies. Well, parts of them, anyway. Their *livers*."

Mrs Hall looks up from her marking, "Girls, girls, settle down! You'll have to stay in if you can't work more quietly."

Sarah, in front of me, is sliding a library book open at a photograph of naked Black men behind the venetian blind so the girls passing in the courtyard outside will see it through the window. I look out of a broken slat at the mountains in the distance. School is sliding off me. I take one of my favourite imaginings: I have finished school. For good. I am on a plane arriving at Heathrow. Any moment now, I will be in my distant father's arms, my face buried in his warm shoulder, in the bald suede that holds the essence of him.

Vignette two: Women of the sun

Today, we are presenting our *Welcome to Our Tribe Handbooks* to the class. We've made up funny names for our tribes. The *Woollygoogooloo* Tribe. The *Babagaga* Tribe. We can earn extra marks for creativity. We participate in an arms race of savageries. Which tribe will be the worst? When Mrs Hall is late for the next class, the girls nominate me to find her. On my way to the staffroom, I hear a voice in the History store cupboard. Nice Mr Randwick. He seems to be taking our class as a stand-by lesson for Mrs Hall, who's away.

"I can't believe I've got to fill in again this week. At least it's a video. Eileen's message says it's called *Against the Wind*. Where is the fucking thing! Why does every stand-by have to be so bloody difficult!"

Mr Gibb, the head of History is in there too. "I thought she took it home to watch. She loves Jon English with his shirt off, splitting that massive log. When he's gone from convict to settler. He's the nearest thing to a pirate we've got in the Year Nine syllabus. Can you do some games with them instead? Play some guitar."

"Eileen needs a good you-know-what, like most of the female teachers in this place. I've got sixty Year 12 practice exams to mark before tomorrow. I haven't got time to play the guitar. What else can I show them?"

"There's this, *Women of the Sun*. It's a series."

"It's not too Aboriginal is it? The common test starts at Early Settlers, so I don't even know why the hell we're doing this token stuff."

"It was Shazza's idea. Sharon Davies. You know. The new young History teacher. Not bad looking. She's into social justice. I've only seen the trailer; I vaguely remember some White men in it. Squatters, maybe? That would work as a link to the test."

"How long does each episode go for?"

"45."

"That's at least six exams marked. It'll do."

Back in the classroom, Mr Randwick inserts the video into the player underneath the television on a trolley at the front of the room. The first episode is called "Alinta," the flame. Alinta is a young Aboriginal girl, around our age, living a traditional Aboriginal life with her family and tribe. It takes us some time to get used to the idea of walking around in a grass skirt with bare breasts. Giggling. Whispers. Glances at Mr Randwick, who is preoccupied with his papers. He doesn't even see the breasts. Then we get caught in the eel trap of story. The tribe. The Elders. The handsome fiancée. The necklace gift. The beautiful, rich, long possum skin cloaks. The White convict escapees. The rape. The spearing. The betrayal we sense is coming. The deep stomach sadness of losing your home. Then the young couple are saying goodbye to the tribe. They are going back to his tribe. Loved ones are rubbing their palms under their arms, and then, oh no, the room cracks open with laughter…they are wiping them ON EACH OTHER'S CHEEKS. Worst horror of horrors!

Every single one of us has a shiny butterfly tube of Impulse body spray in our school bags. Spellbound. Mischief. Inspiration. Temptation. Midnight. Merely Musk. Every single one of us has scrubbed under our own arms with perfumed soap, rolled on deodorant, and then finished with spray that very morning. This is just too gross. This is ugly grubs and pointy bones taken way, way, way too far. This goes beyond the fascinatingly primitive to the just plain disgusting. For everyone but me.

This is where I split. This is where part of me is jumping around the room with everyone else, squealing and trying to escape Sarah, who is touching under her arms and chasing us. The other part is at home on my bed, reliving my fantasy of seeing my dad again, of hugging him, of burying my nose in his underarm jacket seam.

Mr Randwick is dragged back from exam-land.

"You idiots! Sit down! What on earth! Sarah, get back in your seat! And you lot, how dare you climb on those desks. Get down this instant, or you will not be allowed to hear the guest speaker next week!"

The class settles. The film goes on. I am no longer watching.

That second part, the new part of me, is, tentatively, starting to ask what the difference is, ask what is worse about waiting a short time for death in a tree, compared to waiting an age for death in a stark nursing home room that smells of shit and disinfectant. What is the difference between fresh sweat on your face and stale sweat in a seam? What is the difference between eating the liver of your enemy and your own placenta, like my mum did after I was born? What is the difference between a Black child and a White one?

Vignette three: The guest speaker

Before the next History lesson, I catch the flu and spend a week at home in bed. The first assembly back at school addresses something that happened while I was away.

Dr Cutton, the principal, takes off her glasses and leans forward on the lectern. "I regret to confirm that Miss Davies is no longer with the school. We abhor the incident that occurred last week and trust this will be an end to the matter. All guest speakers will, in future, be personally vetted by the vice principal. We acknowledge the enormously valuable contribution made to our nation by all your families, and we do not support a Black Armband view of history. I have the full support of the board on this matter."

History is first period. All the History staff are in a huddle just outside the staff room.

"What happened?" I asked Sarah.

"Miss Davies, you know, the new History teacher who's so into the A***, organised this guest speaker. This woman came in—she didn't even look that black—and she stood up and looked us all in the eye, and she said nothing, just looked and looked. So creepy. She said nothing, and we said nothing, and it was really weird."

"Then she started with, 'How far back in your family tree do you think you have to go to find a rapist or murderer?' Mrs Hall nearly fainted. Mr Gibb wasn't even there; he was teaching, and Mr Randwick was doing marking, so she was there on her own. Then the speaker told us all this stuff about massacres and stolen children and diseases and slavery, and what happened to Black women when White men arrived without White women. Showed us a video on deaths in jail and asked how we felt about that. As if we did it! As if we should be ashamed.

"At the end, some girls tried to argue with her. Isi tried to say she was born in Singapore, and she's only been in Australia five years, and she doesn't have any Aborigine killers in her family. So this woman asked her what she'd done to find out about it all since she arrived. And Isi said, 'I'm here aren't I?' So Miss Davies told her not to be rude, but you could tell she was kind of glad Isi said it. The speaker was getting everyone riled up. Then Leticia Pinker had to get up and say thank you on behalf of the students, and she put in that her family were very religious Christians and would never do anything like that, and they say prayers for Aborigines all the time at her church. And the woman laughed at her and asked her if she knew what a mission was. Then Miss Davies tried to say thank you and make it all nice and *la-di-da, valuable perspectives, grateful for your time* and stuff, but it was too late.

"About twenty parents complained and said they were disgusted and they were considering moving their daughters away from the school to somewhere with Australian values, not lefty politics."

Mrs Hall arrives and silences us with her eyes.

"Girls, today we will debate whether Portugal or Britain discovered Australia. Who has heard of the mahogany ships?"

No more tribes. No more Alinta. No more Miss Davies, creator of the "Welcome to our Tribe" assignment, but who I never actually even met. And me. I wonder what the guest speaker looked like. What her voice sounded like. I seem destined to never quite hear. Never quite know.

Discussion and reflection

These vignettes, with their blatant racism and sexism, are products of my blended learning and teaching experiences of the 1980s and 1990s. At a most obvious level, they demonstrate common discursive abuses of their time, such as paternalism (in pronouns such as 'our' for First Nations Peoples) and persistent denial and dishonesty (in referring to the 'discovery' of an inhabited continent) that serve to justify and ameliorate the theft of land. However, they also echo stories that First Nations university students who attended school more recently, in the 2000s and 2010s, have told me—for example, of Aboriginal students being sent out of the classroom to stand in the corridor for lessons mentioning Aboriginal Peoples.

The vignettes might be reflected on in several ways. First, as a window into curriculum history, they allow for Lowe and Yunkaporta's[25] interrogation of the depth of Aboriginal perspectives in curriculum. They argue that the following must not only be represented but critiqued for the *way* they are represented:

- Land
- Language
- Culture
- Time
- Place
- Relationships

In the storied lessons described here, based on real events, there is no sense of the school existing on Country or of the "Welcome to Our Tribe" project being connected in any way to any Country, except through vague notions of desert in the emptiness of the horizon line behind the man on one leg; there are no First Nations languages heard, and the English language used is not respectful or appropriate; there is no sense of Victorian First Nations histories and diversity, despite 'Alinta' living in what is now known as Victoria; First Nations Peoples are historicised and essentialised, caricatured and homogenised, exoticised and demonised; there is no sense of the interconnectedness of human and nonhuman relations in First Nations cultures or in any collaborative design of curriculum. Madsen et al.'s *Yarns: First Nations Resource Evaluation Tool*[6] also highlights that there is no sense of the Country where the textbook and assignment were produced.

While the educational events of these vignettes are couched as a progressive curriculum by the White teachers involved, this teaching clearly performed work of recolonising, of making accommodations that facilitate the maintenance of colonial fictions such as White entitlement to Country. The work of increased curricular representation here enacts further violence because of the *way* it has been enacted and its denial of the theft of land. These kinds of apparently 'worthy' strategies were naturalised as inclusive initiatives, and they also potentially empowered White Australians to ask questions about what more First Nations Australians could possibly want. Mere salience or prominence is demonstrably not necessarily proof of actual progress, and this functions as a reminder to evaluate what such initiatives achieve in the present.

Decolonising the white self

Yet the more interesting critical reflective work that these vignettes invite is thinking about the self I portray here that I have felt the need to conjure into existence. The literature warns of self-congratulatory narratives and White saviour narratives emerging in these kinds of stories, and reading over this work is uncomfortable for me, as I am forced to confront the way I depict the central persona here as superior to other students and teachers, more sensitive or insightful, seeking more, seeking the truth.

What recuperative work am I doing on the self here? In real life, not fiction, I laughed at the library book in the window when I walked past it after class and admired the daring of the student who put it there, but I also think the vividness of the memory links to a sense of shame that has become stronger over time. Why have I needed to write a White hero student protagonist into the story and portray the one real First Nations Person represented here as a villain, going too far, saying too much, and in effect closing down what might have been a White 'awakening'?

I employ technologies to distance the protagonist, or indeed myself, from the racism around us. Even grammatically, in discussing the vignettes and the practices within them, I avoid using the pronoun 'I' and claiming the problematic language used. Thinking with bell hooks requires me to think how this story itself works to keep structures of domination in place, perhaps by making excuses for my own limitations as an activist in the present or to perform, in a perfunctory way, White guilt. It also makes little attempt to actually challenge my right not to question my colour or even perceive it to any meaningful extent.

If this writing was shared in a professional learning group, there would be much more to talk about, for example, (1) the conflict I describe between teachers, (2) the rhetorical choices made by the guest speaker, and (3) the fate of Miss Davies, the White teacher 'Mummy.' Miss Davies is depicted as a casualty in the 'history wars' because she dared to engage a speaker who asked uncomfortable questions that may alienate students, a genuine risk.[27] There is also the question of the enormity of White Australian history the previous account elides: the personal histories of White British or European families as colonisers.

While writing this chapter, in a chance conversation with a cousin researching our family tree, I heard that my young great-grandfather's male relatives were "not around much," as they were "out east" in the Wurundjeri lands between my home and the Dandenongs "felling trees for felloes." Felloes are the arched wooden inserts inside wheel rims that secure cart or carriage spokes. Not only did my family participate in the destruction of the Country on which Wurundjeri People's lives depended, but they were also *stealing* country to provide the transport machinery that drove colonial power and extended colonial reach. Understanding my own family's role here, so conveniently ignored and 'forgotten,' is a humbling and sobering blow to the arrogance of my own settler-colonial identity and also my crusading History teacher professional identity. Teaching Australian history for years without investigating my own history demonstrates complicity and wilful neglect; these revelations position me in a different way in relation to a more truthful history education, implicated rather than neatly outside.

In all de-colonising educational initiatives, including shifting focus from interrogating Blackness to thinking about Whiteness, White teachers need to be aware of how what is said and done may shut down truth-telling, as demonstrated in and by the vignettes in this chapter. It is this kind of reflexive work on the self that may, ultimately, best represent White courage in the 'history wars.' To begin to de-colonise the self is to try to set aside the colonists' refusal to acknowledge the intimate and everyday colonial violences in our own educational and family histories and present-day practices. It is also to commence the difficult work of trying to understand what this might mean for how we design curriculum and how we teach.

Ideas and strategies for white teachers' history education memory space writing

The practice of memory writing, as demonstrated earlier, can be used in professional learning to give rise to evaluation of curricula, reflections on White educator identities, and further questions about purported 'decolonising' initiatives. This chapter, or the vignettes, could be used as a before or after writing exercise to stimulate discussion and emphasise that there is more to do in the 'history wars,' or in decolonising History, than merely ticking boxes by adding First Nations content.

Memory writing workshop strategies

1. Acknowledge Country and also the country of participants' lived experiences in Australia—for example, where they grew up and went to school.
2. Begin writing on a sentence stem, such as, "In Australian History, I learnt…," or "My Australian History teacher taught me…"
3. Consider how to move from individual writing and reflection to collective writing and reflection following discussion, using stems such as, "In Australian History we learnt…" Explore opportunities to do this in conversation, consultation or collaboration with First Nations Peoples local to the relevant area of Australia.
4. Cultural safety needs to be an important consideration at the outset of all such discussions, with at least basic cultural competence ensured for all White educators involved. For example, First Nations Peoples would potentially be involved in dialogue as experts, interlocutors, and contributors, not as those needing to reflect on race. The Australian Human Rights Commission has a useful resource exploring the concepts of cultural safety and security.[28]
5. Possible questions after reading the chapter and doing the preceding writing include the following:

   1. In what ways, if any, do the experiences described in the vignettes resonate with your own history education?
   2. What other experiences and resources related to teaching with or about First Nations Peoples have been part of your History education?
   3. On whose terms and conditions have these experiences and resources entered the curriculum and classroom?
   4. How has History teaching changed since your own education? What has your role been in any changes?
   5. What is your role in your memory space writing? How do you represent yourself as a White person in a settler-colonial nation?
   6. Is there evidence in your writing of trying to distance yourself, or your family, from racism in Australia's history? Describe how and why you feel this emerges in the writing.
   7. How are Lowe and Yunkaporta's[29] key markers of the depth of First Nations perspectives in a text (see the following) represented (or not) in (a) your writing and (b) your teaching?
      - Land
      - Language
      - Culture

- Time
- Place
- Relationships

8 What are the told and untold stories about your own family's acquisition of and interactions with Country? These may be residually present in paper documents like the *Welcome to Our Tribe Handbook* but in the form of certificates of subdivision or title, leases, letters, diaries, and family history research documentation. How might these stories inform your positioning as a History teacher in a settler colonist nation?
9 What might you take from these vignettes/your own memory space writing to inform your professional learning needs or in decolonising your teaching? How can you access appropriate learning and develop a professional learning plan in this area?

In a follow-up session, teachers could bring curriculum materials to critique, change, or make plans to replace in decolonising moves achieved through appropriate consultation processes.

Notes

1 Lumley, S. (1915). *Daddy, what did you do in the Great War?* (Lithograph on paper laid down on linen). The War Office.
2 British Library. (2023). *Daddy, what did you do in the Great War?* British recruitment poster. https://www.bl.uk/collection-items/daddy-what-did-you-do-in-great-war
3 Hook, G. (2012). Towards a decolonising pedagogy: Understanding Australian Indigenous studies through critical whiteness theory and film pedagogy. *The Australian Journal of Indigenous Education, 41*(2), 110–119. https://doi.org/10.1017/jie.2012.27
4 Samier, E. (2017). Towards a postcolonial and decolonising educational administration history. *Journal of Educational Administration and History, 49*(4), 264–282. p. 11. https://doi.org/10.1080/00220620.2017.1343288
5 Sapto, A., Utami, I. W. P., Leksana, G., Ayundasari, L., & Ramadhan, F. (2023). Recent trends in the decolonisation of history curriculum: A systematic review. In Ridhoi et al. (Eds.), *Embracing new perspectives in history, social sciences and education* (pp. 39–43). Taylor and Francis.
6 Merriam Webster. (2023). *De-Prefix.* https://www.merriam-webster.com/dictionary/DE
7 Lorde, A. (1984). The master's tools will never dismantle the master's house. In *Sister outsider: Essays and speeches* (pp. 110–114). Crossing Press.
8 Bignall, S. (2014). The collaborative struggle for excolonialism. *Settler Colonial Studies, 4*(4), 340–356. https://doi.org/10.1080/2201473X.2014.911651
9 Landsman, J. (2011). Being white: Invisible privileges of a New England prep girl. In J. Landsman & C. W. Lewis (Eds.), *White teachers/diverse classrooms: Creating inclusive schools, building on students' diversity and providing true educational equity* (pp. 11–24). Stylus.
10 Ladson-Billings, G. (2011). Yes, but how do we do it? Practising culturally relevant pedagogy. In J. Landsman & C. W. Lewis (Eds.), *White teachers/diverse classrooms: Creating inclusive schools, building on students' diversity and providing true educational equity* (pp. 33–45). Stylus.

11 Yunkaporta, T. (2019). *Sand talk: How Indigenous thinking can save the world*. Text Publishing.
12 Harkin, N. (2021). *Q&A with Natalie Harkin*. Paper presented at the Summer School, University of Utrecht.
13 Clandinin, D. J., & Rosiek, J. (2007). Mapping a landscape of narrative inquiry. In D. J. Clandinin (Ed.), *Handbook of narrative inquiry: Mapping a methodology* (pp. 35–75). Sage.
14 Kuhn, A. (1995). *Family secrets: Acts of memory and imagination*. Verso.
15 Ibid.
16 Mackinlay, E. (2012). PEARL: A reflective story about decolonising pedagogy in Indigenous Australian studies. *The Australian Journal of Indigenous Education, 41*(1), 67–74. p. 16. https://doi.org/10.1017/jie.2012.10
17 Eisner, E. (2003). Concerns and aspirations for qualitative research in the new millennium. In N. Addison & L. Burgess (Eds.), *Issues in art and design teaching* (pp. 52–60). Routledge. p. 57.
18 Rowland, G., Rowland, S., & Winter, R. (1990). Writing fiction as inquiry into professional practice. *Journal of Curriculum Studies, 22*(3), 291–293. https://doi.org/10.1080/0022027900220306
19 Clough, P. (2002). *Narratives and fictions in educational research*. Open University Press.
20 hooks, cited in Mitchell, C., & Weber, S. (1999). *Reinventing ourselves as teachers: Beyond nostalgia*. Routledge. http://site.ebrary.com.ezproxy-m.deakin.edu.au/lib/deakin/docDetail.action?docID=10054861
21 Ibid., p. 16.
22 Kamler, B. (2001). *Relocating the personal: A critical writing pedagogy*. State University of New York Press.
23 Mitchell & Weber. *Reinventing ourselves as teachers*, p. 173.
24 Lowe, K., & Yunkaporta, T. (2013). The inclusion of Aboriginal and Torres Strait Islander content in the Australian National Curriculum: A cultural, cognitive and socio-political evaluation. *Curriculum Perspectives, 33*(1), 1–14. p. 9.
25 Lowe & Yunkaporta. The inclusion of Aboriginal and Torres Strait Islander content, p. 9.
26 Marsden, B., Perkins, R., & Shay, M. (2021). Critical selection of curriculum materials for embedding Indigenous knowledges and perspectives: tools for teachers. In M. Shay & R. Oliver (Eds.), *Indigenous education in Australia: Learning and teaching for deadly futures* (pp. 133-147). Oxon, UK: Routledge.
27 Race, R., Ayling, P., Chetty, D., Hassan, N., McKinney, S. J., Boath, L., Riaz, N., & Salehjee, S. (2022). Decolonising curriculum in education: Continuing proclamations and provocations. *London Review of Education, 20*(1). p. 12. https://doi.org/10.14324/LRE.20.1.12
28 Human Rights Commission. (2011). Chapter 4: Cultural safety and security. *Social Justice Report*. https://humanrights.gov.au/our-work/chapter-4-cultural-safety-and-security-tools-address-lateral-violence-social-justice
29 Lowe & Yunkaporta. The inclusion of Aboriginal and Torres Strait Islander content, p. 9.

Chapter 8

Acknowledging First Nations perspectives in primary schools

Kate Harvie

Author positioning statement

Acknowledging genealogy is customary in First Nations introductions. As an action of decolonising, it is imperative that I, too, acknowledge my genealogy to position myself for the reader. I introduce myself as a non-Indigenous Australian woman living and working on Wurundjeri Country. My genealogy and qualifications classify me as a non-Indigenous, white, middle-class, teacher, teacher-educator, and researcher. I am a fifth-generation colonised Australian with English, Dutch, and French ancestry. I am a daughter, wife, mother, sister, and aunty.

As a non-Indigenous educator, I acknowledge my white privileged background, which is a contributing factor to how I view the world. Being aware of this, I am conscious that giving advice or guidance to other teachers by a non-Indigenous person needs to be undertaken in a culturally safe way in order to acknowledge my colonial background and to be respectful of self-determination protocols. Rigney (1999) writes how Aboriginal Peoples and communities have been "poked, prodded, measured, tested and compared" by non-Indigenous people, which has resulted in the "extraction, storage and control over Indigenous knowledges,"[1] which also includes stealing intellectual property, such as artworks. I understand that my role as an ally is to acknowledge and honour First Nations voices whilst consistently challenging my own white privilege to disrupt colonisation.

Teacher narrative

I am a teacher. Teachers are knowers of themselves, of children, of situations, of subject matter, of teaching, and of learning.[2] My career in education spans 30 years. Seventeen of those years teaching in primary schools in both Australia and the United Kingdom and 12 of those years lecturing pre-service teachers at an Australian university. My lectures included looking at the Aboriginal and Torres Strait Islander cross-curriculum priority in Humanities Education (Social Studies: History, Geography, Civics and Citizenship). I am currently employed at the Department of Education, Victoria, in the Koorie Curriculum

Clusters project. It is these experiences that provide me with an astute insight into the typical lives and work of other non-Indigenous teachers with similar socio-political positioning as myself, including comparable lived experiences in navigating how to embed First Nations perspectives into curriculum and school culture. In my current role, I work with and alongside First Nations colleagues, Registered Aboriginal Parties, and cluster schools to lead improvement in teacher capability and confidence in partnership with local Registered Aboriginal Party Elders and consultants. This project is informed by the *Marrung Aboriginal Education Plan 2016–2026*[3] and the *Dhelk Wukang 2022–2026 Aboriginal Inclusion Plan*.[4] Exploring partnerships and co-designing resources by Registered Aboriginal Parties and cluster schools is an exciting project to be working on to see how schools can deconstruct colonised curriculum with the knowledge, support, and guidance of their local Registered Aboriginal Parties.

Colonisation in primary schools can be detected not only in the History curriculum but throughout other aspects of the school. It can move beyond the classroom walls to penetrate whole school culture in subtle but significant ways. Examples of colonisation in action are still evident in the use of incorrect or outdated language, such as 'Aborigines'; racist comments, taunts, or slurs allowed within the classroom or the playground; misappropriation or unauthorised use of artwork and art methods (such as dot painting on toilet paper rolls to make 'didgeridoos'); and teaching history with white-washed bias, omitting truth-telling, and favouring a colonised view. Often, schools, teachers, and students are oblivious to colonised practices. Teacher memories, mandated curriculum, inappropriate bias in the classroom, and outdated resources compound the need for new ways to look at curriculum from a different perspective.

Through my research and experiences in education, I have explored common challenges with non-Indigenous teachers planning and teaching First Nations perspectives. Many non-Indigenous teachers lack the capability and confidence in teaching Aboriginal and Torres Strait Islander histories and cultures, resulting in resistance to teaching First Nations perspectives.[5] The consistent message I have found among non-Indigenous teachers is that they "don't want to get it wrong."[6] I position myself "in the midst"[7] of these teachers with similar lived experiences to myself, where I intend to challenge and disrupt stagnant narratives to promote ways to decolonise curriculum, drawing upon my own personal and professional narratives. In my yarns with other non-Indigenous teachers and pre-service teachers, some of the reasons that they are hesitant or reluctant to teach Indigenous perspectives include being

- culturally unfamiliar with First Nations culture and history;
- underprepared to teach First Nations perspectives as a result of lack of knowledge, content, and pedagogical approaches included in their initial teacher education course; and
- under-resourced with current locally anchored teaching and learning resources.

Adding to this is a lack of ongoing professional learning opportunities in First Nations perspectives for teachers and a lack of opportunities to build relationships and partnerships with Traditional Owners, local Elders, and Aboriginal community members.

From my research, I noted that there are teachers who are *culturally unfamiliar* with First Nations history, culture, and knowledge. In one instance, a teacher I spoke to relied on the knowledge and understanding of a relative who had spent six weeks 'visiting' Darwin. Another teacher added that they had a cousin who had worked in a school for five months on Arrente Country, and so they saw them as 'experts' in First Nations culture. Unfortunately, teachers relying on second-hand connections as a way to gain 'advice and permission' to teach a particular cultural or historical First Nation concept provide disjointed constructions of truth and understanding. Non-Indigenous teachers being culturally unfamiliar with Aboriginal Ways of Knowing, Being, and Doing, as well as not understanding protocols around acknowledging contemporary, local culture, and significant peoples and places, is problematic to reducing or eradicating colonised practices in schools.

I know first-hand after teaching pre-service teachers that they are *underprepared* to teach First Nations perspectives with any confidence or authority. I have witnessed many pre-service teachers over the past 12 years relying on their schooling memories and regurgitating this in their own teaching practice assessments. It is promising to see that Australia has introduced a mandatory one-off First Nations 'unit' into every initial teacher education course; however, I argue universities should be looking closely at how First Nations perspectives can be embedded into every individual unit undertaken by pre-service teachers throughout the duration of their course. From my own experiences in teaching pre-service teachers, they revert to 'teacher memories' when tasked with a lesson to present on Aboriginal and Torres Strait Islander histories and cultures as part of their Humanities education unit. When pre-service teachers were asked to present a lesson that included First Nations perspectives, they most often reverted to dot painting, colouring the Aboriginal flag, or reading a Dreaming story: typical examples of what they might have learnt at school. The lack of deep cultural understanding from their own schooling perpetuates what they think is appropriate to plan and teach to future classes of Australian students.

Finding suitable locally anchored resources and translating these into authentic, non-tokenistic teaching experiences can also be a challenge for teachers. Locally anchored resources are those that are unique to the local area and provide significant insight into local First Nations Peoples from that Country. A Naarm (Melbourne) example of a locally anchored resource is the 'Corroboree Tree' located at the Burnley Oval in Richmond, Melbourne, which is "a huge, ancient, dead River Red Gum once served as a marker of clan territories, and also a place for various gatherings and celebrations."[8] Significant sites such as this can be incorporated into local history curriculum to make learning more relevant and experiential for students and challenge the place of colonisation in primary history curriculum.

In my research, I found that schools that prioritised a yearly budget for First Nations teaching resources, such as picture storybooks, artefacts, local First Nations dance groups, visiting artists and incursions, provided their students with current and authentic learning experiences rather than those that relied on old, outdated books, posters, and artefacts, allowing decolonisation to be embedded even further within the curriculum. Prioritising appropriate locally anchored resources where possible to support teaching and learning, ensuring that these resources are current and appropriate, and providing equitable access to these resources for all staff are ways to ensure that these resources are used for the purposes they were intended for.

Context

There are two specific rationales for decolonising approaches in primary schools which are the moral/ethical and curricular imperative. In the next section of this chapter, I highlight the education declarations which inform curriculum, identifying specifically the need for First Nations perspectives to be given priority in schools. Although these declarations provide a 'best-practice' approach, the reality is that there are other factors at play which determine the realities of how curriculum may be decolonised. These factors include educational memories that cloud teachers' judgements, and I frame these within my own lived experiences as a student and teacher in the 1980s and 1990s. Finally, I provide First Nations strategies of Yarning, Dadirri, and Ganma to demonstrate ways that teachers can deconstruct colonial practices in their curriculum, teaching, and whole-school culture.

Curriculum declarations

Curriculum in Australian schools is driven by ministerial education declarations, which ultimately direct the overarching goals and aspirations of Australian education. Such declarations are relevant to decolonising curriculum, as they set out the expectations for schools when embedding First Nations perspectives into the curriculum. However, they do not prescribe exactly how this is to be done in individual schools and classrooms.

The 2008 *Melbourne Declaration on Educational Goals for Young Australians*[9] highlighted the need for all Australian students to "understand and acknowledge the value of Indigenous cultures and possess the knowledge, skills and understanding to contribute to, and benefit from, reconciliation between Indigenous and non-Indigenous Australians."[10] The Australian Curriculum and Assessment Reporting Authority (ACARA) recognised the importance of this and in 2010 wrote Indigenous perspectives into the national curriculum "to ensure that all young Australians have the opportunity to learn about, acknowledge and respect the history and culture of Aboriginal people and Torres Strait Islanders."[11] As a result, the cross-curriculum priority of Aboriginal and Torres Strait histories and cultures was expected to be included across all Key Learning Areas (KLAs) from Foundation to Year 10. In 2008, Harrison wrote, "[A] key point about including Indigenous perspectives in your classroom is to make Indigenous Australia an ongoing reference point for the students."[12] Although the inclusion of First Nations perspectives in the Australian Curriculum had been included to some extent in past curriculum iterations, the cross-curriculum priority approach was a new way to include First Nations perspectives.

An Aboriginal and Torres Strait Islander Advisory Group and Task Force was responsible for writing the content for the Aboriginal and Torres Strait Islander cross-curriculum priority in the Australian Curriculum.[13] This was a significant step towards advocating self-determination, having First Nations perspectives written *by* First Nations Peoples, compared to heavily colonised curricula previously. Having a First Nations voice writing the content for the Aboriginal and Torres Strait Islander cross-curriculum priority in the Australian Curriculum was a positive step towards being able to begin the process of deconstructing and decolonising Australian Curriculum to include more truth-telling history and acknowledgement of significant contributions of First Nations Peoples. The New Zealand Ministry of Education has a similar approach to curriculum construction, with First Nations whānau having input into the design and construction of the Aotearoa New Zealand school curriculum, announcing, "From 2023, Te Takanga o Te Wā and Aotearoa New Zealand's histories will be part of all kura and schools' marau ā-kura and local curriculum," and "there will be opportunities for whānau and communities to contribute to the development of their school or kura local curriculum–marau ā-kura, to include local critical histories."[14]

In the decade prior to the introduction of the Aboriginal and Torres Strait Islander cross-curriculum priority, the Australian federal government had debated and denied the tumultuous and violent history of European invasion and the impact this had on First Nations Peoples and communities. The infamous 'history wars' argued that students in schools were being taught History from a 'black armband' approach and others instead advocated for a more positive narrative. The debate prompted a review of changes to the existing Aboriginal history curriculum, as Clark stated the 'black armband' tag was a "strategic conservative swipe at histories that revealed Australia's past as racist and violent"[15] and that "recognition of illegitimacy in history syllabuses extended the concern about changing approaches to Australian history into the realm of public education."[16]

The Aboriginal and Torres Strait Islander histories and cultures cross-curriculum priority addresses two specific needs:

- Aboriginal and Torres Strait Islander students can see themselves, their identities, and their cultures reflected in the curriculum of each of the learning areas, can fully participate in the curriculum, and can build their self-esteem.
- Aboriginal and Torres Strait Islander histories and cultures cross-curriculum priority is designed for all students to engage in reconciliation, respect, and recognition of the world's oldest continuous living cultures.[17]

Through this cross-curriculum priority, students are encouraged to inquire more deeply about the impact of European invasion on First Nations Peoples, with the inclusion to explore the turbulent history of settler engagement and tragic events that occurred in Australian history. Students also celebrate the personal and significant impacts that individual Aboriginal and Torres Strait people have had on Australian society, culture, sport, art, and communities. Despite these changes, History curriculum was still being censored by bureaucrats, such as this ambiguous recommendation in the 2014 review of the Australian Curriculum[18] in which the reviewers, Donnelly and Wiltshire, indicated that ACARA should reconceptualise the Aboriginal and Torres Strait Islander histories and cultures cross-curriculum priority and embed it into teaching and learning programmes "only where educationally relevant, in the mandatory content of the curriculum."[19] This recommendation was contrary to equipping teachers with direction and guidance in how, when, and what to teach Indigenous perspectives and reneged on the importance of a mandatory, culturally safe curriculum. It reinstated the colonial approach to curriculum that Australian teachers had become accustomed to. Other critiques, such as Salter and Maxwell's, identified flaws in the cross-curriculum priority approach, saying that the 'content' in the Aboriginal and Torres Strait Islander cross-curriculum priority "uses a colonising narrative…which can be discretely identified and inserted into curriculum to conquer 'problems,'" such as social inclusion and equity.[20]

In 2021, ACARA released further draft variations for a range of KLAs in the Australian Curriculum, with the Indigenous Advisory Group proposing changes "to give First Nations culture far greater emphasis in the national curriculum," and to include "truth-telling and inclusive language, including broadening terminology to include First Nations Australians as well as Aboriginal and Torres Strait Islanders."[21] This 2021 review of the curriculum called for "greater connection to Country, land and seas and the impact of colonisation and dispossession."[22] Federal Indigenous Affairs minister Ken Wyatt stated,

> It is important that all Australian students are provided the opportunity to learn about the depth, wealth and diversity of Aboriginal and Torres Strait Islander 65,000 year old history and cultures, and we want to ensure teachers are appropriately supported to embed Indigenous Australian perspectives in their classroom practice.[23]

Not surprisingly, other bureaucrats weighed in on the proposals, with federal education minister Alan Tudge arguing that the new ACARA proposals "painted a negative view of our country, our history, our future."[24] Deakin University Pro Vice Chancellor, Indigenous Strategy, and Innovation, Professor Mark Rose, said Mr Tudge's comments were unhelpful and instead argued, "[T]his is about teachers, who are the greatest judges of education for their kids, and have the right tools to equip the kids of tomorrow with the right tools."[25] I agree in principle with Professor Rose; however, I think Australian non-Indigenous teachers would welcome more whole-school planning and professional learning to support this statement. The National Indigenous Youth Education Coalition (NIYEC) co-ordinator Hayley McQuire also found Mr Tudge's comments unhelpful, stating,

> It's about being honest about our history and how that history has shaped our society today. ... What the federal education minister is saying is that he doesn't actually care about how Aboriginal and Torres Strait Islander people feel when they're learning a history that does not represent the truth of their experiences.[26]

Showing similarities with Australia's education system, Canadian scholar Ugwuegbula argued that Eurocentric education, curriculum, and pedagogy were "founded on principles of colonialism and continue to centre on Eurocentric, or Western, knowledge and theories of teaching and learning, leaving out the diverse knowledge of Black, Indigenous, and other marginalized communities."[27]

The *Mparntwe (Alice Springs) Education Declaration*, introduced in 2019, aimed "to promote excellence and equity and enable all Australians to become confident and creative individuals, successful learners, and active and informed community members."[28] Although this declaration was officially titled the *Alice Springs (Mparntwe) Education Declaration*, I choose to symbolically decolonise this document by placing the emphasis on Arrernte language. The preamble of the Mparntwe Declaration includes this statement:

> We recognise the more than 60,000 years of continual connection by Aboriginal and Torres Strait Islander peoples as a key part of the nation's history, present and future. Through education, we are committed to ensuring that all students learn about the diversity of Aboriginal and Torres Strait Islander cultures, and to seeing all young Aboriginal and Torres Strait Islander peoples thrive in their education and all facets of life.[29]

This claim from Australian education ministers adds, "Our challenge is to turn the aspirations set out in this document into actions."[30] Yet how schools and teachers are expected to implement this into practice with limited funding for professional learning or resources is a considerable challenge. Having a curriculum with mandatory regulations to include Aboriginal and Torres Strait Islander perspectives and education ministers declaring that they are committed to all Australian students learning about First Nations perspectives is one thing, but ensuring teachers have the capability, knowledge, and confidence to actually embed these perspectives is another.

Temporality and teacher memories

As a student in Year 5 in 1982, I remember learning a colonised history curriculum about 'Aborigines' (sic) and how European settlers 'conquered' Australian shores. The hero in this story was Captain Arthur Phillip, and the villains were portrayed as the Aboriginal 'natives' (sic). I recall doing a 'project' on 'Aborigines Yesterday' (sic) which involved buying the 'Aborigines Yesterday project kit'[31] from the local news agency that I (along with everyone else in the Year 5/6 class) cut and pasted onto a large piece of poster paper, to present back to the class. This project kit and the *Encyclopaedia Britannica* (UK publication) were the only reference materials available to my generation in pre-internet days. Forty years ago, this was the way that colonised curriculum was done. 'Dreamtime' stories were presented as the 'religion' of First Nations Peoples, and images of semi-naked men playing didgeridoos or hunting with spears were commonplace. There was an omission of women, colour photography, clothing, or joy in the images we were provided with. Black and white portraits of men with stern faces, standing with an intimidating stance, often with dead animals slung across their backs, were routinely presented, and as I began teaching in the early 1990s, I understood quickly that these were the only teacher resources that were available. First Nations Peoples were also represented as 'nameless' and without any real culture or wisdom. If I was a bureaucrat hoping to instil a Eurocentric, colonised, white-washed, biased curriculum in Australian primary schools, then circa 1993–2008 would tick all of those boxes.

As a graduate beginning teacher in the early 1990s, the goal of colonisation was revealed as I regurgitated my 'teacher memories' and replicated inadequate curriculum and pedagogies that I had encountered during my earlier school days. I did not learn anything of significance about First Nations history, culture, or knowledges that I can recall at teachers' college, apart from some vague cross-hatching painting techniques in a visual art class. Looking back through my teacher work plans from these formative years, I notice 'integrated studies' units of work titled "Australia through Time" and "Aborigines in Australia." These units of work were thematic based, where everything 'First Nations' was thrown into the unit for that particular ten-week school term. No real thought was given to First Nations perspectives once the term was over.

Just like me, many Australians recall that they learnt nothing, or very little about Aboriginal and Torres Strait Islander histories and cultures through their Eurocentric-focused schooldays.[32] Adding to this problem, teachers recall very limited memories about what they learnt during their own school days, often replicating this in their current curriculum design and delivery.[33] The 'teacher memories' that I refer to here are those that teachers recall from their own learning experiences as children and adolescents, either in education settings or in their lived experiences outside of formal learning. The memories that teachers recall as students compared to when they become teachers are not going to have the same context, and they are often unaware of the implications race has on their pre-conceived biases, education, pedagogy, and curriculum.

Using temporality as a lens to explore these teacher memories and drawing on my own personal experience challenges me to critically reflect on these memories of sustained colonising curricular practices. Temporality explores the past and present, and is an expression of something happening over time, "experienced on a continuum."[34] Relying on antiquated information, inappropriate terms, and outdated language is an effect of coloniality, inadequate teacher training, and insufficient professional learning of the Australian teacher workforce. Dewey's concept of continuity and experience explains how teachers' present experiences are a direct result of their past experiences, which interact with and influence their current situation.[35] The recall of teachers' memories and lived experiences has an impact on teacher knowledge and informs their current and future teacher practice. According to Clandinin and colleagues, "temporality draws attention to the past, present, and future of events and people, with a focus on them as always in process."[36] This definition of temporality offers a framing for a continuous narrative which advocates for more relational practices, deep listening, and collaboration in disrupting colonised curriculum into the future.

Memories offer us an opportunity to look back and to look forward, and every memory has a sequence of temporality which places the memory in a particular moment in time. Green writes, "[S]cholars are acutely aware that curriculum work exists in time, in history" and that "the historicity of curriculum work is not temporally fixed."[37] In other words, curriculum adapts and changes and is not static but moves with the times, informed by societal and political expectations. Economic, political, social, and technological trends reflect changing values in society, which drive local, national, and international curriculum change or reform. Bernstein similarly notes, "[C]urricula reform today arises out of the requirements to engage with this contemporary cultural, economic, social and technological change."[38] These observations highlight that we live in a continuous narrative which encapsulates stories from the past, with subtle changes or emphasis each time the narrative is recalled along a continuum of time. We, therefore, need to recognise, reflect on, and respond to these shifts. When we factor in the teaching of history curriculum, based purely on memories of "what we learnt years ago," teachers rely on memories from their past learning and recreate this learning for their own students, despite the time in between.[39]

Some teachers are surprised to realise that the misconceptions and prejudice that they learnt as children are often a result of what was "passed on and accepted without question."[40] This is also an issue in other settler-colonial nations. A recent report titled *Decolonizing Our Schools* from Ontario, Canada, suggests that "students come to school with knowledge premised on their lived experiences, the meanings they make from the lessons that schools provide depend on how this knowledge is acknowledged and respected."[41] In Australian contexts, an example of the exposure to racism and prejudice that students may have been witness to is captured in a media article about Adnyamathanha man Adam Goodes, champion Australian Rules football player with the Sydney Swans. In the article, Goodes was asked about taking his godchildren to football matches after the relentless racial abuse he encountered throughout his career on and off the field left him no choice but to leave his beloved sport. He replied, "Unfortunately not. I've tried to go to games and I haven't enjoyed it. It's really sad, because my godchildren love going to the football."[42] His godchildren and many other Indigenous and non-Indigenous Australian children would have witnessed the impact of this racial abuse unfolding on their television screens and other media sources across Australia. Not only does this demonstrate that students arrive at school with lived experiences as 'memories' already formed from exposure to prejudice and racism, but it highlights the responsibility that schools have in not 'passing and accepting without question' how students acknowledge First Nations Peoples and cultures.

Teacher resistance

With the introduction of the Aboriginal and Torres Strait Islander histories and cultures cross-curriculum priority, there was an expectation that teachers should embed First Nations perspectives wherever and whenever possible across every KLA of the curriculum. This change in the delivery and prioritisation of First Nations histories and cultures meant that teachers could no longer consider an 'ad hoc' inclusion of First Nations perspectives but instead were expected to embed these perspectives organically and seamlessly into every component of the curriculum. It meant that if a school had previously taught a unit of work such as "The History of Australia," this could still be taught, but with a greater focus and exploration of First Nations perspectives through the lens of settler colonisation/invasion. These curriculum changes were met with some resistance by non-Indigenous teachers who had varying degrees of First Nations knowledge and understanding. For some teachers who were schooled in a Eurocentric education system, with minimal regard for First Nations perspectives, it left them feeling uncertain and inadequate about what and how to teach. One specific example where teachers not only had to have knowledge of the frontier wars but also the context of economic, social, and political factors is this in the Year 5 History Knowledge and Understanding elaboration:

[I]nvestigating an event or development and explaining its economic, social and political impact on a colony, for example, the consequences of frontier conflict events such as the Myall Creek Massacre, the Pinjarra Massacre.

If we analyse more deeply the complex layers of knowledge and understanding a Year 5 teacher would need in order to teach this history outcome, we see why some teachers might find teaching this a challenge. In order for teachers to build capability, confidence, and historical context, they need ongoing, locally anchored professional learning opportunities, designed and (ultimately) facilitated in collaboration with local First Nations People, as well as time to reflect, discuss, listen, question, share, and wonder about their current practice.

The Maroondah Framework: Yarning (storytelling), Dadirri (deep listening), and Ganma (knowledge sharing)

I introduce the *Maroondah Framework* as a way for schools to consider future opportunities to collaboratively work towards decolonising the curriculum and culture of their schools, specifically the history curriculum. 'Maroondah' is a Wurundjeri- Woi Wurrung word for 'leaves,' and as a local resident, I use this word not only to represent the beautiful green Country of the eastern suburbs of Melbourne but also as an action against colonisation. In 2022, Jill Gallagher, CEO of Victorian Aboriginal Community Controlled Health Organisation, wrote in *The Age* about Victorian Premier Daniel Andrews proposing to rename the local Maroondah Hospital after Queen Elizabeth II (the recently deceased monarch). Gallagher lamented that "Aboriginal culture is near invisible in Australia. We as a people are nearly invisible. To have things named in Aboriginal language gives us a sense of pride for ourselves and as a people."[43] Renaming a hospital after 47 years from local Woi Wurrung language to that of an English monarch was seen as a 'step backwards,' supporting colonisation. I cannot change the Premier's proposal, but I can take action to keep some aspects of the Woi Wurrung language alive. The Maroondah Framework combines three First Nations methodological concepts: Yarning (storytelling),[44] Dadirri (deep listening),[45] and Ganma (two-way knowledge sharing).[46] This framework assists schools in reflecting upon and deconstructing their current practice. Using these Indigenous methodologies, teachers can consider First Nations Ways of Knowing, Being, and Doing[47] and collaborate through respectful and culturally safe practices to re-design their curriculum and implement new and innovative school culture initiatives to provide rich and authentic learning experiences for their students, which challenge colonised views.

Yarning (storytelling), in its simplest form, is an informal, relaxed conversation between two or more people, discussing experiences and stories about their lives, understandings, thoughts, feelings, and ideas.[48] It is grounded in Australian Indigenous Ways of Knowing, Being, and Doing[49] and is a way that First Nations and non-Indigenous People can "develop and build a relationship that is accountable to Indigenous people."[50] Adelaide Plains Kaurna Aboriginal Elder Aunty Coral Wilson believes that for people to understand and work with Aboriginal ways of living and culture, they need to "work with sheer good heart (understanding), mind (attitude) and hands (skill) to render sharing hands to walk together,"[51] respecting the integrity and values which underpin these First Nations worldviews.

Dadirri (deep listening) is a word from the Ngangikurungkurr (river people) from Daly River in the Northern Territory of Australia, which translates into "inner, deep, quiet listening."[52] Dadirri encourages two-way listening between First Nations and non-Indigenous People, with one not being louder or stronger than the other. Dr Ungunmerr-Baumann, a Daly River Elder, insisted that with Dadirri "listening and learning must go both ways."[53] Dadirri encourages transparency and mutual trust through reflective inner listening and works to strengthen this trust through communication and respectful relationship building. In education contexts, Dadirri encourages a reciprocal deep listening between First Nations Peoples and schools.

Ganma (two-way knowledge sharing) is from the Yolgnu people in Arnhem Land, Northern Territory and describes the intersection where First Nations knowledges (fresh water) and non-Indigenous knowledges (salt water) connect.[54] Ganma is a naturally occurring phenomenon connecting these two bodies of water. The different bodies of water churn beneath the surface, creating a "rich habitat of its own."[55] When these waters connect, they form a white foam that is the result of where "knowledges are shared, coming together in the central space that creates a site of contestation."[56] The foam retains some of its identity and memory as fresh or salt water, but it becomes something new and unique when mixed whilst still holding true to each separate entity. It is also necessary to be quiet and patient, and to "listen deeply to hear the foam's soft sound."[57] In this way, the process of knowledge sharing and dadirri has memory which needs to be nurtured carefully. If the foam is cupped too tightly in the hands, it evaporates, but if it is handled gently, it has great power. Ganma provides a pathway for connections, promoting new knowledge and new ways of working. This knowledge is collaborative and is not 'owned' by a single entity. Yolngu People demonstrate that it is possible for a great sharing to flourish if each person is respectful of the other and open to yarning and dadirri, signifying where there is scope for First Nations and non-Indigenous People to build strong partnerships.[58]

Although these First Nations methodologies originated on the other side of Australia from where I am based in Naarm (Melbourne), the key elements of yarning, dadirri, and ganma are transferable to First Nations cultures throughout Australia, and this recognition enables a cross-cultural community development approach.

Ideas and strategies for decolonising curriculum in primary schools

The Aboriginal and Torres Strait Islander histories and cultures cross-curriculum priority is expected to be embedded throughout all primary KLAs, specifically History, and also through specialist areas such as Dance, Drama, Art, and Physical Education. All primary 'classroom' teachers teach Humanities (which encompasses History, Geography, and Civics and Citizenship), and schools develop a whole-school sequential learning plan across all year levels. Specialist teachers also embed Indigenous perspectives into their programmes where possible. Some primary schools that I have visited are doing amazing work in this space and have prioritised embedding First Nations perspectives into their curriculum and whole-school culture. The following ideas and strategies are to be used as a stimulus for schools undertaking a whole-school approach, to affirm what they are already doing well, or to consider if there are areas which could be improved.

1) **Build local relationships with First Nations Elders and community members**
   Having a yarn or inviting Registered Aboriginal Parties on Country where the school is located to provide (paid) professional learning to teachers is one way to establish a local relationship. Using Ganma as a guide, teachers should consult a Traditional Owner or delegated community member whenever possible, to seek advice before teaching concepts to students. After a school has completed an audit of its whole school curriculum (see point 3), there may be inadequacies, which open opportunities to work more closely with local First Nations Peoples. A school may commit to staff undertaking Cultural Understanding Safety Training (CUST) or an 'on Country' experience, facilitated by local First Nations mob. Teachers can also incorporate Dadirri into these local relationships in order to learn more deeply about First Nations culture and perspectives.

2) **Research local places, names, and significant First Nations sites to be used as local teaching and learning resources**
   Decolonising the places we live, work, and learn using First Nations–approved language is another way to acknowledge commitment to decolonising the curriculum. Teachers can encourage students to yarn with family, friends, and local First Nations Peoples about the importance of place names and local significant Aboriginal sites, discussing how they can respect and care for these places into the future.[59] An example of this is Birrarung Marr on Wurundjeri Country–Naarm (Melbourne). Birrarung Marr is a significant cultural site beside the Yarra River where First Nations Peoples would come together to celebrate eels migrating ('birrarung' means 'river of mists' and 'marr' relates to 'side').[60] Birrarung Marr now includes a family park and meeting place where First Nations Peoples celebrate significant

events, such as a Welcome to Country smoking ceremony at the beginning of NAIDOC week. The realisation of local site importance is a way for students to understand the importance of Country and the Ways of Knowing, Being, and Doing, and to learn more about how First Nations local communities have cared for land, sea, and skies for millennia before colonisation. Acknowledging traditional language of places and local sites also provides opportunities for First Nations students to see themselves represented in the communities they live and go to school in.

3) **Audit school curriculum to show evidence of where First Nations perspectives are being included, in which discipline, and at what year level**
An important first step for primary schools is to start with a whole-school curriculum audit to identify where First Nations perspectives are being planned and taught across year levels, KLAs, and specialist classes. Yarns and self-reflections drawing on Dadirri principles provide schools with insights into current practices and identify whether further support is required. This assists leadership in understanding and prioritising professional learning for teachers, including employing First Nations Peoples in this process, drawing on Ganma to collaborate and co-design resources and learning experiences.

4) **Commit to a yearly budget to purchase First Nations resources or experiences made, written, or designed by First Nations Peoples for learning**
Supporting local First Nations artists, writers, businesses, landscape designers, dance companies, or garden nurseries shows that schools are repositioning colonisation and desiring a need to support First Nations Peoples and the significant contribution they make to the school and local community.[61] One example of this is the Djirri Djirri dancers.

> Djirri Djirri are the only Wurundjeri female dance group and are Traditional Custodians of Narrm (Melbourne) and surrounds. Djirri Djirri means Willy Wagtail in Woiwurrung…the Spirit's Messenger. … We are all connected by blood through one woman, Borate, Berak's (William Barak's) sister. We dance together as cousins, nieces, aunties and mothers with daughters. We teach our dancers to also sing in Woiwurrung language, our Mother Tongue.[62]

Schools can ensure that they prioritise a budget towards buying resource materials for teachers and students to use in the classroom. There are many excellent picture storybooks and young adolescent novels published by First Nations authors which share insights into traditions, culture and ways of life. Aunty Joy Murphy and Lisa Kennedy's *Welcome to Country*[63] and Aunty Joy Murphy, Andrew Kelly and Lisa Kennedy's *Birrarung Wilam—a Story from Aboriginal Australia*[64] are two local and personal favourites.

5) **Promote best practice in terms of appropriate language use, zero tolerance of racism, and misappropriation of First Nations art and culture**
Although a standard expectation in schools, schools can support decolonising practices by properly addressing racism and protecting the intellectual property and integrity of First Nations art and culture. One example of a programme that teachers can use to address prejudice and racism in schools is the *Racism No Way* programme—an anti-racism programme designed for Australian schools.[65] Their website provides teachers with resources and ideas to teach anti-racism and prejudice at all year levels. Acknowledging First Nations artists by name is a simple but significant way that schools can protect the integrity of First Nations art and culture.
6) **Share teacher memories to disrupt the colonisation of these memories and bring about change in future teaching practice**.
Reflecting on teacher memories is something I have often done with teacher groups as a way to identify and disrupt why they rely so heavily on what they learnt at school. Using Dadirri, school staff can self-reflect on their own schooling memories and identify how they can move beyond these in their current practice. Critically self-reflecting on what teachers learnt at school and providing peer feedback through this process is an important part of acknowledging colonisation and deconstructing ways that can challenge current practice to prevent repetitive patterns of colonisation.

Conclusion

I have offered some reasons why teachers still grapple with the challenges of decolonising primary curriculum and have also offered some strategies through the *Maroondah Framework*, which could be considered by schools as a way to affirm and improve current practice. The first steps for schools are identifying, acknowledging, self-reflecting, and disrupting the factors which influence the implementation of First Nations perspectives, such as teacher memories, being culturally unfamiliar, academically underprepared and under-resourced, lacking professional learning, and the absence of relationships between local Elders, community members, teachers, and schools. If these elements are explored and addressed, then Australian primary schools can establish a more inclusive and culturally safe curriculum which not only highlights but also prioritises First Nations perspectives.

Notes

1 Rigney, L.-I. (1999). Internationalization of an Indigenous anticolonial cultural critique of research methodologies: A guide to indigenist research methodology and its principles. *Wicazo Sa Review: Emergent Ideas in Native American Studies*, *14*(2), 109–121. https://doi.org/10.2307/1409555

2 Clandinin, D., & Connelly, F. (1992). Teacher as curriculum maker. In P. Jackson (Ed.), *Handbook of research on curriculum* (pp. 363–401). Macmillan Publishing Company.
3 Department of Education and Training (DET). (2016). *Marrung: Aboriginal education plan 2016–2026*. Department of Education and Training, Melbourne, Victoria.
4 Department of Education and Training (DET). (2022). *Dhelk Wukang: Aboriginal Inclusion Plan 2022–2026*. Department of Education and Training, Melbourne, Victoria.
5 Pete, S., Schneider, B., & O'Reilly, K. (2013). Decolonizing our practice: Indigenizing our teaching. *First Nations Perspectives*, 5(1), 99–115.
6 Harvie, K. (2021). *Indigenous perspectives, Australian curriculum and teacher practice: The dynamic interplay*. [Unpublished doctoral thesis]. Deakin University, Burwood, Australia.
7 Clandinin, D. J., & Connelly, F. M. (2000). *Narrative inquiry: Experience and story in qualitative research*. Jossey-Bass.
8 Wurundjeri Land and Compensation Cultural Heritage Council Incorporated & City of Yarra. (2003). *The Aboriginal history of Yarra*. Sites of Significance – The Aboriginal History of Yarra. https://aboriginalhistoryofyarra.com.au/sites-of-significance/
9 Ministerial Council on Education, Employment, Training and Youth Affairs (MCEETYA). (2008). *Melbourne Declaration on Educational Goals for Young Australians*. http://hdl.voced.edu.au/10707/73935
10 Ibid.
11 Australian Curriculum, Assessment and Reporting Authority (ACARA). (2023). *ACARA – Development of the Australian Curriculum*. https://www.acara.edu.au/curriculum/history-of-the-australian-curriculum/development-of-australian-curriculum
12 Harrison, N. (2008). *Teaching and learning in Indigenous education*. Oxford University Press.
13 ACARA (2023). *ACARA – Development of the Australian Curriculum*.
14 New Zealand Government Ministry of Education. (2023). *Te Tāhuhu o te Mātauranga* establishment of Te Mahau within a redesigned Te Tāhuhu o te Mātauranga | Ministry of Education – Education in New Zealand. https://www.education.govt.nz/our-work/changes-in-education/establishment-of-te-mahau-within-a-redesigned-te-tahuhu-o-te-matauranga-ministry-of-education/
15 Ibid., p. 1.
16 Ibid., p. 5.
17 Australian Curriculum, Assessment and Reporting Authority (ACARA). (2023). *ACARA – Curriculum*. https://www.acara.edu.au/curriculum
18 Donnelly, K. (2015). Review of the Australian curriculum: A view from a member of the review team. *Curriculum Perspectives*, 35(1), 8–19. https://www.researchgate.net/publication/278412459_Review_of_the_Australian_Curriculum_A_view_from_a_member_of_the_Review_Team
19 Australian Curriculum, Assessment and Reporting Authority [ACARA]. (2021). *Australian curriculum review consultation*. https://www.australiancurriculum.edu.au/consultation/cross-curriculum-priorities/
20 Salter, P., & Maxwell, J. (2016). The inherent vulnerability of the Australian curriculum's cross-curriculum priorities. *Critical Studies in Education*, 57(3), 296–312. https://doi.org/10.1080/17508487.2015.1070363
21 Collard, S. (2021). 'We're ecstatic': Indigenous educators welcome proposed changes to educational curriculum. *NITV News*, 29 April 2021. https://www.sbs.com.au/nitv/article/were-ecstatic-indigenous-educators-welcome-proposed-changes-to-educational-curriculum/6c1vnkf8v#

22 Ibid., n.p.
23 Ibid., n.p.
24 Jenkins, K. (2021). 'A farce': Federal education minister's views on draft curriculum slammed. *NITV News*, 22 October 2021. https://www.sbs.com.au/nitv/article/a-farce-federal-education-ministers-views-on-draft-curriculum-slammed/fo92qgkw8
25 Ibid., n.p.
26 Jenkins (2021). 'A farce'.
27 Ugwuegbula, L. (2020). *The role of education in perpetuating racism and white supremacy: Rethinking the Eurocentric curriculum*. The Samuel Centre for Social Connectedness.
28 Council of Australian Governments Education Council. (2019). *Alice Springs (Mparntwe) education declaration*. https://www.dese.gov.au/alice-springs-mparntwe-education-declaration/resources/alice-springs-mparntwe-education-declaration
29 Ibid., p. 3.
30 Ibid.
31 Leyden, P. (circa 1980). *Resource material for school project 'Aborigines Yesterday.'* Publishing House Pty. Ltd. "Leyden House" N.S.W.
32 Craven, R. (2020). *Teaching Aboriginal studies: A practical resource for primary and secondary teaching*. Routledge.
33 Harvie (2021). *Indigenous perspectives, Australian curriculum and teacher practice*.
34 Clandinin, D. J., & Connelly, F. M. (2000). *Narrative inquiry: Experience and story in qualitative research*. Jossey-Bass.
35 Dewey, J. (1997). *Experience and education*. Free Press.
36 Clandinin, D. J., Cave, M. T., & Berendonk, C. (2016). Narrative inquiry: A relational research methodology for medical education. *Medical Education*, *51*(1), 89–96.
37 Green, B. (2003). Curriculum inquiry in Australia: Toward a local genealogy of the curriculum field. In W. F. Pinar (Ed.), *International handbook of curriculum research* (pp. 123–141). Routledge.
38 Bernstein, B. (2000). *Pedagogy, symbolic control, and identity*. Rowman & Littlefield Publishers.
39 Harvie (2021). *Indigenous perspectives, Australian curriculum and teacher practice*.
40 Craven, R. (2020). *Teaching Aboriginal studies: A practical resource for primary and secondary teaching*. Routledge.
41 Dion, S. D. (2010). Decolonizing our schools: Aboriginal education in the Toronto distric board. York University.
42 McRae, D. (2020). Adam Goodes: 'Instead of masking racism, we need to deal with it day-to-day'. *The Guardian*, 3 March 2020. https://www.theguardian.com/sport/2020/mar/02/adam-goodes-interview-racism-walk-away-afl
43 Gallagher, J. (2022). Maroondah hospital name change is a step backwards. *The Age*, 22 September, 2022. Maroondah Hospital name change is a step backwards (theage.com.au)
44 Bessarab, D., & Ng'Andu, B. (2010). Yarning about yarning as a legitimate method in Indigenous research. *International Journal of Critical Indigenous Studies*, *3*(1), 37–50. https://doi.org/10.5204/ijcis.v3i1.57
45 Ungunmerr, M.-R. (1988). *Dadirri: Inner deep listening and quiet still awareness*. https://www.miriamrosefoundation.org.au/about-dadirri/dadirri-text
46 Muller, S. (2012). 'Two Ways': Bringing Indigenous and non-Indigenous knowledges together. In J. K. Weir (Ed.), *Country, native title and ecology*. ANU E Press and Aboriginal History Incorporated; Aboriginal History Monograph 2459–80.

47 Martin, K. L., & Mirraboopa, B. (2003). Ways of knowing, being and doing: A theoretical framework and methods for Indigenous and indigenist research. *Journal of Australian Studies, 27*(76), 203–214. https://doi.org/10.1080/14443050309387838
48 Bessarab & Ng'Andu (2010). Yarning about yarning as a legitimate method in Indigenous research.
49 Martin & Mirraboopa (2003). Ways of knowing, being and doing.
50 Bessarab & Ng'Andu (2010). Yarning about yarning as a legitimate method in Indigenous research.
51 Sharmil, H., Kelly, J., Bowden, M., Galletly, C., Cairney, I., Wilson, C., … & de Crespigny, C. (2021). Participatory action research-Dadirri-Ganma, using yarning: Methodology co-design with Aboriginal community members. *International Journal for Equity in Health, 20*(1), 1–11. https://doi.org/10.1186/s12939-021-01493-4
52 Ibid.
53 Ungunmerr-Baumann, M. R., Groom, R. A., Schuberg, E. L., Atkinson, J., Atkinson, C., Wallace, R., & Morris, G. (2022). Dadirri: An Indigenous place-based research methodology. *AlterNative: An International Journal of Indigenous Peoples, 18*(1), 94–103. https://doi.org/10.1177/11771801221085353
54 Marika, R. (2000). Milthun Latju Wana Romgu: Valuing Yolŋu knowledge in the education system. *TESOL in Context, 10*(2), 45–52.
55 Bat, M., & Guenther, J. (2013). Red dirt thinking on education: A people-based system. *The Australian Journal of Indigenous Education, 42*(2), 123–135. https://doi.org/10.1017/jie.2013.20
56 Ober, R., & Bat, M. (2007). Paper 1: Both-ways: the philosophy. *Ngoonjook, 31*, 64–86.
57 Sharmil et al. (2021). Participatory action research-Dadirri-Ganma.
58 Yunupingu, M. (1994). Yothu Yindi: Finding balance. *Race & Class, 35*(4), 113–120. https://doi.org/10.1177/030639689403500412
59 Wurundjeri Land and Compensation Cultural Heritage Council Incorporated & City of Yarra. (2003). *The Aboriginal history of Yarra.* https://aboriginalhistoryofyarra.com.au
60 City of Melbourne. (2023). *Birrarung Marr.* https://whatson.melbourne.vic.gov.au/things-to-do/birrarung-marr
61 Sharmil et al. (2021). Participatory action research-Dadirri-Ganma.
62 *Djirri Djirri Wurundjeri women's dance group.* https://djirri-djirri.com.au
63 Murphy, J., & Kennedy, L. (2016). *Welcome to country.* Walker Books Australia.
64 Murphy, J., Kelly, A., & Kennedy, L. (2020). *Birrarung Wilam – A story from Aboriginal Australia.* Walker Books Ltd.
65 NSW Department of Education. (2000). *RacismNoWay: Anti-racism education for Australian schools.* Australian Government. https://racismnoway.com.au/teaching-resources/anti-racism-activities/

Chapter 9

Doing intercultural history
A framework for history teachers

Kerri Anne Garrard

Author positioning statement

I am a non-Indigenous woman who grew up in the northern suburbs of Melbourne before moving to the Mornington Peninsula on Bunurong/Boon Wurrung Country. My PhD explored the relationship between interculturality and history education because, after teaching history in schools for about 28 years, I was aware that history teachers are given little support to question/develop certain aspects of what they are asked to teach. In particular, the agents of dominant historical narratives that successfully continue to 'colonise' students of Australian history. Now, I use my work teaching pre-service teachers and researching history education to grow my understanding of the power embedded in the discourse of colonialist curriculum and its persistence to resist change.

Introduction

Cultural diversity is a defining feature of Australian society, with approximately 30% of the population born overseas and over 300 different languages spoken in our homes and across communities.[1] The First Nations Peoples of Australia exemplify this, being "diverse in culture and language, not only between groups, but within groups as well."[2] However, learning to live with cultural difference and diversity has presented ongoing challenges to the "colonial systems and structures"[3] of education in Australia.

This chapter explores how we can better prepare aspiring History teachers and current practitioners, and therefore the students they teach, to interpret, understand, and question the absence or visibility of cultural difference and diversity in historical narratives related to the invasion/colonisation of Australia. This is a challenging and undeniably complex area for History educators; however, catalytic change, in my view, best stems from school history. The 'history wars' disrupted the historical linchpins of history and the 'order' it is told in Australia because, at its height, it was an ideological attack on developing school history to teach about First Nations Peoples and dispossession.

I consider the questions this chapter raises and potential teaching methods as a natural progression from this.

During the late 1990s to mid-2000s in Australia, the political climate fuelled by the 'history wars' in Australia was 'hot' and reactionary. In 2007, Prime Minister John Howard's coalition government, in the lead-up to the federal election, tied the increased compulsory teaching of Australian history to the projected 2009–2012 state funding and placed its faith around what should be taught in the hands of a conservative reference group led by Geoffrey Blainey. However, the Howard government was defeated in December 2007, and the incoming Labor government, led by Kevin Rudd, called for an end to the 'history wars': "Any truthful reflection of our nation's past is that these [truths about the past] are all part of the rich fabric of our remarkable story called Australia."[4] In April 2008, the Rudd government established the independent National Curriculum Board to take on the challenge of engaging the community in developing Australia's first national curriculum in English, Mathematics, Science, and History for implementation from 2011. The first national History curriculum has sustained close attention from politicians, teachers, and academics. In 2021, then Education Minister Alan Tudge repackaged Mr. Howard's 'root and branch' approach—a reference to British policy to stamp "potent cultural authority"[5] on History curriculum—during the review of the Australian Curriculum (AC) when he called for a more 'patriotic' approach to the AC: History. This reified that Australian history education always sits "at the most volatile point on the interface between politics and education"[6] in Australia.

The Western perspective and colonial narrative that conservative politicians sought to embed in the nation's historical consciousness whilst trying to sustain the multiculturalist ideology of the '80s and '90s were most formidable and remain so today. Thirty or 40 years later, the centrality of First Nations Peoples histories and cultures to debates concerning History curriculum, usually around Invasion Day, is testament to the ongoing problems we have in this country. We continue to practice what W.E.H. Stanner described as "the Great Australian Silence" in his Boyer lecture in 1968 and the "cult of forgetfulness" on a national scale, whereby Australians do not just fail to acknowledge the atrocities of the past but choose to not think about them at all, to the point of forgetting that these events ever happened.[7] There is an ambivalence towards decolonisation of history education fuelled not only by this forgetfulness but also by the memory of extraordinary contentions made by senior politicians such as former Prime Minister Tony Abbott. In 2013, Abbott claimed that the "putative failure to properly acknowledge 'the Western canon' amounts to a new version of the 'great Australian silence.'"[8] Even as I write this chapter, hopeful of the capacity of school history to bring change to carefully crafted narratives of colonialism, the broader historical imaginary of Australia in 2023 is characterised by the Indigenous Voice to Parliament referendum and remonstrations about the value of First Nations People's cultures and histories as inherent to Country.

Everything about how we teach History has to do with identity, and like history itself, a sense of belonging to the past is an essential cultural factor which orients our lives.[9] However, based on the cultural identities of teachers and the Eurocentric nature of schooling in Australia, since colonisation, a normalising of "false, negative stereotypes in education"[10] of many marginalised cultures, but particularly First Nations Peoples, has been permitted to grow. Since Federation in 1901, the teaching of Australian history has driven dominant narratives that influence dominant and marginalised cultural groups, with the aim of shaping their beliefs, values, and social structures. A key aspect of iintercultural history is to challenge the exertion of colonial influence and engage students in 'other' histories that ensure a comprehensive past. It seeks to give voice to First Nations narratives, which are historically silenced by carefully constructed language, and celebrate the exchange of histories between cultures: both positive and negative, violent and non-violent, Indigenous, settler, and migrant.

If we are committed to decolonising history education, then our starting point must be the positioning and relationality between First Nations Peoples and the colonialist narrative in history. For example, when a narrative of the colonisation/invasion of Australia is included in prescriptive curriculum, how First Nations Peoples are positioned in relation to that narrative cannot be taken for granted. It is essential to ask what is the relationality of cultures in the story told, and what is positioned as an accountable past? Is the relationality 'obedient' or 'disobedient'[11] to the dominant culture, and how does this reinforce the strength of the dominant narrative? These questions can also be raised in relation to the assemblage of the ideological story of colonisation in resources such as history textbooks and the visual and digital production of historical narratives used in the classroom.

History curriculum in Australia

> We're still pedalling a colonial narrative, to take at [sic] the Year 9 curriculum. There has been moves within that colonial life, the different cultures within that ... But certainly, just the Aboriginal narrative in the Year 9 text was virtually non-existent. It wasn't anything new, it wasn't anything that I wasn't aware of from when I was learning at secondary school colonial history.
>
> (History teacher, 2017)

History curriculum policy often serves as a nation's mirror, which at times is implicit and at others explicit in settler nations like Australia. For some history teachers, as the previous vignette illustrates, history curriculum in this country remains "designed on a narrow understanding of the nation"[12] that lacks connection to its intercultural imaginary and historical cultural diversity. The perennial nature of colonialist history curriculum in Australia began with the introduction of free compulsory secular education in 1872 under the Education

Act. Since then, school history has presented students with vivid visual, written, and spoken examples of different and similar cultures located across time and around the world,[13] albeit through a Eurocentric lens that often contrasts differences in 'other' histories to strengthen Western, Christian, and colonialist discourses. Linear progress has long been linked to the nation's progress in the past, and this often focuses on the building of the nation-state supported by traditional narratives[14] at the expense of bringing the contribution of 'others' in from the peripheral.

One unit taught in Year 9 in the AC entitled *Making and Transforming the Australian Nation (1750–1914)* is an example of this. Even the title of this unit orients the teacher to think everyone in their history classroom maintains a Western view of the world. It could be argued that this misconception is impacting our young people's interest in Australian history. Anna Clark's (2008) research showed students believed Australian history to be 'boring,'[15] and more current research shows the status of Australian history at the senior secondary level to be in decline across the country.[16] More concerning is the token inclusion of Australian history in the national senior secondary curriculum and the propensity to construct a strident discourse of colonialism characteristic of homogenising the population through the "power of institutional practices such as [history] education."[17]

As much as we might like to think the 'decolonisation' of Australia's Eurocentric and dominant historical narrative to mean simply 'swapping' a colonial historical narrative for an Indigenous one, we know this is not the case. As Tuck and Yang (2012) tell us, this approach is often more detrimental to the true meaning of decolonising history education because it simply "move[s] the 'settler' to innocence"[18] and drives deeper the entangled histories of settler nations. However, as I suggested in the opening of this chapter, it is warranted and timely that school history can look to 'breaking out' of the 'order' of how the story is told, without compromise, to emancipate the historical thinking of our teachers and students. This is where the concept of interculturality can help because the prefix 'inter' negates dominance by accepting—not tolerating—difference. This is not to suggest that Australia's colonial beginnings are not significant, in fact, as you will read in the following explanations, the role of traditional narratives orient people of all cultures in time and place. However, the "unequal plays of histories and power over time"[19] that remain captured in the discourse of school history prevent the genuine support of History teachers and their resources to combat the consequences of this power. Therefore, the theoretical framework I outline in this chapter is one means of *doing* intercultural history.

Defining interculturality in the Australian curriculum context

Interculturality refers to the interaction and exchange of cultures, promoting respect, understanding, and dialogue between different cultural groups. It is different to principles of multiculturalism in education, which in Australia have often seen difference and diversity as a deficit, rather than a normative aspect of the past that should be celebrated. The concept is translated in the AC as Intercultural Understanding (ICU) and is embedded in other state and territory curricula in various ways. For example, in Victoria, it is known as the Intercultural Capability curriculum.

In the AC, ICU is one of seven General Capabilities included across the eight key learning areas. By its own definitions, the national History curriculum aims to engage students in the study of lives, cultures, values, and beliefs of people within and beyond their own culture in other periods of time so they can develop a deeper understanding of similarities to and difference from their own lives,[20] which aligns strongly with the language, intentions, and principles of ICU. A quick search of the current version of the AC (v9), 7–10 History curriculum shows that out of the seven General Capabilities, ICU is included the most in the History curriculum. However, this alignment is not as evident in schools. Educational research shows that ICU is mainly taken up by schools as a whole-school approach[21] or "good intention"[22] characterised by international food and costume days rather than from within a specific discipline. Nevertheless, the key premise of interculturality, to recognise the power dynamics and unequal relationships between cultures inherent in how we teach history, cannot be underestimated.

A brief word about history teachers, interculturality, and decolonising history education

Theoretical preparedness to challenge dominant historical narratives has several implications for history educators. Simply introducing discussion about topics such as Australia Day/Invasion Day and what this brings to telling the story of the nation's past can trigger guilt-induced feelings for their students. This comment is by a history teacher in a predominantly 'white' secondary school:

> I most recently just had a conversation with kids, and I thought about doing a different angle before introducing our 'white shame.' Like kids shut down about their own history because they feel like they're being blamed— and we are very one culture here [in this school], so a lot of them take on one side of the story rather than considering the other side because they don't see themselves aligned with that.

In my research, history teachers also noted the need for continuous professional development to stay in touch with how they might improve their educational practices using ICU. In some interviews, which focused on teaching Australian history, interculturality immediately challenged ethnocentric and traditional Eurocentric approaches to their teaching, creating some tension.

Despite this, the following comment reflects the opportunity of ICU to facilitate a more accurate teaching of Australia's past:

> I think a lot of it [how we teach history] will change if all Australian's and all Australian students start to perceive that that [Indigenous history] is part of their history as well, it's not just the European side of it and the colonisation side of it, it's actually trying to have some blending of those ideas rather than keeping them separate I think is really important too.

My point here is that teachers' interpretation and conceptualisation of interculturality for their history teaching, supported through professional development, will 'realistically' contribute more to decolonising history education and shifting the narrative of the nation's past than almost anything else.

'Doing intercultural history': Explaining the framework

> It will be a great day when all our children know the story of our indigenous [sic] history, as well as they know the story of Captain Cook and white settlement in Australia.
> (The Gippsland Times, 2015)

'*Doing* Intercultural History' is a theoretical tool, adapted from Jörn Rüsen's typologies of historical narration and historical consciousness, that uses interculturality to intersect with these fundamental acts of historical thinking.[23] Figure 9.1 is a visual representation of the four stages of this tool: traditional, exemplary, critical, and transformative. Each stage uses linguistic devices to interpret and analyse narratives. The fine lines of the prism represent the interconnected nature of each stage, and the thicker lines drive key concepts. Whilst each of the four stages serves a distinct purpose, they are not mutually exclusive. Each can incorporate elements of the others, offering nuanced insights into cultural practices and societal issues. For example, the 'critical' concept must draw upon traditional or exemplary elements; otherwise, it is simply used to negate other perspectives.

The four stages of doing intercultural history

Traditional

It is human nature to hold onto 'traditional' narratives passed down to us through time. The traditional stage of *Doing* Intercultural History highlights the complicit nature of traditional historical narratives to construct stereotypes and foster dominance through distinct discourses. An example of this is the story of 'terra nullius,' which remains a pillar of the Western narrative of

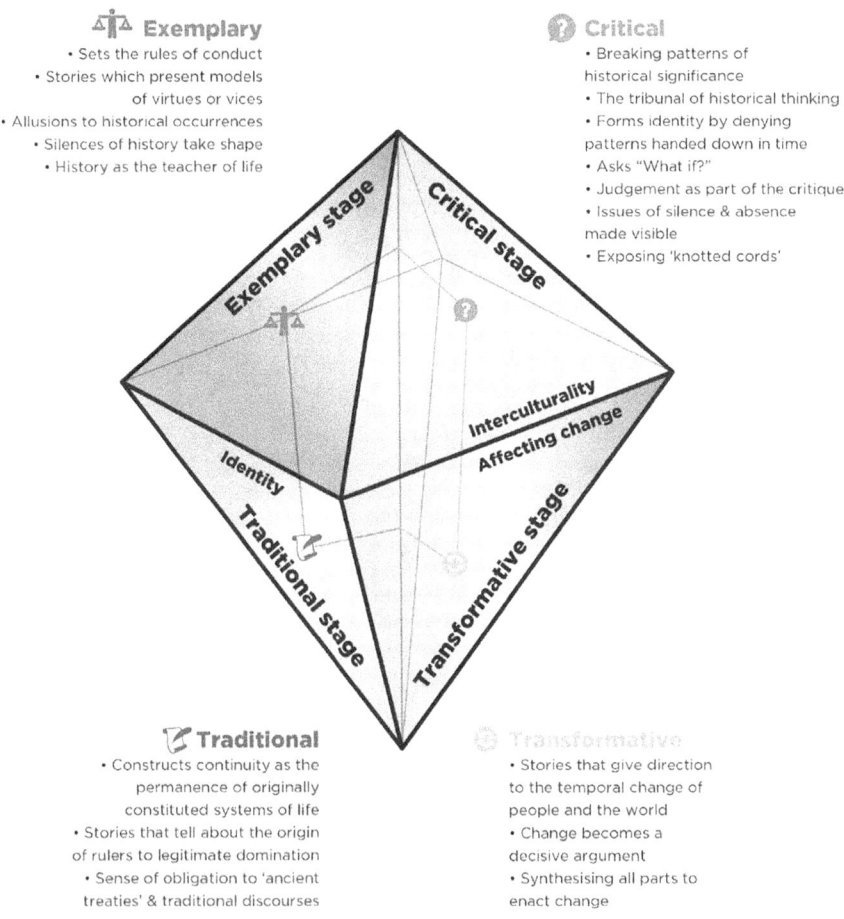

Figure 9.1 'Doing intercultural history': A theoretical framework Garrard © 2018

colonisation and successfully resists the narrative of invasion in our schools and in Australia's history politics. Over time, 'terra nullius' has been made significant through powerful language that associates the term with a 'system of life' established by the rulers/invaders. Despite historical evidence in protest, this traditional narrative is entrenched in the historical consciousness of History curriculum and its agencies.

Exemplary

Exemplary narratives play a vital role in connecting the past with the present, enabling students to understand the values and principles that continue to shape Australian society. These narratives highlight stories that showcase the resilience, innovation, and diverse experiences that have contributed to the development of Australia. We can use the exemplary stage of the framework to recognise these characteristics which also uphold the continuity of experiences and innovations that have been deemed significant by more traditional accounts.

For instance, let's consider the concept of 'terra nullius' once again. While this story is traditionally portrayed, its significance as an exemplary narrative lies in its ability to reflect shared values and virtues that are attributed to the dominant culture. Similarly, the hero worship of war in the Year 9 and 10 national History curriculum can be seen as a generalising experience. Although there have been efforts to incorporate the perspectives of First Nations Peoples into this narrative, it is important to note that their story is not given the same level of exemplification.

Critical

In this space, we use the principles of interculturality—exchange of and respect for the histories of other cultures and valuing their histories—as a tool to detect signals and symbols (mechanisms of language) that reinforce cultural dominance. This is not intended as a *free-for-all all* of unsubstantiated storytelling. Rather, the critical stage of the framework is a space to legitimise a challenge to cultural norms, power structures, and social injustices maintained through traditional and exemplary historical narratives. It is here that the hopes reflected in the vignette at the beginning of this section might come to fruition. For example, the primary function of this stage is to shed light on how distinct discourses construct Australia's history as a homogenous experience.

Transformative

The transformative stage aims to affect change by utilising the judgements made in the critical stage to disrupt the traditional and exemplary narratives. Its ultimate goal is to move historical thinking beyond the conventional methods of teaching history. Transformative narratives ask teachers and, therefore, their students to explore new perspectives, question established identities, values, and vices, and offer an ICU of history. Engaging with transformative narratives encourages teachers and students to think creatively, embrace diversity, and develop fresh approaches to understanding and relating to different cultures.

With all of this in mind, it is a good time to give some examples that put the framework into practice and support the main interest of this chapter: intercultural history teaching.[24]

Intercultural history teaching—From theory to practice

After speaking with both pre-service teachers and current history teachers, I found their own experience of how they were taught history remains with them as a reference point. For example, one teacher said, "So my history experience was the Captain Cook story and the idea of heroes and conquerors, and the noble savage and that sort of aspect" (participant's words). This account gives testament to how difficult it is to shift deep-seated historical consciousness because it has temporal power. However, the most important aspect of doing intercultural history is that teachers believe their history teaching can be transformative.

The following are two examples of how *Doing* Intercultural History might be used. The first focuses on selected History curriculum (AC). I see prescriptive History curriculum as a powerful narrative in itself, based on the inclusion and exclusion of historical content knowledge. It is often seen, as explained earlier, as a nation's mirror. The second example focuses on how visual language is used to construct a historical imaginary based on a 'traditional' colonialist narrative. The aim of these examples is to provide aspiring and current teachers of history in Australian schools with the impetus—and confidence—to move toward teaching intercultural history.

Example 1: Curriculum

You might work through this example independently or discuss it with your teaching colleagues. I also envisage it might be a useful exercise with pre-service teachers. Let's take the Year 9 History curriculum (AC) because it engages students in some of the narratives being highlighted in this chapter. For example, the impact of settlement on First Nations Peoples. My purpose is to highlight how the *Doing* Intercultural History might facilitate serious consideration regarding the positioning of First Nations Peoples within the specific curriculum and how they are framed as the cultural 'other' through colonialist language.

Australian Curriculum: History/ Year 9/Knowledge & Understanding/ Making and Transforming the Australian nation (1750–1914)
Content descriptor (AC9HH9K03): Students learn about the causes and effects of European contact and extension of settlement, including their impact on the First Nations Peoples of Australia.
Elaboration: Examining the effects of colonisation, such as frontier conflict and massacres of First Nations Australians, the spread of European diseases, and the destruction of cultural lifestyles
Sub-elements of ICU: (1) Engaging with cultural and linguistic diversity and (2) reflecting on culture and cultural diversity
Refer to Figure 9.1 to ask, *Where is the above content descriptor positioned within 'Doing Intercultural History'?*

The language of the content descriptor functions within the traditional stage of the framework because it establishes the identity of the rulers and their origins of power. It positions the identity of First Nations Peoples within a constituted system of destruction to create two stereotypes: the conqueror and the conquered. This is an example of how a traditional discourse arranges us to meet the stereotype of the 'other' before we meet the people.

Suggestion: Consider how difficult it is for your students to develop historical empathy from within the traditional stage of the framework, a position of continuity of a dominant narrative and how this lack of empathy or absence of respectful exchange of historical experiences might affect marginalised groups.

Simply offering a counter descriptor to affect a temporal change to the identities described earlier is a small step towards decolonising history curriculum. One that makes the identity of First Nations Peoples independent of the rulers. For example, *"Examining the cultural lifestyle of First Nations Peoples, as a prominent cultural identity in Australia's history of invasion"*. Present this as part of students' learning, asking them to find evidence—both primary and secondary sources—to substantiate what they find.

Example 2: Decolonising visual language

This example refers directly to the functions of *Doing* Intercultural History and could be used in discussion with teaching colleagues, pre-service teachers, or simply for your own professional development toward a decolonising project in your classroom. My aim here is not to suggest that these visuals be dismissed or erased from the timeline. Rather, as a decolonising project, draw attention to how the historical concept of 'chronology'—one of seven historical concepts within the national History curriculum—and the inclusion and exclusion of cultural contributions create a powerful colonial narrative.

What follows is a specific analysis of three visuals from a timeline which constructs a chronological narrative of Australia's past from 1750 to 1914. This timeline appears in a popular Year 9 History textbook[25] used widely in Australia for teaching the deep study of Australia at Year 9: *Australian Curriculum: History/ Year 9/Making and Transforming the Australian Nation (1750–1914)* (ACARA, v9), and denotes "some key events and developments related to the making of the nation Australia."[26] For context, there are nineteen entries on this timeline and two references to First Nations Peoples. The first in 1750: "First Nations Australians lived in harmony with the natural environment" and the second: "Myall Creek massacre, New South Wales 1838."

The three visuals appear here in the order they take on the timeline. Note the sequence is important because it builds the momentum of the traditional and exemplary narrative, orienting the familiar and recognisable story of colonisation for the reader, a seamless unfolding of peaceful European settlement (Figure 9.2).

Doing intercultural history 151

Figure 9.2 Visual 1: Artist's impression of the home of George Prideaux Robert Harris, Hobart Town 1806[27]

An artist's impression of Van Diemen's Land, the first settlement at Risdon Cove on the Derwent River plotted in 1803,[28] is the first visual on the timeline. The visual sits comfortably within the parameters of the traditional stage of *Doing* Intercultural History. It is a Eurocentric representation of peaceful 'order,' which was prevalent in early nineteenth-century art, to make the 'other' and their world intelligible to a European audience.[29] The focus on colonial architecture, a cottage complete with fireplace and chimney, provincial windows, and door, safely gated by a picket fence against the rugged bushland, draws on deep-seated stories of the 'origins' of the 'rulers' taming the new world. It captures a picture of 'colonial success' and the historical imagination of an ordered environment where people live peacefully and work hard at the expense of any other cultural lifestyles and achievements (Figure 9.3).

The ancient pathways in the Blue Mountains were travelled by First Nations Peoples long before Blaxland, Wentworth, and Lawson. The geographic features and the intense flora and fauna of the region had been recorded by the Darug and Gundungurra people. However, the 'inclusion' and placement of

Figure 9.3 Visual 2: Artist's impression of explorers Gregory Blaxland, William Wentworth, and William Lawson crossing the Blue Mountains in 1813[30]

Figure 9.4 Visual 3: *Zealous diggers at Bendigo* by ST Gill, 1854[31]

visual two on the timeline speaks to, rather than back at, the 'allusion' of white settlers and explorers as 'discovering' and *taming* the country, making the discrete position of a singular cultural identity *exemplary*. By making the crossing of the Blue Mountains by Blaxland, Wentworth, and Lawson significant, the visual functions within the exemplary concept of the framework. There is no other claim to exploration on the timeline; therefore, it builds on the familiar trope of the traditional discourses of European discovery to create a dichotomy of strength and weakness. The inclusion of this visual, at the expense of all others, uses the story of the European explorers as a model of *virtues and vices*, which 'silences' the identity of the Darug and Gundungurra people who had already recorded these discoveries without destruction (Figure 9.4).

With reference to Figure 9.1, the third visual is another example of exemplary rules of conduct. It denotes 1851 and the Australian Gold Rush. By the time the Gold Rush officially started in Victoria in 1851, the Port Phillip Aboriginal Protectorate (1838–1850) had been disbanded.

However, First Nations Peoples had already been dispossessed of their land by squatters and sheep, and they were now facing a second invasion from gold-seekers from across the globe. Consider the cultural 'hegemony' that lingers behind the decision to place the painting 'Zealous Diggers at Bendigo' on the timeline. It constructs a cultural identity of whiteness that is disproportionate[32] and reinforces a set of *virtues*—namely, Christian family values—where the man stands as a tower of strength above the female who nurses the babe in her arms. The linguistic devices of the exemplary concept of the framework illuminate a reward for settlement and conquering of the wilderness by the dominant culture.

So, what do we (history teachers or pre-service teachers) do now?

Once attention is drawn to how the positioning and sequence of the visuals construct a Eurocentric narrative of making the nation, take the opportunity to enact interculturality and its principles through the critical stage of the framework. Discuss how your students can build their ICU by sharing, negotiating, accepting, or rejecting the story of the visuals. There are further strategies at the end of this chapter that might help you further.

In a discussion of this kind, you will find that some teachers will be prepared to dive in with unfettered stories of Indigenous history as the 'alternative' perspective, others will remain loyal to the foregrounding of Australia as a nation through the lens of white Australian history. It is at this point that the leading teacher must be well informed about the purpose of the framework and, in particular, how the critical stage interacts with the other stages. Again, these small steps towards decolonisation are not about swapping one perspective for the other—which is often an immediate response of teachers—nor is it about blind acceptance of a narrative because of its 'colour.'

Based on your understanding of the functions of each stage of the framework, some questions for each teacher involved to consider with their students in mind might be: *How well do my students know the story constructed by the visuals? What happens if we take the three visuals out of the timeline? What are the important parts of the traditional narrative that need to be retained/replaced? Why? What do students see about themselves in the timeline? What don't they see? How might they add to the story of the 'timeline'?*

Suggestion: Using a timeline that you are currently using with your students, test the functions of the *Doing* Intercultural History. Use the visual language of the timeline you have chosen. Keep in mind that what can be achieved by the critical stage is only dynamic if it moves the development of your students' historical thinking toward change. This is about listening and adjusting how you yourself think about the narrative constructed—again, not to discard what we don't agree with or is too familiar or traditional—but to challenge the historical content knowledge included or absent from the narrative.

Conclusion

This chapter has attempted to respond to the propensity of history education to continue to position First Nations Peoples as 'other' in narratives of the colonisation/invasion of Australia and that these narratives have remained dominant due to the perennial nature of history education to celebrate settlement in Australia as a symbol of progress and success. However, unless there are new theories to support history pedagogy in everyday history classrooms, pre-service teaching programmes and agentic resources, instrumentalist approaches to historical narratives will remain difficult to shift. *Doing* Intercultural History[33] was developed by the author to take aim at the "deep structure of historical narration"[34] to wield power and speak back to instrumental ethnocentric and Eurocentric narratives.

I have argued that school history and the delivery of prescriptive History curriculum has a great responsibility in decolonising Australian history education. Hence, this is why I have raised questions about how we are to celebrate cultural difference and diversity in Australia if we remain troubled by the discrete articulation of First Nations Peoples cultures as integral to the nation's past. In response, I have presented the broader concept of interculturality, which already exists within the national curriculum, as essential and integral to addressing some of these contemporary issues through the lens of the past. The intercultural relations that have shaped Australia should be central to how we design, resource, and teach Australian history. It is imperative that we nurture cultural diversity in Australian society, that those bestowed with the responsibility of teaching complex and troubled histories to all young Australians are theoretically prepared to move beyond myths of peaceful settlement and the cultural stereotypes this has produced.

This chapter has advocated teaching intercultural history as a tool for fostering critical thinking skills so that through their own development, teachers can encourage their students to question dominant historical narratives and develop a more engaged and holistic understanding of Australian history. *Doing* Intercultural History is offered in good faith as one means of achieving this because it is grounded in research based on the analysis of discourses of history teachers in Australia and resources that are fundamentally used in history classrooms across the country. Teaching intercultural history needs to be developed and perfected in this country in the hope that we empower young Australians to be active participants in the construction and interpretation of their own histories. Then we may inherently tell the stories of the nation rather than the nation's 'story.'

Strategies to support intercultural history teaching

These strategies intend to provide further understanding of positioning Intercultural History teaching by enacting the three sub-elements of ICU in the AC (ACARA, v9): Reflecting on culture and cultural diversity, navigating intercultural contexts, and engaging with cultural and linguistic diversity.

Strategy 1: This strategy engages the sub-element of ICU, 'Reflecting on culture and cultural diversity.'

Simple preparation around the construction of texts that are **complicit** in entrenching **traditional** identities is one way of reflecting on culture and cultural diversity found in the past. In this example, I take an excerpt from a history textbook currently used in Australia.

A nation is a group of people united by a common language, history and culture that live in a clearly defined area. The story of Australia's journey from convict dumping ground to democratic nation is a dramatic and exciting one. In 1901, after more than 100 years of European settlement, the six separate British colonies across the continent joined together to create the Commonwealth of Australia—a process known as Federation. Each colony shared many common characteristics—culture, language, political systems, and religion. They also shared a belief that the Indigenous people of Australia had no claim over the land they had inhabited for tens of thousands of years. The characteristics and beliefs of people from each of the original colonies heavily influenced the new formed nation of Australia and continue to do so to this day.[35]

1 Where does the excerpt fit within the framework–traditional, exemplary, critical, or transformative?

   a Traditional to exemplary

2 How are First Nation Peoples histories positioned in this excerpt?

   a *As part of a system of destruction*
   b *To reinforce terra nullius*

3 Who is made significant in the description?

   a *The six colonies*

4 Which 'group' is made 'exemplary'?

   a *The colonists*

5 What virtues or vices are made exemplary?

   a *culture, language, diet, political systems, and religion (Virtues)*
   b *They also had a similar lack of recognition for the rights of the original inhabitants of the country (Vices)*

6 What would this excerpt look like written through the lens of the critical stage of the framework?

   a *What is a counter narrative, using a primary/secondary source as evidence, that (re)thinks what is handed down here?*
   b Ask students what words might be used to shift the position of First Nations Peoples as independent of the story they already know.

7 Replace the excerpt above with a story or narrative currently being used in your History classroom and take to a discussion with a colleague or group of history teachers and work through each step.

Strategy 2: This strategy engages the sub-element of ICU, 'engaging with cultural and linguistic diversity.'

Consider the position of the simple linguistic devices such as the collective pronoun 'our' and how it is used. The traditional and exemplary concepts of the framework draw attention to how/when the collective pronoun is used to support the strength of the dominant group. This can help with students' engagement with oral, written, and visual texts that position the power of the collective pronoun to belong to First Nations Peoples or when terms such as 'invasion' are used as part of truth-telling rather than as a divisive term. For example, online resources such as *Deadly Story*[36] are an example of how specific language and the collective pronoun are used to counter dominant positioning.

Strategy 3: This strategy engages the sub-element of ICU, 'navigating intercultural contexts.'

Align the third sub-element of ICU with the critical and transformative functions of the framework by seeking out intercultural contexts for study. Within the prescriptive historical content knowledge, consider where/when intercultural contexts might provide a more accurate and comprehensive narrative of a period of time. For example, evidence of intercultural trade that is independent of British trade in the past or why it could not be. Or the teaching of the Frontier Wars that show the strength and resilience of this culture.

- First, ask students to find these *inter*cultural contexts in the history texts provided to them.
- Imagine your checklist for what makes the evidence or interpretation they find intercultural or not. Can this be inherited by your students?
- Using *Doing* Intercultural History to support your students' historical thinking: present the framework with the four stages highlighted on the screen. After explaining the function of each stage, use the word 'sovereignty' or 'ceded' as topics for inquiry and ask students what it means when you place the word (visually) within each stage of the prism. For example:
    - Traditional stage establishes sovereignty in relation to terra nullius.
    - Exemplary stage affirms/alludes to sovereignty and ceded as rights to the land and its discovery as new and British.
    - Critical stage asks, *What if there is another meaning for these words?*

    > "A spiritual notion: the ancestral tie between the land, or 'mother nature'"
    > (Uluru Statement from the Heart)

- Transformative learning about these meanings.

Notes

1 Australian Bureau of Statistics, 2021. https://www.abs.gov.au/statistics/people/people-and-communities/cultural-diversity-census/2021
2 Australian Institute of Aboriginal and Torres Strait Islander Studies [AIATSIS]. (n.d.). *Living languages.* https://aiatsis.gov.au/explore/languages-alive
3 Davies, T. (2022). 'But we're not a multicultural school!': Locating intercultural relations and reimagining intercultural education as an act of 'coming-to-terms-with our routes'. *The Australian Educational Researcher*, 50(3), 991–1005. https://doi.org/10.1007/s13384-022-00537-0

4 Mark, D. (2009). *Rudd calls for end to 'history wars'*. "Any truthful reflection of our nation's past is that these are all part of the rich fabric of our remarkable story called Australia."
5 Woodpower, Z. J. (2013). *The Australian national history curriculum: Politics at play*. University of Sydney.
6 Cooper, H., Dilek, D., & Nichol, J. (2009). History education, identity and citizenship in the 21st century. *International Journal of Historical Learning Teaching and Research, 8*(1), 4–6.
7 Australian Museum. (n.d.). *Curator's acknowledgement: The Great Australian silence*. Australian Museum. https://australian.museum/learn/first-nations/unsettled/healing-nations/the-great-australian-silence/#:~:text=Stanner%20talked%20in%20his%20Boyer,all%2C%20to%20the%20point%20of
8 Moore, R. (2015). *Whiteness threatened? A content analysis of Australian social science texts, 1950–2010*. University of Tasmania.
9 Rüsen, J. (2005). *History: Narration – Interpretation – Orientation*. Berghahn Books.
10 Australian Museum. (n.d.). *Curator's acknowledgement*.
11 Rivera, I. (2023). Undoing settler imaginaries: (Re)imagining digital knowledge politics. *Progress in Human Geography, 47*(2), 298–316. https://doi.org/10.1177/03091325231154873
12 Gundara, J. S. (2014). Global and civilisational knowledge: Eurocentrism, intercultural education and civic engagements. *Intercultural Education*, 1–14. https://doi.org/10.1080/14675986.2014.888802
13 Gilbert, R. (2019). General capabilities in the Australian curriculum: Promise, problems and prospects. *Curriculum Perspectives, 39*(2), 169–177. https://doi.org/10.1007/s41297-019-00079-z
14 Fozdar, F., & Martin, C. A. (2021). Making history: The Australian history curriculum and national identity. *Australian Journal of Politics & History, 67*(1), 130–149. https://doi.org/10.1111/ajph.12766
15 Clark, A. (2008). *History's children: History wars in the classroom* [Bibliographies]. University of New South Wales Press.
16 Cairns, R., & Garrard, K. A. (2020). Flatlining? National enrolment trends in senior secondary history. *Agora, Sungrapho, 50*(3), 59–67.
17 Bekerman, Z., & Zembylas, M. (2011). *Teaching contested narratives: Identity, memory, and reconciliation in peace education and beyond*. Cambridge University Press. p. 29.
18 Tuck, E., & Yang, K. W. (2012). Decolonization is not a metaphor. *Decolonization: Indigeneity, Education & Society, 1*(1), 1–40.
19 Bardhan, N., & Sobré-Denton, M. (2015). Interculturality, cosmopolitanism, and the role of the imagination: A perspective for communicating as global citizens. In M. J. Rozbicki (Ed.), *Perspectives on interculturality: The construction of meaning in relationships of difference* (pp. 131–160). Palgrave Macmillan. p. 151. https://doi.org/10.1057/9781137484390_8
20 Gilbert, R., Tudball, L., & Brett, P. (2019). *Teaching humanities and social sciences*. Cengage. p. 51.
21 Halse, C., Mansouri, F., Moss, J., Paradies, Y., O'Mara, J., Arber, R., & Denson, N. (2015). *'Doing diversity' an Australian Research Council linkage project final report*. Deakin University.
22 Gorski, P. C. (2008). Good intentions are not enough: Decolonizing intercultural education. *Intercultural Education, 19*(6), 515–525. https://doi.org/10.1080/14675980802568319
23 Rüsen (2005). *History*, p. 15.
24 Note: *'Doing* Intercultural History' is not exclusive to teaching Australian history, but these examples are specific for the purposes of this chapter.

25 Carrodus, G., Delaney, T., Howitt, B., & Smith, R. (2012). *Oxford Big Ideas. History 9: Australian curriculum*. Oxford University Press. p. 309.
26 Carrodus, G., & Smith, R. (2016). *Oxford Big Ideas. History 9: Victorian curriculum*. Oxford University Press. pp. 94–95.
27 Author unknown. (1806). G. P. Harris' cottage, Hobart Town, V. D. Land, Aug. 1806. Trove. https://nla.gov.au/nla.obj-135214475/view (Public Domain).
28 Carrodus et al.(2012). *Oxford Big Ideas*. A cottage in early Hobart 1803, Oxford Big Ideas History 9. Oxford University Press.
29 Grishin, S. (2014). *Australian art: A history*. The Miegunyah Press.
30 Ulm, M. E. (1880). The Blue Mountain pioneers at the summit of their expedition, lithograph, Sydney Mail 1880, Mitchell Library, State Library of New South Wales and Wikimedia Commons, Public Domain.
31 Gill, S.T. (1852). Zealous gold diggers, Bendigo July 1st 1852. Macartney & Galbraith, State Library of Victoira, Public Domain.
32 Moore, R. (2015). *Whiteness threatened? A content analysis of Australian social science texts, 1950–2010*. University of Tasmania.
33 Garrard, K. A. (2019). *Interculturality and secondary history education: A contemporary study of history pedagogy*. Deakin University.
34 Rüsen (2005). *History*, p. 15.
35 Carrodus, G., & Smith, R. (2016). *Australia (1750–1918)*. Oxford University Press.
36 Unknown. (n.d.). *Deadly story*. Department of Families, Fairness and Housing. https://deadlystory.com/page/about/about-us

Chapter 10

Examining invasion and possession narratives through Asia-related history

Rebecca Cairns

Author positioning statement

As a non-Indigenous settler of mostly Irish and Scottish ancestry, I acknowledge I have experienced history education and settler colonialism from a comfortable and unearned position of privilege while living on the unceded, ancestral lands of the Boonwurrung, Wurundjeri, Wadawurrung, and Gimuy-walubarra Peoples. Recognising that the inherently racist and unjust structures and ideologies of coloniality—that have disproportionately advantaged me as a white settler while disadvantaging First Nations Peoples—continue to be perpetuated through educational and knowledge-making practices means I am committed to addressing the (de)colonising practices that shape history education. This includes critically reflecting on my own practice that has spanned 13 years teaching in secondary schools and 10 years in higher education.

Introduction

Invasion narratives are unevenly woven into Australian history, depending on whose stories are being told, who is telling them, and for what purpose. Despite First Nations People's resistance and enduring connection to Country, the brutal processes and structures of colonisation—also described as settler colonialism—continue to deny First Nations sovereignty while benefiting non-Indigenous people living on unceded lands. The fact that the Australian Curriculum still positions 'invasion' as a 'contested' term despite multiple curriculum descriptions recognising that First Nations Peoples see the 'settlement' of their lands as an invasion, highlights how history curriculum perpetuates the sort of binary 'history wars' discourses discussed in the opening chapter of this collection. Settler denial of the violent and invasive processes of settler colonialism clings to the untroubled 'three cheers' view of the continent's supposed peaceful and progressive settlement. Yet, since the nineteenth century, white settlers have actively maintained invasion narratives to describe the perceived threat of 'Asian invasion' for the purposes of reasserting white sovereignty.

With its focus on exploring decolonising approaches to Asia-related Australian history, this chapter seeks to do three things. First, it problematises the way 'Asia' has traditionally been imagined by the Eurocentric knowledge production practices we can describe as *West as method*, a concept expanded upon in this chapter. By introducing Taiwanese Cultural Studies scholar Chen Kuan Hsing's[1] conceptualisations of *Asia as method* and *deimperialisation*, the chapter offers teachers and students some analytic tools to critically reflect on the historical imagination of 'Asia' and the extent to which the agency and diversity of historical actors in and from Asia are recognised through historical narratives and sources. Second, the chapter draws in Goenpul scholar and Indigenous rights activist Aileen Moreton-Robinson's conceptualisation of *possessive logics*, which act to rationalise and reaffirm "the nation-state's ownership, control and domination."[2] Third, it then demonstrates how history educators might apply these concepts to the analysis of common nineteenth-century anti-Chinese political images to critically reflect on the ways these sources represent an explicit Asian invasion narrative embedded within an implicit possession narrative. The questions and ideas discussed aim to identify ways forward for decolonising history curriculum.

At its broadest, I understand the goal of decolonising history curriculum as seeking to recognise and redress the way colonial powers (i.e., Euro-American powers) have controlled the knowledge production practices of disciplinary History and therefore presented distorted views of historical processes, especially the ongoing effects of the invasion of the lands of Indigenous Peoples across the world. In response, decolonising approaches seek to diversify the narratives, knowledges, voices, experiences, and perspectives that contribute to historical knowledge-making practices and amplify the voices that have been systematically marginalised by colonialism and racism. This includes recognising the limitations of the Western-centric disciplinary traditions that shape history education. More specifically, the decolonisation of history curriculum should be approached differently according to the specifics of national and local contexts.

In settler-colonial Australia, decolonising history curriculum recognises the rights of First Nations Peoples to exercise sovereignty and self-determination, promotes teaching and learning about First Nations Peoples histories and cultures in ways that re-centre First Nations Peoples perspectives, uses but also problematises historical inquiry as a means to interrogate settler colonialism, and seeks opportunities for critical self-reflection on one's own historical positioning in relation to Australia's colonial past and decolonising present and future. Acknowledging people have differing views on the term *settler colonialism*, I use it throughout this chapter as a way of articulating the specific form of colonialism that aggressively and systematically sought to replace the sovereignty of First Nations Peoples with the authority of the settler-colonial nation-state. As noted in Tuck and Yang's definition, settler colonialism "is different from other forms of colonialism in that settlers come with the intention of making a new home on the land, a homemaking that insists on settler sovereignty over all things in their new domain."[3] By making the land their home, a source of capital, and disrupting Indigenous relationships to land, settlers have and continue to inflict "profound epistemic, ontological, cosmological violence";[4] in other words, they continue to inflict violence on Indigenous ways of knowing and being.

Overall, this chapter seeks to provide History educators with some concepts and strategies that can help to develop more complex understandings of sovereignty when exploring Asia-related Australian history topics. As discussed elsewhere, the capacity of educators to take up decolonising approaches can be in tension with the shortcomings of current disciplinary approaches of History.[5] Language usage and author positionality are also important to decolonising approaches. Acknowledging the shortcomings of homogenising terms like *Indigenous*, I use the term First Nations Peoples to refer to Aboriginal and Torres Strait Islander Peoples as the first peoples of the lands and waterways of what is now called Australia and use specific language group names where possible. The term 'Indigenous' is used in direct quotes and in relation to Indigenous or non-Indigenous people worldwide. I have also noted the positionality of key authors in terms of cultural background where the authors have acknowledged this themselves.

The possessive logics of Alfred Deakin

I come to this research as a school History teacher who now works with pre-service teachers as they prepare to teach History in Australian primary and secondary schools. My institutional positioning, coupled with the personal positioning outlined in the statement earlier, provides the ethical and professional impetus to adopt decolonising approaches to history education, curriculum inquiry, and research methodologies. The research on which this chapter is based was conducted at Deakin University, which has campuses located on unceded Wadawurrung Country (Geelong—where I live and work), Eastern Maar Country (Warrnambool), and Wurundjeri Country (Burwood).

The university was named after Alfred Deakin, Australia's inaugural attorney-general and three-time prime minister. The following quote from Deakin in 1901 underscores his racist vision and legacy:

> In another century the probability is that Australia will be a White Continent with not a black or even dark skin among its inhabitants. The Aboriginal race has died out in the South and is dying fast in the North and West even where most gently treated. Other races are to be excluded by legislation if they are tinted to any degree. The yellow, the brown, and the copper-coloured are to be forbidden to land anywhere.[6]

Fortunately, Deakin's vision was not realised, but he was instrumental in the enactment of Federation-era policies based on racial purity and racial discrimination—particularly those that have come to be called the White Australia policy. Moreton-Robinson articulates the intentions of Deakin and his peers as possessive logics:

> At the turn of the twentieth century, the founding white fathers of Australia's federation feared that non-white races would want to invade the country. They were concerned with white racial usurpation and dispossession and took action to ensure that Australia would be a nation controlled by and for whites. Their possessive logics were embedded in the law through the passage of the Immigration Restriction Act 1901, which the new federal government implemented in the form of the White Australia Policy.[7]

These racialised ideologies and laws exemplify Moreton-Robinson's notion of the white possessive, a conceptualisation that will be explored below. The divisive effects of the legislation or policies that are collectively known as the 'White Australia policy' were intentionally harmful to First Nations Peoples and continue to be felt in the present, significantly influencing how Australia has imagined itself in relation to its Asian neighbours for more than a century. Although not supported by everyone, the idea of 'Australia for the white man' was substantially motivated by fear of Asia and fed by invasion narratives,[8] examples of which we will explore in this chapter.

West as method

Version 9.0 of the Australian Curriculum's cross-curriculum priority states, "Knowing, understanding and growing engagement with Asia are foundational for young people as Australia seeks to strengthen its ties in the Asia region."[9] The subject of History has been central to the national project of 'knowing' Asia for decades. In the post-war period, Australia was surrounded by Asian nations undertaking decolonisation: the political processes of becoming independent from former colonial powers. Australia was now compelled to get to know nearby nations as neighbours rather than enemies if it was going to become more integrated in the region. In the late 1960s Asian History was introduced as a subject in Victoria in Form 4 (Year 10)[10] and in Forms 2–4 (Years 8–10) in New South Wales.[11] By 1968, Asian History became the most popular Form 4 History subject in Victoria, and by 1970, 50% of schools taught it.[12] Interest in Asian history prompted reflection on significant historiographical issues. At the time, critiques noted that History courses were seen to be too focused on "the relationship of Western nations to Asia"[13] and tended to perpetuate tokenism and simplistic Western cliches of Asian history.[14] One of the reasons these issues remain nearly 50 years on relates to the power of *West as method*.

The term 'Asia-related Australian history' is ambiguous because it is premised on a highly contestable term. *How do we define 'Asia'?* Ask a group of students to make a list of countries they consider to be part of Asia, and the exercise will soon have them reflecting on the limitations of geo-political, linguistic, cultural, and other definitions. Historically, 'Asia' is an idea that has largely been constructed through a Eurocentric imagination. Etymologically, the term can be traced back to the ancient Greeks, who used it to name the lands and people to their east—that is, not Europe to the west.[15] Emerging with the Enlightenment and colonial expansion during the eighteenth and nineteenth centuries, new knowledge about race theory, historiography, political economy, modern geography, theories of state, and the natural sciences influenced European worldviews.[16] These ideas reinforced beliefs that Europe or the 'West' was the most advanced society on earth, supposedly symbolising sophistication, modernity, progress, industrialisation, and power. In contrast, Asia or the so-called East represented a backward, undeveloped, uncivilised place that needed colonising and Christianising.[17] Into the twentieth century, the idea of Asia continued to be fixed to a narrative of European modernity that was sustained by the scaffolds of empire, nation-state, and capitalism.[18]

These enduring categorisations have given rise to simplistic yet familiar binaries that include East/West, Orient/Occident, coloniser/colonised, self/other, and white/other. Such understandings are problematic because they continue to position Asia primarily as a product of Western imperialism and colonialism and maintain the knowledge practices of West as method. Although there is increasing awareness about the ways West as method is privileged through Eurocentric content in official curriculum documents, we can still see evidence of it in recent History curricula. For example, my analysis of VCE History Study Designs—the documents that comprise the senior secondary curriculum in the Victorian Certificate of Education (VCE)—indicates that Asia still gets predominantly viewed through Western-centric reference points: imperialism, colonialism, cold-war structures, the nation-state, and Western intervention.[19] With a few exceptions, these units rarely take pre-colonised societies as their starting points or make time to examine the long-term impact of colonisation.

We can also see the tendency to take the imperial powers or colonialism as the starting point in the Australian Curriculum History V9.0 topic: *Making and transforming the Australian nation.* For example, by prefacing the topic with "the causes and effects of imperial expansion and the movement of peoples in the late 18th and 19th centuries and the different responses to colonisation and migration" (AC9HH9K01),[20] the curriculum implicitly sets up a narrative that empowers Europe. As Indian subaltern studies scholar Dipesh Chakrabarty has noted, this reinforces a dominant narrative whereby "Europe works as the silent referent."[21] We can also see instances of European powers being prominent in the curriculum descriptors of the *Asia in the world*

1750–1914 depth study in Australian Curriculum: History V9.0, such as examining the "causes and effects of European contact, including colonisation, on an Asian society" (AC9HH9K20).[22] As a result, these knowledge practices tend to position European colonial powers as the central reference point from which to view the processes of world history, which positions Asia as inferior and overlooks Asian imperialism.[23]

Concerns about such patterns were expressed by VCE History teachers I interviewed a few years ago, quoted here using pseudonyms.[24] Bryce commented, "The only Asian studies we do are things that are Western topics that lend themselves or are related to Asia." Mark reflected, "[A] lot of the time when Asia comes into the curriculum it is because of some conflict or the negative connotation." Similarly, Penny said, "I couldn't spot a time when Asia is covered in a positive way." While investigating the negative effects of colonialism or Western intervention is an important part of historical inquiry, West as method tends to position Asian societies and First Nations cultures in a negative light and as passive rather than agentic participants of world history.[25] As I explore elsewhere, West as method also gets reproduced in the disciplinary structures of History and historiography, as well as the way it is enacted by teachers.[26] The effects of these knowledge production practices are summed up by Fijian, Chinese, and British descent Australian historian Tracey Banivanua Mar: "History has been central to the denial of the presence, let alone the independence, of Indigenous and colonized peoples, making its production a fraught political exercise."[27] The subject of History should therefore be accountable for scrutinising how historical actors are positioned within narratives about imperialism and colonialism, how they have been reproduced, and how they might be reimagined.

Asia as method

Asia as method offers a strategy for destabilising West as method. In the case of Asia-related history, this does not mean rejecting the label of Asia altogether. Rather, instead of only imagining Asia and world history from a central Western-centric axis or reference point, it requires more complex conceptualisations that reimagine Asia and world history from alternative axes or multiple reference points. With the aim of moving beyond outmoded conceptualisations of Asia and world history, Chen's notion of Asia as method seeks to recognise Asia as an active agent of world history:

> If Asia is to have analytical value, it does indeed have to be placed in the frame of world history, but if world history is understood as Euro-American imperialism and capitalist expansion, the agency and subjectivity of Asia are stripped away. ... Asia as method recognises the need to keep a critical distance from uninterrogated notions of Asia. ... It sees Asia as a product of history, and realises that Asia has been an active participant in history.[28]

Chen uses the notion of *deimperialisation* to describe the sort of critical reflexivity required to action Asia as method. For those who have inherited the privileges of Euro-American colonial expansion, it requires "the colonising or imperialising population to examine the conduct, motives, desires and consequences of the imperialist history that has formed its own subjectivity."[29] In other words, as a white settler of European descent, I need to reflect on how I have directly and indirectly benefited from the structures of settler colonialism here in Australia and the colonial project across the Asia region more broadly. This includes reflecting on how these power relations shape my own historical interpretations, individual subjectivity, and experience of the world but also how coloniality continues to shape the collective subjectivity of the Australian nation.

In regard to decolonising Australian history education, the Asia as method framework can assist all curriculum actors—teachers, students, curriculum leaders, publishers, etc.—to evaluate curricular constructions of Asia and utilise historical inquiry as an opportunity for critically reflecting on our self-understandings, worldviews, and ways of seeing self and other.[30] Drawing on Chen's notions of deimperialisation, I have formulated a set of questions that can be used as an analytic tool by educators and students for decolonising Asia-related Australian history (see Table 10.1). The student questions could be differentiated to suit individual needs or adapted to a specific topic or source, as illustrated in the table.

Table 10.1 Critical questions for engaging Asia as method[31]

Reflective questions educators can ask in relation to Asia-related history content and curriculum	Reflective questions students can ask in relation to Asia-related history
• To what extent do these representations recognise Asia as an active agent of world history? • How do these representations provide opportunities to view Asia as diverse, relational, and dynamic? • To what extent do these representations include points of reference that break away from the East/West binary? • How do these representations offer opportunities to look at Asia-related history through but also beyond the prisms of imperialism, colonialism, cold-war structures, and the nations-state? • Are there opportunities to consider decolonisation and deimperialisation as ongoing concerns for both former colonised and former colonising societies?	• Who is seen as the winners and/or losers? Who is seen to have power, and who lacks power? • Are people, groups, or developments related to Asia seen to have power or be important? • Are people or places related to Asia generalised about or based on negative stereotypes? • Are people or places related to Asia seen to be diverse, complex and ever-changing? • What might be some of the problems with always viewing Asia-related history from the perspective of Western colonisers? • What sorts of historical narratives or topics are common in the study of Asia-related history? How could they be different?

(Continued)

Table 10.1 (Continued)

Reflective questions educators can ask in relation to Asia-related history content and curriculum	Reflective questions students can ask in relation to Asia-related history
• Are the voices of diverse historical actors represented? • To what extent do these representations encourage historical interpretations and perspectives from a range of positions or represent a range of narratives? • How do these histories, including the long-term impact of imperialism and colonialism, relate to my own positioning, world view, or experiences? • How do these histories, including the long-term impact of imperialism and colonialism, relate to students' positionings or experiences?	• What sort of narratives or stories are provided about the people who did the colonising and the people who were colonised in Asia or Australia? • Why is it important to find out about the long-term or lasting impact of colonisation on the people who were colonised and the people who did the colonising? What are the impacts? • From whose perspectives are historical narratives being told? Whose voices are included and whose are not? • How do these histories connect with your own ideas and experiences? How might this compare to other people or groups in the past and the present?

Applying Asia as method to the Australian Curriculum: History

I will now consider how the Asia as method framework might be applied to the depth study *Making and transforming the Australian nation (1750–1914)* in Version 9.0 of the Australian Curriculum: History. One of the curriculum descriptions states:

> AC9HH9K06: different experiences and perspectives of colonisers, settlers and First Nations Australians and the impact of these experiences on changes to Australian society's ideas, beliefs and values.[32]

As an example of the sort of content that might be covered, one of the elaborations suggests

> examining the experiences of non-Europeans in Australia prior to the 1900s such as Japanese pearlers in Darwin, Chinese people in the goldfields, South Sea Islanders on sugar plantations in Queensland and Afghan cameleers in central Australia.[33]

Prior to investigating these 'non-European' experiences teachers could use the questions in Table 10.1 to tailor questions for students that prompt discussion about the way that groups of Asian heritage people are positioned: Who are considered non-Europeans? What sort of historical narratives reproduce categories like European/non-European? How does the category non-European relate to the categories of colonisers, settlers, and First Nations Australians? What might be some problems with viewing a large group of people as non-European? Who is seen to have power and who lacks power in these categorisations? Are there any problems with the other categories: Japanese pearlers, Chinese people, South Sea Islanders, and Afghan cameleers?

Such questions can challenge students to develop more complex knowledge and also connect with the skills descriptions, including questioning and researching. Reflecting on the way these labels simplify the cultural and linguistic complexity of people with Asian heritage could inform students as they develop historical inquiries or encourage them to take up the theme of diversity through their research: *Where did cameleers come from? Were all cameleers 'Afghans?' What were the experiences of culturally and linguistically diverse groups of cameleers? What do we know about the intercultural relations between cameleers themselves and other groups of people?* Students would soon discover the term 'Afghan' or 'Ghan' is a homogenising misnomer. Many cameleers were Muslim and came from what is today called Afghanistan, but many represented different ethnic and religious groups from across what might be broadly described as Central Asia, India, Persia, and the Middle East. Although its MA15+ rating may limit school-based screenings to students 15 years and older, the 2020 film *The Furnace*—filmed on Yamatji Country and featuring Badimaya language—is set during the West Australian gold rush of the 1890s and exemplifies a text that moves towards an Asia as method reading of a cameleer's experience and intercultural relations.[34]

Historical inquiry about Chinese people in the goldfields, as suggested in the previous elaboration, is a common topic covered in Year 9 History. To move towards an Asia as method or a decolonising approach, the experiences of Chinese Australians could be explored in ways that afford them agency as historical actors rather than victimising or demonising them. Drawing on curriculum resources and historical sources that are informed by contemporary developments in Australian and transnational historiography can help history educators counter stereotypes of marginalised groups. Historian of Chinese-Australian history, Sophie Couchman notes, "[O]ver the past two decades scholars have been exploring in more detail the lives of Chinese Australians, the communities they formed and the nature of the economic, social and spiritual contribution they made within particular states, regions or cities."[35] Despite these historiographical developments, Couchman also argues that "Australia needs to do more than simply describe the activities of Chinese Australians as an 'exotic' immigrant group oppressed by white racism who have since overcome these challenges to 'thrive' in wiser, more tolerant Australia today."[36] This points to a challenge for Australian history educators: helping themselves and students understand the nuances of exclusionary and inclusionary practices over time.

Historian Marilyn Lake points to the way earlier histories of Chinese Australians focused on histories of racial hostility and harassment, exemplified by school curriculum resources that focus on depictions of Chinese in racist cartoons and magazines—such as those discussed later in the chapter. This focus, she argues, "tended to be on white attitudes towards Chinese Australians, who were represented in terms of racial stereotypes, rather than on the political activities, viewpoints and writings of Chinese colonists themselves."[37] Lake instead suggests viewing these histories and sources through a world history approach "is necessary to illuminate the four-way struggle between the British and Chinese empires, the self-governing colonies of Australia, and local Chinese communities."[38] Significant to these struggles are the relations non-white migrants had with First Nations communities. As noted by the editors of a recent issue of *Australian Historical Studies*, "analysis of heterogeneous migrant perspectives on Aboriginal Australia represents an important challenge for Australian history."[39] Here they highlight the need for more diverse narratives and perspectives about interactions between non-white migrants and First Nations Peoples. A resource that explores such intercultural relations is the *Gold* digital resource produced by SBS[40] that accompanied the 2021 production of *New Gold Mountain* (MA15+), set on Dja Dja Wurrung and Taungurung Country in the Bendigo goldfields in 1855.[41] The section of the resource titled *Voices* "turns the spotlight onto some of the lesser known narratives, sourced from a broad range of perspectives."[42]

Possession as method

In the book *White Possessive: Property, Power and Indigenous Sovereignty*, Aileen Moreton-Robinson argues, "Australian national identity is built on the disavowal of Indigenous sovereignty because the nation is socially and culturally constructed as a white possession."[43] Throughout, Moreton-Robinson demonstrates how "white possession disavows Aboriginal sovereignty through racist techniques, conventions, laws, and knowledges, each shaping and affecting the lives of Aboriginal people."[44] The idea that the nation has been constructed as a white possession is a powerful and challenging idea to explore in the decolonising history classroom and one that can be used in dialogue with Asia as method.

The conceptualisation of white possession draws attention to what Morton-Robinson describes as disproportionate differences between Indigenous and non-Indigenous ways of being and knowing:

> Indigenous ontological relations to land are incommensurate with those developed through capitalism, and they continue to unsettle white Australia's sense of belonging, which is inextricably tied to white possession and power configured through the logic of capital and profound individual attachment.[45]

This highlights how white settler associations with place are quantified by the economic value of owning land. Moreton-Robison[46] provides an illustration of this stark difference by comparing how traditional owner of Kakadu National Park in the Northern Territory, Bill Neidjie of the Bunitj clan and Gagudju language group, sees land, place and belonging, with the sort of colonial view of attachment and ownership represented by the lyrics of *I still call Australia home*, by white entertainer Peter Allen (a song that continues to be revived by advertisements for Qantas airlines). This distinction moves me, as a white settler, to recognise that my own worldview about place, land, ownership, and sovereignty is embedded within the mainstream settler-colonial ontology or way of being. Among other things, my ownership of a small piece of stolen Wadawurrung Country means I am complicit in maintaining the structures that have sought to erase and replace Wadawurrung sovereignty. The historian Ann Curthoys underscores this inheritance: "All non-Indigenous people, recent immigrants and descendants of immigrants alike are beneficiaries of a colonial history. We share the situation of living on someone else's land."[47] While history education cannot easily resolve such deep ideological fissures, as my colleagues argue elsewhere in this book, non-Indigenous teachers have a responsibility to grapple with them as part of the work of decolonising history education and decolonising self. This can involve looking for new opportunities to critically reflect on worldviews about invasion and sovereignty—not just at the beginning of the school year in the wake of Invasion/Australia Day—but across a range of history topics.

Rethinking the 'Mongolian octopus'

The aim of this final part of the chapter is to bring the concepts of Asia as method and white possession into dialogue to interrogate the use of historical sources related to Chinese immigration in the nationalist/Federation period from the 1880s to the beginning of World War I. These images—often propagandistic cartoons inciting fear of the 'yellow peril' or 'Asian invasion'—have deliberately not been reproduced here for some of the following reasons. Having been widely reproduced in school history textbooks and online resources, they are readily accessible. One of the most well-known—"The Mongolian Octopus–Its Grip on Australia" published in 1886 by *The Bulletin*[48]—depicts a racist caricature of a human-headed octopus and the so-called eight crimes the Chinese/Mongols will bring. As I will argue, the usage of these images and the suggested activities warrant a decolonial rethinking.

While it is important to provide evidence of the xenophobic attitudes that fuelled nationalism at the time, these images of Chinese invasion are rarely accompanied by alternative images that represent Chinese immigrants as agentic or heterogenous, let alone actual Chinese perspectives. The negative connotations of this sort of imagery are illustrated by a comment from Janette, an Australian history teacher, as she reflects on a recognisable pattern: "[E]ven with Australian history around Federation—fear of the Asian invasion, the Mongolian Octopus, all those—you look at those images and it is all those negative sort of things." Such knowledge production practices reaffirm that in the Australian imaginary, historical Asia tends to be constructed as menace and monster.[49] This does not mean that such imagery should not be critically evaluated in history classes; rather, it needs to be contextualised and historicised within a multiplicity of perspectives and sources. It can also be utilised to reflect on the underpinning possessive logics driving such representations and in dialogue with the experiences of First Nations Peoples.

The term 'John Chinaman', now considered derogatory and homogenising, is often used in the language of these cartoons and to describe this common caricature of Chinese labourers and merchants in the nineteenth century—'John' being the generic name given to all 'Chinamen.' The caricature is prominent in newspapers and magazines in Australia and other settler colonies, particularly the United States, which like Australia, attracted large numbers of Chinese labourers following the Californian gold rush. During the second half of the nineteenth century, more than 100,000 Chinese came to the Australian colonies. Owing to China's proximity and large population, many feared that Australia might be overrun by Chinese, an anxiety that nationalist politicians could manipulate as the colonies debated the merits of federating.[50] Historicising these representations is something that can be done with students as part of their analyses of historical sources.

Students are often asked to analyse the anti-Chinese attitudes expressed in political cartoons to learn about the experiences of Chinese immigration and the arguments for Federation. The online resource titled *Chinese Migration*, published by Education Services Australia as part of the Scootle repository of resources, is composed of four such images. The accompanying descriptions of the first two indicate these images convey warnings about Chinese violation:

1 Wake, Australia! Wake, 1888: This black-and-white cartoon depicts a caricatured Chinese man with 'CHINESE INVASION' printed on his clothes. He is climbing with a knife in his mouth into the bedroom of a sleeping young woman identified as 'AUSTRALIA.'
2 Anti-Chinese immigration cartoon, 1888: This buff-rendered cartoon depicts five young women, representing the self-governing Australian colonies, straining at a lever labelled 'FEDERATION.' They are attempting to topple a huge rock, caricatured as a Chinese man's head, off the edge of a cliff. The head is labelled 'THE CHINESE PEST.'[51]

Similarly, the Asia Education Foundation has an activity that draws on almost the same set of invasion images.[52] As Ouyang[53] and, more recently, Zhang and Lin[54] have noted in their historical analyses, Australian literature and writing from this period is also littered with visions of 'Chinese invasion' and distorted representations of Chinese people. Zhang and Lin suggest that in this period of heightened

Australian nationalism, "Australian intellectuals and writers were eager to voice Australian-ness—an anti-imperialist national identity which was exclusionary and predicated on binary opposition between white and non-white."[55]

We can therefore draw on these sources to evaluate the ways these sorts of historical narratives and binaries acted to "naturalise and legitimise settler sovereignty" while "affirming metanarratives of *terra nullius*."[56] In addition to using the Asia as method questions in Table 10.1 to prompt questions about the racist attitudes reflected in these visual and written texts, Moreton-Robinson's articulation of white possession stimulates new questions: What does this imagery say about Australian-ness at the time? What does it say about the way white Australia viewed invasion, ownership, and possession? How do these sorts of images tie national identity to whiteness, landownership, and defending Australia's borders? Based on what we know about the century of Australian history prior to these images being published, how realistic is it to represent Australia as an innocent, young, white woman? How could these sorts of images be interpreted as expressions of the denial of First Nations sovereignty? How do these representations of ownership contrast with First Nations perspectives on belonging and connection to Country? How do these cartoons connect to global processes of imperialism and colonialism at the time? From here, these questions could also be posed in relation to the present and the lasting effects of coloniality on different groups of people, including the individual teacher and student.

In the context of school history, the 'Mongolian Octopus' cartoon has come to exemplify a classic source for exploring Chinese migration and thus the doing of Asia-related Australian history. However, the aforementioned sorts of questions challenge history educators to rethink its use and remind us that it does not actually reflect a Chinese perspective. As Anna Kyi, a historian at Sovereign Hill (a Victorian gold rush attraction) highlights, "[O]ne of the challenges facing researchers of nineteenth-century Chinese-Australian history is the dearth of sources reflecting the Chinese perspective."[57] Given the 'Mongolian Octopus' cartoon has been included as a source representing Australia's defining moments on the National Museum of Australia's Digital Classroom[58] (with little context or suggestions for use), history educators might critically reflect on what makes it a "defining moment." Perhaps it presents a moment in which we can see what Moreton-Robinson describes as "whiteness operat[ing] possessively to define and construct itself as the pinnacle of its own racial hierarchy."[59] The eight tentacles represent the so-called crimes that threatened to grip Australia: cheap labour, pak-ah-pu (gambling game), immorality, smallpox and typhoid, opium, bribery, fan-tan (gambling game), and customs robbery. These crimes could be interpreted within the broader context of Australian settler-colonial history: To what extent have invaders/settlers committed such crimes against First Nations Peoples since 1788? To what extent were similar crimes committed by British imperialists and colonists in the colonies and elsewhere in the region? The arrival of smallpox and its decimation of First Nations populations offers a concrete point of comparison, as does the illegal importation of opium to China by the British. The notion of customs robbery might be compared to the Victorian Government's anti-Chinese legislation 1855–1862, which required an immigration poll tax to be paid only by Chinese people when arriving at the colony's ports. Students might also consider the prevalence of gambling in the colonies. The image could also be used to raise questions about the assumptions made about Chinese arrivals. For example, historian Greg Watters[60] argues that there is little evidence to suggest that Chinese labourers brought and spread smallpox during the 1881–1882 Sydney smallpox epidemic; rather, these fears of contamination were manipulated by politicians and acted to consolidate support for non-white immigration.

Conclusion

Throughout the chapter, I have explored some concepts and strategies that may support educators to infuse their pedagogical and curricular practices with decolonising approaches. Helping young people develop more complex understandings of how colonisation operates in the past is essential to "understanding what is at stake in identifying as Indigenous today" [61] in settler-colonial societies like Australia and across our region, as well as fostering *makarrata*, "the coming together after a struggle"[62] as envisaged in the *Uluru: Statement of the Heart*. Being able to recognise and resist dominant modes of knowledge-making practices and historical narratives in relation to Asia-related history in Australian schools is an important part of this endeavour.

As this chapter has shown, key concepts that offer lenses for doing this include settler colonialism, West as method, Asia as method, and white possession. I have also argued that keeping abreast of contemporary historiographical debates can help history educators develop more complex understandings of the ways dominant colonial narratives can be decentred through greater emphasis on a plurality of voices, perspectives, and sources. However, the enduring dominance of West as method on knowledge production practices means that the scarcity of non-Anglo and translated sources representing diverse historical perspectives and interpretations will continue to impact on the range of educational resources available. As the project of decolonising history education gathers further momentum, the expansion and accessibility of quality curriculum resources will be essential to supporting decolonising approaches to learning and teaching. The onus is, therefore, on the history education community to call for resources that engage students in intercultural and decolonial approaches to history education, a point also explored by Fricker and Garrard in this collection. We can draw inspiration from the conceptual contributions of decolonising scholars like Chen and Moreton-Robinson to assist us in posing and investigating new questions about agency, power, narrative, and sovereignty. In doing so, we can challenge ourselves and the young people we work with to articulate the ways history constructs and distorts stories about invasion and encourage critical reflection on how we are positioned in relation to them.

Ideas and strategies for deimperialising Asia-related history

- Examine the way West as method operates in curriculum documents, content choices, the discipline of History, learning and teaching resources, textbooks, the availability of historical sources, and the voices represented within them. Ask, How might these be otherwise? What can I do to diversify and multiply the knowledges, voices, perspectives, narratives, and interpretations within these history education texts and spaces?
- Use the Asia as method–inspired questions in Table 10.1 when working with Asia-related histories and content. This can prompt new ways of interpreting familiar historical sources and narratives.
- Seek out topics and perspectives within the curriculum, texts, and sources that privilege historical voices that have been marginalised in dominant historical narratives.
- Engage with recent work of historians, especially those that take a decolonising approach to history, and the communities whose voices and experiences are central to these histories.
- Articulate and critically reflect on your own positioning in relation to settler colonialism in Australian and regional contexts (see the chapters in this collection that expand on this).
- Help students to explore the notion of Australia as a white possession.

Notes

1. Chen, K. H. (2010). *Asia as method*. Duke University Press.
2. Moreton-Robinson, A. (2015). *White possessive: Property, power and Indigenous sovereignty*. University of Minnesota Press.
3. Tuck, E., & Yang, K. W. (2012). Decolonization is not a metaphor. *Decolonization: Indigeneity, Education & Society*, (38), 1–40. p. 5.
4. Ibid.
5. Cairns, R. (2020). Deimperialising Asia-related history: An Australian case study. *Curriculum Inquiry*, 50(2), 126–148. https://doi.org/10.1080/03626784.2020.1747936; Keynes, M. (2021). Engaging transitional justice in Australian history curriculum: Times, temporalities and historical thinking. *Curriculum Inquiry*, 51(4), 413–436. https://doi.org/10.1080/03626784.2021.1938972
6. Deakin, A. (1901). Cited by McGregor, R. (2011). *Indifferent inclusion: Aboriginal people and the Australian Nation*. Aboriginal Studies Press. p. 19.
7. Moreton-Robinson (2015). *White possessive*, p. xii.
8. Walker, D. (1999). *Anxious Nation*. University of Queensland Press.
9. ACARA. (2023). Asia and Australia's engagement with Asia cross-curriculum priority. *Australian Curriculum Version 9.0*. https://v9.australiancurriculum.edu.au/f-10-curriculum/cross-curriculum-priorities/asia-and-australias-engagement-with-asia?organising-idea=0

10 Education Department of Victoria. (1968). *Teacher's guide: History 1. The use of sources.* Education Department of Victoria.
11 *The Bulletin.* (1968). What do we know about Asia? *The Bulletin,* pp. 28–32.
12 Crean, D. R. (1975). Letters. *Agora, 9*(2), 2; Education Department of Victoria. (1968). *Teacher's guide.*
13 Auchmuty, J. J. (1970). *Teaching Asian languages and cultures in Australia* Commonwealth Advisory Committee on the Teaching of Asian Languages. p. 33.
14 Martell, W. H. T. (1970). Presenting Asian history. *Agora, 4*(4), 6–10; Russo, P. (1969). Avoiding the Western cliches of Asian history. *Agora, 3*(3), 1–5.
15 Knight, N., & Heazle, M. (2011). *Understanding Australia's neighbours: An introduction to East and Southeast Asia.* Cambridge University Press.
16 Wang, H. (2011). *The politics of imagining Asia* (T. Huters, Trans.). Harvard University Press.
17 Ibid.
18 Ibid.
19 Cairns, R. (2021). Recognizing, reproducing and resisting West as method discourse: An analysis of senior secondary Asia-related history curriculum enactment. *Journal of Curriculum and Pedagogy, 18*(1), 21–44. https://doi.org/10.1080/15505170.2020.1764413
20 ACARA. (2023). History 7–10. *Australian Curriculum V9.0.* https://v9.australiancurriculum.edu.au/f-10-curriculum/learning-areas/history-7-10/year-9_year-10?view=quick&detailed-content-descriptions=0&hide-ccp=0&hide-gc=0&side-by-side=1&strands-start-index=0&subjects-start-index=0
21 Chakrabarty, D. (2000). *Provincializing Europe: Postcolonial thought and historical difference.* Princeton University Press. p. 28.
22 ACARA. (2023). History 7–10: Year 9. *Australian Curriculum V9.0.* https://v9.australiancurriculum.edu.au/f-10-curriculum/learning-areas/history-7-10/year-9?view=quick&detailed-content-descriptions=0&hide-ccp=0&hide-gc=0&side-by-side=1&strands-start-index=0&subjects-start-index=0
23 Chen (2010). *Asia as method.*
24 Cairns, R. (2018). *The representation of Asia in Victorian senior secondary history curriculum.* [Doctoral thesis, Deakin University]. Deakin Research Online. https://dro.deakin.edu.au/articles/thesis/The_representation_of_Asia_in_Victorian_senior_secondary_history_curriculum/21112357/1
25 Chen (2010). *Asia as method.*
26 Cairns, R., & Weinmann, M. (2023). *The Asia literacy dilemma: A curriculum perspective.* Routledge.
27 Mar, T. B. (2012). Settler-colonial landscapes and narratives of possession. *Arena Journal, 37–38*(Jan), 176–198. p. 197.
28 Chen (2010). *Asia as method,* pp. 214–215.
29 Ibid., p. 4.
30 Cairns, R. (2020). Deimperialising Asia-related history curriculum. *Curriculum Inquiry, 50*(2), 126–148. https://doi.org/10.1080/03626784.2020.1747936; Lin, A. M. Y. (2012). Towards transformation of knowledge and subjectivity in curriculum inquiry: Insights from Chen Huan-Hsing's 'Asia as method'. *Curriculum Inquiry, 42*(1), 153–178. https://doi.org/10.1111/j.1467-873X.2011.00571.x
31 Chen (2010). *Asia as method*; Cairns (2020). Deimperialising Asia-related history curriculum.
32 ACARA. (2023). History 7–10: Year 9.
33 Ibid.
34 MacKay, R. (2020). *The Furnace.* Umbrella Entertainment.

35 Couchman, S. (2015). Introduction. In S. Couchman & K. Bagnall (Eds.), *Chinese-Australians: Politics, engagement and resistance* (p. 6). Brill.
36 Ibid., p. 6.
37 Lake, M. (2015). The Chinese empire encounters the British empire and its 'colonial dependencies': Melbourne, 1887. In S. Couchman & K. Bagnall (Eds.), *Chinese-Australians: Politics, engagement and resistance* (p. 100). Brill.
38 Ibid., p. 101.
39 Piperoglou, A., & Simic, Z. (2022). Their own perceptions: Non-Anglo and Aboriginal Australia. *Australian Historical Studies, 53*(4), 519–530. https://doi.org/10.1080/1031461X.2022.2122268
40 SBS. (n.d.). *Gold*. https://www.sbs.com.au/gold/
41 Cox, P. (2021). *New Gold Mountain*. Goalpost Television.
42 SBS. (n.d.). Voices. *Gold*. para 1. https://www.sbs.com.au/gold/voices/
43 Moreton-Robinson (2015). *White possessive*, p. xxi.
44 Ibid., pp. xix–xii.
45 Ibid., p. xxi.
46 Moreton-Robinson, A. (2020). "Our story is in the land": Why the Indigenous sense of belonging unsettles white Australia. *Religion & Ethics*. ABC. https://www.abc.net.au/religion/our-story-is-in-the-land-indigenous-sense-of-belonging/11159992
47 Piperoglou & Simic (2022). Their own perceptions, p. 519.
48 May, P. (1886, 21 August). The Mongolian Octopus – Its grip on Australia. *The Bulletin*.
49 Walker, D., & Sobocinska, A. (2012). *Australia's Asia*. UWA Press. p. 1.
50 Macintryre, S. (2016). *A concise history of Australia*. Cambridge; Watters, G. (2012). Contaminated by China. In D. Walker & A. Sobocinska (Eds.), *Australia's Asia* (pp. 27–49). UWA Press.
51 Education Services Australia.
52 AEF. (2023). *Year 9 – Attitudes towards Chinese migrants*. https://www.asiaeducation.edu.au/curriculum/history/details/year-9-attitudes-towards-chinese-migrants
53 Ouyang, Y. (1995). *Representations of Australia and Australians in China and Hong Kong*. Griffith University.
54 Zhang, J., & Lin, B. (2023). Images of Chinese in Australian nationalist literature. *Neohelicon*. https://doi.org/10.1007/s11059-022-00682-6
55 Ibid.
56 Mar (2012). Settler-colonial landscapes and narratives of possession.
57 Kyi, A. (2009). Finding the Chinese perspective. Locating Chinese petitions against anti-Chinese legislation during the mid to late 1850s. *Provenance, 2009*(8). para 1.
58 National Museum of Australia. (2023). An anti-Chinese cartoon titled 'The Mongolian Octopus', published in the *Bulletin* in 1886. *Australia's Defining Moments Digital Classroom.* https://digital-classroom.nma.gov.au/images/anti-chinese-cartoon-titled-mongolian-octopus-published-bulletin-1886
59 Moreton-Robinson (2015). *White possessive*.
60 Watters (2012). Contaminated by China.
61 Stewart, G. T, Hogarth, M., Sturm, S., & Martin, B. (2022). Colonization of all forms. *Educational Philosophy and Theory*, 1–5. https://doi.org/10.1080/00131857.2022.2040482
62 First Nations National Constitutional Convention. (2017). *Uluru: Statement from the heart*. https://ulurustatement.org/the-statement/view-the-statement/

Chapter 11

Decolonising the teaching of local history using cinematic virtual reality

Will King

Author positioning statement

As a white settler researcher from an English, German, and Scottish background, I acknowledge that my ancestors and I benefitted from the dehumanising policies enacted under settler colonialism. I am a guest on the lands of the Peek Wuurong and Kirrae Wuurong People, and I am fortunate to have the privilege of working with Uncle Rob Lowe, a Peek Wurrung Elder who has generously shared his stories, thus allowing me to see the history of Warrnambool and South-West Victoria from a First Nations perspective. My friendship with Uncle Rob has inspired me to work with him as an ally to help decolonise Warrnambool's history, and together, we have developed some much-needed teaching resources that have revealed to many history students the existence of a vibrant First Nations history in their local area.

Introduction

> And then my grandfather always kept saying to me don't ever tell your stories, Rob, our story, don't tell them, because no one is going to believe what you say. So that's the reason why we were told never to tell what took place.
>
> — Uncle Rob Lowe

Uncle Rob Lowe's words convey a key challenge in teaching about First Nations histories and cultures in local communities: the silencing of First Nations voices. The history of many local communities has been written without the inclusion of First Nations Peoples or their perspectives. History teachers in local communities often find it challenging to develop First Nations history syllabuses because they cannot locate either historical accounts written from First Nations perspectives or local histories that focus specifically on First Nations Peoples. Decolonising the teaching of local history means producing teaching and learning resources that privilege First Nations voices, that are created in collaboration between First Nations and non-Indigenous People, and that are easily accessible for use in the History classroom.

DOI: 10.4324/9781003435617-11

Uncle Rob is a Wundjit, or senior Elder, of the Peek Wuurong People. He was born in 1947 and brought up on the Framlingham Aboriginal Reserve outside Warrnambool. On many occasions, while living on the Reserve, Uncle Rob and his family reported to the police how they had been physically and sexually abused in violent encounters with settler citizens. The police refused both to believe these allegations and to act on them because the perpetrators of the violence were settler Australians. Uncle Rob's grandfather and other Elders, therefore, began to instruct members of their communities not to tell their stories of life as First Nations Peoples in Warrnambool. They believed that revealing their stories placed them at risk of violent reprisal from both the police and Warrnambool's settler citizens.

Decolonising local First Nations history syllabuses involves filling in the silences of local settler histories to reveal the truth about the impact of colonisation. Loss of culture due to colonisation has also been significant for many First Nations communities.[1] Gubbi Gubbi scholar Kevin Lowe found that non-Indigenous teachers' lack of knowledge about the history of local First Nations communities contributed to a limited understanding of the connection between First Nations culture and "community well-being."[2] This highlights the need for schools and teachers to adopt a decolonising pedagogical approach when teaching local First Nations histories in the classroom. Decolonising pedagogical work makes "First Knowledges visible and valid"; it foregrounds a consideration of "the history and deep knowledge of this Country outside of colonial conceptions"; it critiques and questions the ongoing impact of colonialism; it brings together First Nations and non-Indigenous students and teachers in cross-cultural learning collaborations.[3] Adopting a decolonial pedagogical approach that privileges First Nations knowledges and culture will help students explore the First Nations histories of their community in an inclusive and culturally safer manner.[4]

Bates and Bowry have argued that the practice of teaching local history creates a sense of immediacy and a "powerful sense of connection" for students, increases their interest in History as a subject, and makes students more responsible citizens within their local community.[5] If students are to become socially conscious community citizens, then they must study the place-based history of their community through First Nations perspectives. Lummi scholar Michael Marker emphasises the salience of place and locality as the key pillars of teaching history from a First Nations perspective, arguing that "a local history that includes First Nations voices has the potential to challenge old assumptions about the community's identity [and] (re)frames the community's relationship to the traditional territory."[6] However, Warrnambool's local history continues to be framed through settler colonial ways of knowing, underpinned by the "terra nullius myth of peaceful settlement of an unowned land."[7] Much of Warrnambool's violent colonial past remains unacknowledged and unknown by its non-Indigenous community.

Massacre sites, the Frontier wars, the Stolen Generations, segregation policies enforced under assimilation, and even the existence of the Framlingham Reserve have yet to be properly recognised or included as part of Warrnambool's historical narrative.

This chapter draws on findings from my doctoral research and collaborations with Uncle Rob Lowe to co-design a cinematic virtual reality film called *The Crossing*.[8] In the first half of the chapter, I identify how settler local histories occlude First Nations Peoples, erasing them from the historical consciousness and public memory of Warrnambool's settler population. I then examine how cinematic virtual reality (CVR) film experiences could contribute to the decolonisation of history teaching in secondary school classrooms through stimulating historical empathy and understanding local First Nations perspectives as part of Australian history curriculum. In the second half of the chapter, I describe key principles from the co-design process for *The Crossing* that could serve as a possible model for constructing decolonising alliances between schools and First Nations communities for local history syllabuses that are First Nations–led and foreground Indigenous epistemologies.

Writing settler colonial local histories

This section provides a brief chronological summary of Warrnambool's local settler historiography. I have included this summary to show how the production of multiple local histories devoted mainly to chronicling white settler progress has created a paucity of written historical texts focusing on First Nations Peoples. I want to highlight how colonisation has forcibly replaced First Nations oral traditions of knowledge transmission by codifying the production of local history through the hegemony of the written text.

The foundational texts of Warrnambool's history have been written from a male settler perspective constructed within the paradigm of the nineteenth-century frontier myth. The writing of many rural histories made use of the imagery associated with the frontier myth of "the heroic struggle between the forces of good and evil" from which the settler emerges "transformed and upholding the values of self-reliance, democracy and competition."[9] These frontier histories represent First Nations Peoples as "hostile, threatening people to be conquered and annihilated; at other times they are presented in more noble terms, as helpers of the colonial project or as childlike people to be patronized or protected."[10] Davison has argued that the practice of writing local history evolved from the writing of pioneer histories using a series of common tropes:

> [A] triumphant history of territory gained, settled, and subdued. Its endless lists of firsts–the first discovery, the first river crossing, the first station, the first church service–were the genealogy of the communities still striving to establish a sense of legitimacy in a newly settled land.[11]

The use of these pioneer history tropes in producing Warrnambool's local history has been instrumental in erasing First Nations Peoples from the historical record. Warrnambool's history has thus been written to foreground settler narratives that have supplanted the deep-time histories of First Nations Peoples. The early pioneer histories of Warrnambool, such as Richard Osburne's *The History of Warrnambool* published in 1887, use the imagery of the frontier myth to describe the inevitable heroic triumph of settler colonialism over easily subdued First Nations Peoples as "survival of the fittest."[12] Osburne's frontier history perpetuates the image of the Peek Wurrung and Kirrae Wurrung Peoples as a dying race spending their "declining days" in the "peace and comfort" of the Framlingham Aboriginal Station.[13] The next iteration of Warrnambool's official history, *By These We Flourish*, was commissioned by the town council and written by a settler journalist in 1969.[14] By developing an exclusive settler narrative in which there is no mention of First Nations Peoples, this local history suggested the end of the frontier and the successful completion of the colonial project.[15]

Until the 1980s, there were few local texts produced in Warrnambool that were specifically devoted to documenting the history and culture of First Nations Peoples. James Dawson's *Australian Aborigines: The Languages and Customs of Several Tribes of Aborigines in the Western District of Victoria*,[16] published in 1881, was an exception. Dawson and his daughter Isabella worked with several Peek Wuurong and Kirrae Wuurong Elders to record information about cultural practices, history, and language that would otherwise have been lost due to colonisation.[17] This history constitutes a very important resource that is used by members of the local First Nations community in language and cultural revitalisation programmes.

The decolonising of Warrnambool's history was further nourished by the publication of several revisionist histories in the early 1980s that described the deleterious impact of colonisation on First Nations Peoples. These revisionist histories sought to counter the historical amnesia prevalent in Warrnambool's local historiography. These texts were researched in collaboration with the Peek Wuurong and Kirrae Wuurong communities and produced narratives that privileged First Nations agency. Jan Critchett, a non-Indigenous historian, produced a history of the Framlingham Aboriginal station, *Our Land till We Die*, in conjunction with the local First Nations community. She then wrote *A Distant Field of Murder*, an examination of the frontier conflict in South-West Victoria, which foregrounded the resistance of First Nations Peoples to white settlement.[18] Historical works by local First Nations people, such as Uncle Rob Lowe's autobiography *The Mish*, published in 2002, also contributed to making the recent history of First Nations Peoples under colonialism more visible, chronicling his life under the assimilation policy in the 1950s and 1960s.[19] Unfortunately, these texts are often difficult for teachers to access, as they are either out of print, as in the case of *Our Land Till We Die* and *The Mish*, or located as single copies in university libraries and thus are often out on loan. James Dawson's book *Australian Aborigines: The Languages and Customs of Several Tribes of Aborigines in the Western District of Victoria* is still in print but remains expensive to purchase. These difficulties in accessing local historical texts devoted to First Nations histories have made it challenging to teach a decolonised local history of Warrnambool in the classroom.

Using CVR to stimulate historical empathy

This chapter section examines how CVR films could be used as a resource to help teach local First Nations histories in the History classroom. I suggest that the affordances of CVR provide new modes for students to engage with and analyse local First Nations experiences using the historical perspectives skill descriptor at Years 9 and 10 in Version 9 of the Australian Curriculum. The film *The Crossing* is considered a case study for demonstrating how CVR can create empathetic connections between students and local First Nations experiences of life under colonialism, thus furthering their understanding of the impact of discriminatory legislation and policies in the post-war period.

CVR presents the viewer with a 360-degree space that is usually experienced inside a Head Mounted Display (HMD) or headset such as the Oculus Quest 2. A CVR film is captured with a 360-degree camera and allows the viewer to experience it in a format known as three degrees of freedom (3DoF). In the 3DoF format, the viewer is only able to look up and down and rotate their head from left to right. CVR creates an immersive experience that can transport the viewer into a particular historical narrative or event by placing them within it so that they are surrounded by 360-degree film and can look in multiple directions, often guided by sounds and the actions of people or characters within the space.[20]

Immersion relies on the concept of presence or 'being there,' where the user becomes aware only of what is happening in the virtual world, forgetting about the real world and any technology used to simulate what they are experiencing. The CVR world takes place around the viewer, and the direction of their gaze controls the narrative in which they are immersed.[21] By having agency in where to look, the user can manipulate how the real-life event they are experiencing will take place. Traditional close-up shots cannot be used in a CVR film, as the 360-degree camera has no zoom function. Creating close-up shots using a 360-degree camera requires the use of character proximity, where characters will either remain distant from the camera or move very close to the camera to elicit an affective response from the user.[22] This technique also simulates a real-world interaction, as the closer the character is to the camera, the more the character becomes present in the scene. Characters who address the camera or make eye contact with the camera seem to be interacting with the user, thus drawing the user further into a feeling of presence.

What is perspective-taking, and how does it relate to historical empathy?

Perspective-taking is a key concept in developing historical thinking and requires students to demonstrate historical empathy.[23] The definition of perspective-taking is hotly debated among many history education scholars, with a confusing set of different terms being offered. Scholars often conflate perspective-taking with historical empathy and use the two terms interchangeably—for example, treating perspective-taking as a component of historical empathy and vice versa.[24] Endacott and Brooks define historical empathy as "the process of students' cognitive and affective engagement with historical figures to better understand and contextualize their lived experiences, decisions, or actions."[25] In other words, teaching historical empathy means taking the perspective of historical figures by understanding both how they thought and felt about the time period that they were living in and how these thoughts and feelings may have shaped their decisions and actions.[26]

First Nations perspectives in the Australian curriculum—Years 9 and 10

In version 9.0 of the Australian Curriculum, the historical perspectives skill descriptor asks students to "compare perspectives in sources and explain how these are influenced by significant events, ideas, locations, beliefs, and values."[27] First Nations perspectives are included as a content descriptor at Year 9 within the *Knowledge* and *Understanding* section under *Making the Australian Nation*, for example, "different experiences and perspectives of colonisers, settlers and First Nations Australians and the impact of these experiences on changes to Australian society's ideas, beliefs and values."[28] At Year 10, First Nations perspectives are included as an elaboration of the historical perspectives skill descriptor, for example, "explaining the links between the continuities over the period, such as the experiences and treatment of First Nations Australians, women, and migrants."[29] Teaching First Nations histories in a local context will allow teachers to connect to all First Nations content and skills descriptors in Years 9 and 10 of the Australian Curriculum: History.

Perspective-taking and stimulating historical empathy in CVR

CVR offers multiple affordances for helping students engage in historical empathy using First Nations perspectives. Perspective-taking in CVR involves taking either a first-person embodied perspective, where the user assumes the body of a participant in the narrative, or a third-person spectator or witness perspective, in which the user views the action from outside as an observer. The first-person experience often involves the user being inside a character's body and seeing the unfolding narrative from their perspective and is described as realising the real immersive potential of CVR.[30] CVR films can help to stimulate historical empathy in an engaging manner and support students in approaching historical empathy writing tasks that involve understanding and analysing First Nations perspectives. Empathising with people in the past is a "complex historical reasoning competency"[31] that many students find difficult because they cannot comprehend that they have more knowledge than was available to people in the past.[32] This sense of presentism is a barrier to being able to place yourself in the shoes of someone in the past.[33] Many teachers are also reluctant to teach First Nations perspectives in the classroom "because they are not comfortable speaking about someone else's experiences" and that "by speaking for Aboriginal people they may in fact be maintaining the very silence that they had hoped to overturn."[34]

How can CVR first- and third-person perspective experiences help invoke historical empathy?

Endacott and Brooks have described three components of historical empathy:

1 Historical contextualisation: an understanding that the past was different and a deep knowledge of the particular time period's political, social, and cultural norms.
2 Perspective-taking: understanding what a historical actor in the past may have been thinking about their time period and being able to articulate these beliefs and attitudes.
3 Affective response: how might emotions have influenced the actions or thoughts of a historical actor, and how do we relate this to our own experiences.[35]

Historical contextualisation

In the CVR film *The Crossing*, students are immersed in Warrnambool during the historical context of the 1950s and 1960s when the lives of First Nations Peoples were controlled under the policy of assimilation. The film presents a mostly third-person perspective where students experience events as spectators viewing the action from the edge of the scene. In one scene students witness acts of segregation that take place in the old Warrnambool cinema and in another they travel across paddocks with Uncle Rob and family as they attempt to avoid the authorities on the way to the Framlingham Aboriginal Reserve. Being present in many of the scenes allows students to directly experience how the racist political, social, and cultural norms of the assimilation policy impacted the lives of First Nations Peoples. *The Crossing* allows students to see their local community as a decolonised space, in which First Nations histories are visible and the racism that First Nations Peoples endured is revealed. Students are then prompted to question why they may not know this history and why understanding and acknowledging this history is important for their community.[36]

Perspective-taking

Throughout *The Crossing* students are guided by Uncle Rob's voiceover, which communicates his perspective on the events that are depicted. The voiceover adds to the sense of immersion as Uncle Rob's words make sense of each scene and explain to students the colonial harms that he and his family were forced to experience. When his family is forced to sleep under a bridge the night before visiting his grandfather on the Framlingham Reserve, Rob explains that this was because First Nations Peoples needed a permit to enter the Reserve at the time. This gives students some understanding of the strict level of colonial regulation that governed the lives of First Nations Peoples during this time. By listening to Uncle Rob as he narrates his experiences, students can hear First Nations voices, many of which were erased from the local historical record by colonialism. They are thus able to understand Warrnambool's history as multi-perspectival[37] and encounter First Nations perspectives that challenge the racist settler thinking that underpins policies such as assimilation.

Affective response

Understanding the emotions that people in the past were feeling when they confronted difficult situations is an important aspect of teaching historical empathy. In one scene, students take on a first-person perspective as Uncle Rob so they can see the world from his viewpoint. As two menacing drunk white settlers approach the students, they are positioned to experience the fear and terror of Uncle Rob's confrontation with these men during the "nightly raids." The nightly raids involved settler men driving out to the Framlingham Reserve in search of young First Nations girls.[38] Uncle Rob's family is a central focus of *The Crossing*, so the camera has been positioned to bring the user into proximity with his family members so that they can feel the strong affective connections between each of them. Using a first-person perspective, CVR can stimulate moments of historical empathy by collapsing the distance of the past and helping students to see connections between their own experiences and those of First Nations Peoples.[39] This is not to say that CVR will ever provide a complete understanding of the dehumanising racism that First Nations Peoples were forced to endure, but it can allow students to see that colonialism is not only in the past but also ongoing in their present.

How can CVR be used in the history classroom?

In the previous section, I provided examples of how CVR might be used to help students invoke historical empathy. In this section, I show how a CVR experience like *The Crossing* could be integrated into a History classroom study of First Nations historical perspectives in Years 9 and 10 using Endacott and Brooks'[40] instructional model. This model presents four key phases for teaching a historical empathy task:

1 An introductory phase designed to introduce the historical situation and/or the historical figure(s) with whom the students will engage in historical empathy
2 An investigation phase in which students study primary and secondary source material in-depth to develop a deeper understanding of historical context, historical perspective, and related affective considerations
3 A display phase in which students demonstrate the understanding they have developed
4 A reflection phase in which students are invited to make connections between the past and the present while considering how their personal views may have changed as a result of engaging in historical empathy.[41]

A CVR experience could be most effective in the first introductory phase, where it can allow students to immerse themselves in the period of First Nations histories that they are studying. By feeling present in the time period, students' historical imagination is triggered, allowing them a greater understanding of the historical context and the political, cultural, and social problems that confronted First Nations Peoples. This could help students to begin to form empathetic connections in a way that is engaging and could assist them in analysing primary and secondary source material in the investigation phase. This experiential understanding of the historical context gives students a secure grounding for their interpretation of primary and secondary source material. Students now have prior knowledge that would allow them to connect their own experiences with those of the First Nations historical actors in each source, thus creating a pathway into the source material. This prior knowledge may be helpful in the second and third phases, in which students investigate and display their knowledge of primary and secondary sources. *The Crossing*, which involves Uncle Rob narrating his own story, could also be classed as a primary source, which could be used in the investigative phase, especially when local primary sources are difficult to locate.

In the reflection phase of the instructional model, students are "guided through the process of using their understanding of the past to inform their thoughts, emotions, and actions in the present."[42] This phase can be used to further unsettle students' understanding of Warrnambool's local history as a setter colonial narrative. Students could see the need for local truth-telling mechanisms as they recognise how the past connects to the present and that past colonial harms and unjust policies that impacted First Nations Peoples continue into the present through ongoing racism and structural inequality. Students in this phase can reflect on their digital and textual encounters with First Nations perspectives and use what they have learned to produce historical writing that re-frames their local histories as First Nations histories. These counter-narratives that they have created work as examples of decolonial truth-telling to reverse the silences that have determined local histories. They might also begin to question their settler privilege and how this is contributing to the continued disadvantaging of First Nations Peoples in the present.[43]

Decolonising the co-design of local First Nations history syllabuses

In this section, I examine how First Nations concepts of relationality, reciprocity, seeing and reading Country, and yarning can become embedded in decolonising co-design processes to produce local First Nations History syllabuses. I draw on learnings about First Nations methods of collaboration that have been shared with me by Uncle Rob during the co-design of our CVR movie *The Crossing*.

Relationality

First Nations scholars emphasise the importance of relationships for making connections between local First Nations communities and non-Indigenous people. For example, Anishinaabe scholar Patty Krawec has argued that First Nations Peoples and settlers have lived in isolation for too long and that forming relationships is the best way to connect communities. She argues that "we are all related" and that both First Nations Peoples and settlers need to ask the question, "[H]ow can we become better kin?"[44] She contends that to become kin, we must learn and live in relationships that are not formed through settler colonial paternalism but through responsibility and reciprocity.[45] We need to "reimagine the relationships we have inherited" to build a "shared past" that is founded on "unforgetting" histories of colonisation.[46]

What does it mean for schools to see themselves in relation to their local First Nations communities so they can form collaborations that are based on responsibility, respect, and reciprocity? It is important to note that there is no universal First Nations way of knowing, being, and doing. Each First Nations community will have its specific worldviews that are connected to cultural and historical sites located on their Country. When Uncle Rob tells his stories in schools, he places students and teachers in relationship with those stories. This involves the sharing of knowledge and an invitation to the students, teachers, and the school to help him to tell his story. Uncle Rob's stories centre around his family and show how they were impacted by colonial policies, such as assimilation, but also how they resisted these policies. In exchanging this knowledge Uncle Rob connects students, teachers, and schools with his family. By creating this connection, he is making students, teachers, and schools responsible for telling his family's story and thus creating a shared and interconnected history. His invitation reimagines colonial relationships that segregated First Nations and settler communities to establish new relational connections that produce shared understandings of local histories.[47]

Shared knowledge created through relational knowledge transmission should underpin local history partnerships, which become relational collaborations when they involve schools enacting protocols such as responsibility, respect, and reciprocity.[48] When Uncle Rob tells his stories, teachers and students in the school are charged with the responsibility for continuing to re-tell these stories in a culturally appropriate manner and calling out the previous and ongoing impacts of settler colonialism. Importantly, they also become responsible for the way in which this knowledge becomes part of the curriculum that is valued in the classroom and broader community. Each student and teacher becomes responsible to Uncle Rob for representing the First Nations Peoples in his story in a respectful manner. Uncle Rob's encounters with students and teachers in schools are just one aspect of the enactment of local history education. These encounters would ideally lead to the development of a relational curriculum model[49] as the basis for teaching local First Nations histories from Years 7 to 10.

Reciprocity

Reciprocity is a strong cultural protocol in First Nations communities to share and give back. In the process of decolonising history teaching, taking up the notion of reciprocity around knowledge production and transference is critical to co-designing local First Nations history syllabuses. Colonisation saw the theft of the traditional cultural knowledge, practices, and artefacts of Australia's First Nations Peoples by white institutions, often without permission, compensation, or acknowledgement. This has led First Nations Peoples to be wary of entering into collaborations with non-Indigenous peoples, in which the benefits of these collaborations only seem to flow towards non-Indigenous peoples. When First Nations Peoples can see that non-Indigenous people recognise and accept the outcomes of historical interactions, then cross-cultural relationships based on reciprocity are promoted.

Reciprocity has been characterised as "moving backward and forward" so that both First Nations communities and teachers benefit from a mutual exchange of knowledge as they work together to co-design local First Nations history programmes.[50] In return for the knowledge that Uncle Rob has provided schools, teachers, and students need to understand that whatever they create through the collaboration must involve giving back to the local Peek Wuurong/Kirrae Wuurong community. Reciprocity involves giving back in a substantial manner that is not just flying the Aboriginal and Torres Strait Islander flag, performing an Acknowledgement of Country, or organising *National Aborigines and Islanders Day Observance Committee* (NAIDOC) week celebrations.[51] Substantial reciprocity means engaging schools, teachers, and students in educational reciprocity, which starts by improving cultural intelligence through learning about local Peek Wuurong and Kirrae Wuurong history and culture and how these cultures were impacted by colonisation.[52]

Schools in Warrnambool also need to enact educational reciprocity to improve cultural safety for First Nations Peoples by creating safe spaces for cross-cultural collaboration and working with First Nations community organisations to ameliorate educational and social disadvantage amongst First Nations Peoples.[53]

A shared understanding of Country

Country is the core of First Nations ways of knowing but the meaning of this concept is often unfamiliar to, or, is misunderstood by non-Indigenous educators. Developing an understanding of Country and its significance to First Nations Peoples can be a starting point for non-Indigenous educators wanting to co-design decolonising local history curriculum with First Nations communities. Trawlwulwuy scholar Lauren Tynan describes how Country acts as a site of First Nations knowledge production:

> Country inhabits all relationality and is used widely across Australia to describe how all land is Aboriginal land, Aboriginal Country; Country is agentic and encompasses everything from ants, memories, humans, fire, tides and research. Country sits at the heart of coming to know and understand relationality as it is the web that connects humans to a system of Lore/Law and knowledge.[54]

Teachers and students could learn how First Nations Peoples see and read Country as a way of remembering the past. They can experience Country by walking it with First Nations Elders or community members. Seeing and reading Country as a memoryscape is important when local historical sources provide limited evidence of events and encounters involving First Nations Peoples. The First Nations concept of memoryscape is defined by Keith Thor Carlson and Sxweyxwiyam scholar Naxaxalhts'i Albert "Sonny" Jules McHalsic as the "deeply personal ways that individuals interact with their environs to create memoried places."[55] Memoryscapes are landscapes onto which First Nations Peoples "attach and invest" memory so that Country becomes a repository where memories are stored and then invoked.[56] When Uncle Rob actualises his stories about his early life on the Framlingham Reserve, he invokes memoryscapes to bring the past into the present. In my work with Uncle Rob, we spent considerable time walking Country visiting the old sites of the Framlingham Aboriginal Reserve, as he taught me to try to see it as he saw it and to read it as a palimpsest, a historical text with many layers of memory that were remembered and revealed as he narrated his memories.

The memoryscapes that Uncle Rob invokes are valuable historical encounters for students so that they can see First Nations Peoples as active historical agents who have always been present on Country. The Peek Wuurong and Kirrae Wuurong Peoples were not passive in the face of the racist, dehumanising policies that were enacted by institutions such as the Board for the Protection of Aborigines. They enacted multiple forms of resistance to the constant threats of dispossession of land and housing, sexual assault, and ongoing racism. Seeing and reading Country as a site of First Nations knowledge production disrupts settler memoryscapes that view Country through the narrow lens of resource extraction and colonial erasure.[57] When co-designing local history units, teachers can enlarge the focus given to Country as a site of local historical significance that is brought into being through First Nations ways of knowing.

Yarning

A successful decolonising co-design process for developing local First Nations syllabuses will be underpinned by culturally safer practices that initiate and sustain dialogue between First Nations and non-Indigenous project partners. Yarning is a First Nations method for transferring and sharing knowledge in a relational manner that can be used to develop culturally safe communication between schools, teachers, and First Nations communities.[58] Yarning is described as an effective method of communication because it "enables the unfolding of information through the process of storytelling (narrative) in a relaxed and informal manner that is culturally safe for Indigenous people."[59] Yarning is culturally safer because it is a First Nations methodology that has been widely adopted by First Nations communities across Australia. It is relational in that it is "reliant upon relationships and thus the integrity of the process requires responsibility, accountability among the participants, Country, culture and Knowledges."[60] Yarning can help teachers to decolonise their teaching of local First Nations history by developing productive, culturally safe relationships with First Nations communities that are underpinned by a two-way dialogue.

Conclusion

In this chapter, I have provided a model to show how local history curriculum can be decolonised through the inclusion of First Nations perspectives. Historical narratives produced by settler colonial historians have shaped the local history of towns such as Warrnambool, eliding First Nations histories through the privileging of white settlement. I have explained that this has resulted in a paucity of resources on First Nations histories for teachers to use in History classrooms, which may result in local First Nations perspectives becoming too challenging to teach. CVR films, such as *The Crossing*, constitute a new resource for decolonising the teaching of Australian History by including local First Nations histories in the classroom. It is only one example of a teaching resource and needs to be used in conjunction with other primary and secondary historical sources to stimulate immersive historical empathetic connections between students and First Nations perspectives on life in colonial post-war Australia. I have highlighted how historical empathy is difficult to teach and how CVR can assist students in developing the core skills of historical contextualisation, comprehending the thinking of historical actors, and analysing their emotional responses to historical events. Through the teaching of historical empathy, students come to realise that colonialism persists in the present and the need for local truth-telling mechanisms that can reveal this. I have argued that the decolonising of local History curriculum can be a process of co-design that is built on the creation of strong relationships between local First Nations communities, schools, teachers, and students. The development of these relationships should be underpinned by First Nations ways of being and knowing such as relationality, Country, reciprocity, and yarning. The decolonisation of History teaching will only occur when schools abandon the usual ways of working with First Nations Peoples and instead engage them in respectful dialogue through yarning, understand how to share knowledge with them through relationships, and ensure that the creation of any local First Nations history curriculum will benefit First Nations communities.

Ideas and strategies for decolonising the teaching of local history to include First Nations perspectives:

- Collaborate closely with local First Nations communities when devising local First Nations history curriculum using First Nations ways of being and knowing discussed in this chapter.
- Reflect on the way in which settler colonial histories may have shaped the local histories of your community and how they may have excluded First Nations Peoples.
- Seek out historical texts that use local First Nations perspectives.
- Seek out CVR films such as *The Crossing* that focus on First Nations historical content and experiment with them in the classroom using Oculus Quest 2 headsets if possible. YouTube VR[61] is a great starting point for finding CVR films. The CVR films *Collisions*[62] and *Carriberrie*[63] feature Australian First Nations content.

Notes

1 Broome, R. (2010). *Aboriginal Australians: A History since 1788* (4th ed.). Allen and Unwin.
2 Lowe, K. (2017). Walanbaa warramildanha: The impact of authentic Aboriginal community and school engagement on teachers' professional knowledge. *Australian Educational Researcher, 44*, 35–54. https://doi.org/10.1007/s13384-017-0229-8
3 Bishop, M., Vass, G., & Thompson, K. (2019). Decolonising school practices through relationality and reciprocity: Embedding local Aboriginal perspectives in the classroom. *Pedagogy, Culture and Society, 29*(2), 193–211. https://doi.org/10.1080/14681366.2019.1704844

4 Ibid.
5 Bates, N., & Bowry, R. (2021). 'That's next to my Gran's house': Building local history into the curriculum. *Teaching History*, 185, 34–43.
6 Marker, M. (2011). Teaching history from an Indigenous perspective – Four winding paths up the mountain. In P. Clark (Ed.), *New possibilities for the past: Shaping history education in Canada* (p. 105). UBC Press.
7 Krichauff, S. (2017). *Memory, place and Aboriginal-settler history*. Anthem Press. p. 23.
8 King, W. (Director). (2021). *The Crossing* [Film].
9 Furniss, E. (1997). Pioneers, progress, and the myth of the frontier: The landscape of public history in rural British Columbia. *BC Studies: The British Columbian Quarterly*, 115(6), 7–44. p. 10.
10 Ibid.
11 Davison, G. (2000). *The use and abuse of Australian history*. Allen and Unwin. p. 200.
12 Osburne, R. (1980). *The History of Warrnambool capital of the western ports of Victoria, from 1847 (when the first government land sales took place) up to the end of 1886*. Chronicle printing Company, ld., 1887. p. 194.
13 Ibid.
14 Sayers, C. E., & Yule, P. L. (1987). *By these we flourish – A history of Warrnambool*. Warrnambool Institute Press.
15 Ibid.
16 Dawson, J. (2009). *Australian Aborigines – The languages and customs of several tribes of Aborigines in the Western district of Victoria, Australia*. Cambridge University Press.
17 Ibid.
18 Critchett, J. (1992). *Our land till we die. A history of the Framlingham Aborigines*. Deakin University Press; Critchett, J. (1990). *A distant field of murder – Western district frontiers 1834–1848*. Melbourne University Press.
19 Lowe, R. (2002). *The Mish*. University of Queensland Press.
20 Dooley, K. (2021). *Cinematic virtual reality: A critical study of 21st century approaches and practices*. Palgrave Macmillan.
21 Ibid.
22 Ibid.
23 Endacott, J., & Brooks, S. (2013). An updated theoretical and practical model for promoting historical empathy. *Social Studies Research and Practice*, 8(1), 41–58. https://doi.org/10.1108/SSRP-01-2013-B0003
24 See, Barton, K. C., & Levstik, L. S. (2004). *Teaching history for the common good*. Routledge; Huijgen, T., Van Boxtel, C., van de Grift, W., & Holthuis, P. (2017). Toward historical perspective taking: Students' reasoning when contextualizing the actions of people in the past. *Theory & Research in Social Education*, 45(1), 110–144. https://doi.org/10.1080/00933104.2016.1208597
25 Endacott, J., & Brooks, S. (2013). An updated theoretical and practical model for promoting historical empathy. *Social Studies Research and Practice*, 8(1), 41–58. https://doi.org/10.1108/SSRP-01-2013-B0003
26 Ibid.
27 ACARA. (2023). *History 7–10*. https://v9.australiancurriculum.edu.au/f-10-curriculum/learning-areas/history-7-10/year-7_year-8_year-9_year-10?view=quick&detailed-content-descriptions=0&hide-ccp=0&hide-gc=0&side-by-side=1&strands-start-index=0&subjects-start-index=1
28 Ibid.
29 Ibid.
30 Dooley, K. (2021). *Cinematic virtual reality: A critical study of 21st century approaches and practices*. Springer Nature. pp. 35–36.

31 Huijgen, T., Boxtel, C., van de Grift, W., & Holthuis, P. (2016). Toward historical perspective taking: Students' reasoning when contextualizing the actions of people in the past. *Theory & Research in Social Education, 45*(1), 110–144. https://doi.org/10.1080/00933104.2016.1208597
32 Ibid.
33 Ibid.
34 Clark, A. (2007). *History's children: History wars in the classroom.* UNSW Press. pp. 80–81.
35 Endacott, J., & Brooks, S. (2013). An updated theoretical and practical model for promoting historical empathy. *Social Studies Research and Practice, 8*(1), 41–58. p. 46. https://doi.org/10.1108/SSRP-01-2013-B0003
36 Huijgen et al. (2016). Toward historical perspective taking, p. 114.
37 Bartelds, H., Savenije, M., & van Boxtel, C. (2020). Students' and teachers' beliefs about historical empathy in secondary history education. *Theory & Research in Social Education, 48*(4), 529–551. https://doi.org/10.1080/00933104.2020.1808131
38 The scene depicting the "nightly raids" contains no re-creations of violence. It is instead implied.
39 Bartelds, H., Savenije, M., & van Boxtel, C. (2020). Students' and teachers' beliefs about historical empathy in secondary history education. *Theory & Research in Social Education, 48*(4), 529–551. https://doi.org/10.1080/00933104.2020.1808131., p.43.
40 Ibid.
41 Ibid.
42 Ibid., p. 53.
43 Miles, J. (2018). Teaching history for truth and reconciliation: The challenges and opportunities of narrativity, temporality, and identity. *McGill Journal of Education, 53*(2), 294–311. https://doi.org/10.7202/1058399ar
44 Krawec, P. (2022). *Becoming Kin: An Indigenous call to unforgetting the past and reimagining our future.* Broadleaf Books. p. 14.
45 Ibid.
46 Ibid., p. 19.
47 Ibid.
48 Burgess, C., Thorpe, K., Egan, S., & Harwood, V. (2022). Learning from Country to conceptualise what an Aboriginal curriculum narrative might look like in education. *Curriculum Perspectives, 42,* 157–169. https://doi.org/10.1007/s41297-022-00164-w
49 Ibid.
50 McGregor, H., & Marker, C. (2018). Reciprocity in Indigenous educational research: Beyond compensation, towards decolonizing reciprocity. *Anthropology and Education Quarterly, 49*(3), 318–328. https://doi.org/10.1111/aeq.12249
51 Bishop, M., Vass, G., & Thompson, K. (2019). Decolonising schooling practices through relationality and reciprocity: Embedding local Aboriginal perspectives in the classroom. *Pedagogy, Culture and Society, 29*(2), 193–211. https://doi.org/10.1080/14681366.2019.1704844
52 Meissner, S. N. (2022). Teaching reciprocity: Gifting and land-based ethics in Indigenous philosophy. *Teaching Ethics, 22*(1), 17–37. https://doi.org/10.5840/tej2022221118
53 Meisnner (2022). Teaching reciprocity; Bishop et al. (2019). Decolonising schooling practices through relationality and reciprocity, p. 15.
54 Tynan, L. (2021). What is relationality? Indigenous knowledges, practices and responsibilities with kin. *Cultural geographies, 28*(4), 597–610. https://doi.org/10.1177/14744740211029287

55 Thor Carlson, K., &. Albert 'Sonny' McHalsie, N. (2019). Stó:lO⁻ memoryscapes as Indigenous ways of knowing – Stó:lO⁻ history from stone and fire. In S. De Nardi, H. Orange, S. C. High, & E. Koskinen-Koivisto (Eds.), *Routledge handbook of memory and place*. Routledge. p. 10.
56 Ibid.
57 Ibid.
58 Bessarab, D., & Ng'Andu, B. (2010). Yarning about yarning as a legitimate method in Indigenous research. *International Journal of Critical Indigenous Studies, 3*(1), 47. https://doi.org/10.5204/ijcis.v3i1.57
59 Ibid.
60 Barlo, S., Boyd, W. E., Hughes, M., Wilson, S., & Pelizzon, A. (2021). Yarning as protected space: Relational accountability in research. *Alternative – An Alternative Journal of Indigenous Peoples, 17*(1), 42. https://doi.org/10.1177/11771801 20986151
61 @360. (n.d.). Virtual Reality. YouTube. https://www.youtube.com/@360/featured
62 Allen, D. (Director). (2018). *Carriberrie* [Film]. Reddogs VR.
63 Wallworth, L. (Director). (2016). *Collisions* [Film].

Chapter 12

Decolonial futures for history in Australian schools

Sara Weuffen, Rebecca Cairns, and Aleryk Fricker

Authors' positioning statements

Sara Weuffen

As a non-Indigenous woman of German, Scottish and Welsh decent who grew up on Gundijtmara Country in Warrnambool, and currently lives on Wadawurrung Country in Ballarat, I champion the need to find new and integrated ways of working with First Nations and non-Indigenous knowledges in Australian education. Coming from a low socio-economic background, over the past 13 years, I have continued my social justice efforts by listening and learning from First Nations Peoples and colleagues, and non-Indigenous comrades, to unpack the ongoing conditioning effects of settler-colonialism, and adopt decolonial ways of thinking, being, and doing.

Rebecca Cairns

As a non-Indigenous settler of mostly Irish and Scottish ancestry, I acknowledge I have experienced history education and settler-colonialism from a comfortable and unearned position of privilege, while living on the unceded, ancestral lands of the Boonwurrung, Wurundjeri, Wadawurrung, and Gimuywalubarra Peoples. Recognising that the inherently racist and unjust structures and ideologies of coloniality–that have disproportionately advantaged me as a white settler while disadvantaging First Nations Peoples–continue to be perpetuated through educational and knowledge making practices means I am committed to addressing the (de)colonising practices that shape history education. This includes critically reflecting on my own practice that has spanned 13 years teaching in secondary schools and 10 years in Higher Education.

Aleryk Fricker

I have been working in the education sector for over ten years. During that time, I have been a primary and a secondary teacher, as well as an academic, and even spent some time coordinating programmes designed to support

DOI: 10.4324/9781003435617-12

university engagement for secondary First Nations students in Victoria as well. I have done all of these roles as a sovereign and a proud *Dja Dja Wurrung* man. My research focuses on decolonising education and First Nations education contexts, with a view to incorporating as much as possible with the confines of Australia's neo-colonial education structures. I recognise that what is good for First Nations students is good for all students, regardless of their own cultural contexts. This chapter details my efforts to move beyond the abstract and theorising of my research into the applied to have a real-world impact on teachers and classrooms across Victoria.

Introduction

In the discipline of History, more so than any other disciplinary area, the minutia of what knowledge is taught to students has been, and continues to be, a socio-political battlefield worldwide.[1] In 2021–2022, the *Australian Curriculum: History* (F-10) underwent its second review in ten years, resulting in version 9.0.[2] Throughout the nine iterations, ideologies of western civilisation and heritage have been celebrated to instil a *love* of Australia, and encourage the next generation of citizens to take up colonial nationhood narratives.[3] For History educators, and out-of-discipline teachers who have been allocated History classes, there are professional pressures, and assumptions held, that the official curriculum should be presented as written so that the arguably whitewashed version of Australian history prevails.[4] While mandated reporting against the national curriculum for student learning assessment standards is required, educators are afforded the professional autonomy to decide *how* students reach these standards.[5] Thus, there are opportunities for empowered pedagogical practices which speak back to the socio-politically and sanitised version of Australian history. We argue that by taking up a decolonial mindset, and perhaps drawing on some of the strategies suggested throughout this edited collection, educators may be guided to tackle socio-political contestation and present a more truthful picture of Australian history to the next generation of citizens.

The need to shift pedagogical practices towards decoloniality is long overdue. In Australia, unlike many other settler-colonial contexts where an invading force has systematically taken over sovereign lands and enforced a foreign governmental structure, there is an absence of Voice, Treaty, or Truth.[6] Despite a seven-year consultation process of 12 dialogues across the Australian continent, where governmental and First Nations representatives argued that change was needed to empower a "fair and truthful relationship with the people of Australia and a better future",[7] just under 40% (6.26 million) of Australian citizens–of which First Nations Peoples make up 3.8% (984,000) of the population–voted for constitutional recognition and a First Nations voice to parliament; ultimately the October 2023 referendum did not pass.[8] Unfortunately, the denial of First Nations voices for truth-telling has been a salient feature in

Australian history discourses since European invasion.⁹ Yet, in this edited collection, we declare that the time has come to challenge the status quo, speak back against silencing, and move education practices towards working *with* others and critiquing knowledge to decolonise the nation-making story of Australia's history.

In this final chapter of the edited collection, we shine light on the sociopolitical foundations underpinning the 'history wars' tropes and debates to expose the imperialistic enculturing metanarratives so cleverly contained within the history curriculum. In doing so, we demonstrate how First Nations narratives have consistently been positioned in deficit to western perspectives, broken up, and dispersed throughout the curriculum to uphold such metanarratives. From there, we illustrate how, despite a strong record of cultural activism by both First Nations and non-Indigenous scholars and educators for the past 40 years, there remains a paucity of knowledge and guidance about how to push back against such blatant racial inequalities in history education. We then illustrate the possibility of decoloniality, as both theory and practice, to actualise change in ways that trouble the imperialistic metanarrative and associated pedagogical practices of history. From these arguments we propose that decoloniality, by its very nature, is a multi-dimensional and multi-disciplinary undertaking that, at least in the immediate future and in the absence of systematic educational reform, will require individual educators and schools to do the heavy lifting. We conclude the chapter by arguing that the fresh perspectives and strategies provided in this edited collection, based on first-hand experiences and empirical research, suggests that the discipline of History is the most opportune space to actualise truth-telling.

The need for a decolonial education future

The scholarship provided in this book, and that already existing in the field, indicates a critical need to shift educational debates and practices that are so rudimentarily focused on race and culture, and concealed within a reconciliation agenda–that is, in reality, a conflation of apologetic ruminations.[10] We suggest that decolonial schooling "troubles [the] colonial system and [promotes] pedagogies [that] requires an ethos of mutual respect and care"[11] throughout all education spaces, places, and practices. This requires the development of a new metalanguage that evolves out of the unlearning/relearning processes of educators' feeling, doing, and practicing decolonial pedagogies. It also requires leaning into the discomfort associated with proactive assertions of First Nations sovereignty and examinations of policies and practices that have underpinned and legitimated the purposeful genocidal acts committed in the pursuit of a settler-colonial nationhood. Since the 1980s,[12] even though there has been consistent cultural activism for decolonial approaches that espouse truth-telling, there has been consistent socio-political anxiety about narratives of Australia's history bring conveyed to students via education.[13] While it is beyond the scope of this chapter to explore this in depth, understanding that socio-political tensions at the heart of history curriculum debates in Australia have been cemented in notions of race and power is critical to unpacking why such conversations have had limited impact in education curriculum.[14]

Prior to 2013, each state and territory in Australia was an authority unto themselves and developed History curriculum that presented different narratives about nationhood, particularly where First Nations Peoples and perspectives were concerned.[15] For example, Victoria had a, now defunct, Year 11 Koorie History unit, whereas Western Australia and Queensland still have standalone Aboriginal studies units. In 2009, after consistent contestations "about the nation's soul, it's values, and it's beliefs"[16] the process for creating a national History curriculum began, one where a cohesive narrative could be controlled by the educationally, racially, and sexually privileged.[17] The national curriculum was designed and implemented on the argument that all Australian students should be afforded the same opportunities to learn the same historical knowledge and develop "the capacity to think historically"[18] regardless of their socio-economic location or assigned teacher. Students were used as the emotional catalyst for why a cohesive nationalistic story was needed; it hooked into the consciousness of what it means to be Australian – the value of a 'fair go for all'.[19] Yet, this mentality was employed as an artful deception to ensure western ideologies maintained power in the national curriculum.

The narrative of the Australian continent as a piece of land ripe for exploration and civilisation based on the presumption that no structured civilisation existed has persisted since the introduction of formal schooling and continues to underpin historical narratives.[20] Despite social recognition that First Nations Peoples on the Australian continent and surrounding islands are the oldest living continuous cultures on Earth, and continued endeavours by First Nations Peoples to be actively engaged in curriculum consultation, the official Australian History curriculum centres imperialism, white supremacy, and is pervasively anti-Indigenous which entrenches inequitable opportunities for learning.[21] Furthermore, while the study of Aboriginal and/or Torres Strait Islander histories and cultures has been a cross-curriculum priority area for over a decade, there continues to be preoccupation with the outmoded 'history wars' tropes that (re)enforce colonial ways of thinking and being aligned to whiteness, as discussed by Ficker and colleagues in the opening chapter for this book.

A public-facing desktop review of the Years 7–10 overview and depth studies of the *Australian Curriculum: History* (Version 8.0) highlights a linear timeline inextricably tied to notions of imperialism which represents a meta-narrative focused on a European way of life. Such imperialistic subterfuge can be seen in statements around the aim of the curriculum to assist students in developing "understanding of history, First Nations peoples and perspectives, and build[ing] a cohesive and culturally diverse society,"[22] and through thematic analysis of statements within the curriculum. The primacy of imperialism can be observed in Figure 12.1 where key words and statements have been

Decolonial futures for history in Australian schools 197

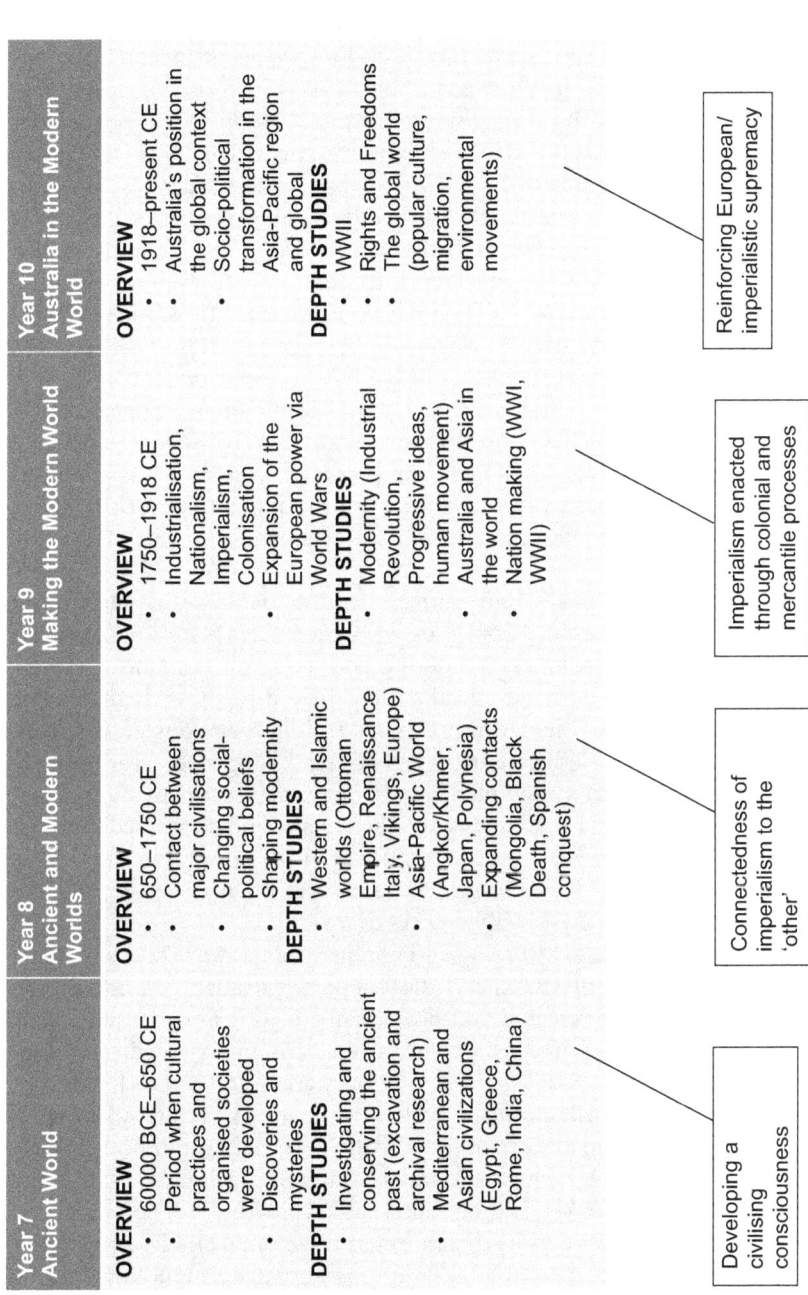

Figure 12.1 The Imperialistic narrative uncovered in the Australian Curriculum: History

identified and extracted from the year level, content, and depth study descriptions for Years 7–10 of the Australian curriculum and placed in a table.[23] A summarising statement about the underpinning narrative was identified by subsequent readings of these extractions using principles of thematic analysis viewed through the lens of the overarching focus of the year level (i.e. *The ancient world*).[24] Even with the inclusion of content descriptions about ancient Australia, the curriculum conveys that life on the Australian continent was/is peripheral to the development of a civilising consciousness (Year 7), European expansion necessitated the fertilisation of colonisation (Year 8), social cohesion is only possible when reflecting colonial processes (Year 9), and colonial power and authority is considered superior to other structures (Year 10).

Drawing connections between individual year level narratives, the overarching metanarrative cleverly asserted across the History curriculum is that:

> With the backing of the political super-power at the time – England – the Australian nation rose from the darkness of ancient civilisation to create a better world. In this world, the rise and power of whiteness was logical, is evidenced by the primacy of western scientific thought and governance, and serves as the legitimate foundation for Australianness.

Critical examination of this metanarrative uncovers ideologies of Darwinism and Christianity. First Nations Peoples are constructed in a historical past tense as operating in passive societies, wandering and living off the land aimlessly, and just waiting until a more advanced society arrived to show them a better way of life. Furthermore, the deficit positioning of First Nations perspectives, subtly hidden in acknowledgements that 'bad' stuff happened – for example systematic genocidal warfare and race-based differential treatment and punishment – legitimises the guise of 'giving of a better life' and continued segregation and/or silencing of First Nations narratives in the history curriculum. In light of the revised *Deep Time History of Australia* in the new Version 9.0 and its enactment, further analysis will be needed.

In order to have such a colonising and conquering narrative and legitimate imperialistic ideologies of whiteness, the counter/narrative of passive First Nationhood needs to be created and firmly embedded.[25] For example, while First Nations perspectives are included in the curriculum – via dedicated topics, elaborations and the cross-curriculum priority area – it is always in contrast to imperialistic onto-epistemologies with investigations orientated towards the deficit and focused on questioning the civility of First Nationhood.[26] While appearing to be inclusive, such positioning is a strategic technique of assimilation "covered by the blanket of friendliness and sympathy."[27] The primacy of discovery, colonisation, and industrialisation in the Australian historical narrative is what Green et al.[28] describes as "representational epistemology" which is "inherently and inescapably political." It is used–whether acknowledged or not–as a justified foundation for the settler-colonial invasion and possession of sovereign and unceded lands.[29] Under this regime, First Nations presence is acknowledged and tolerated in the historical narrative only so long as it does not challenge the ontological validity of settler-colonialism.

While changes have been made to content within the History curriculum that is reflective of the majority ideologies of various governments, and a fluctuating degree of in/exclusion of First Nations perspectives throughout, time and again the metanarrative remains: *The Australian nation should be proud and celebrate the civilising futures bought about by their settler-colonialist ancestors*. This is exemplified in both the 2014 review commissioned by the Coalition government where Wiltshire and Donnelly[30] touted the sanctity of western traditions and then Education Minister Alan Tudge's comments in 2021 that while Australian history should honour First Nations perspectives it should not come at the expense of dishonouring western heritage. However, such statements exist in juxtaposition with Moodie[31] and colleagues' study where 80% of participants affirmed that First Nations histories and perspectives are an important component of compulsory schooling. Interrogation of such foundational beliefs and proclamations is precisely why a decolonial education future is needed to step beyond the constraining binaries of the 'history wars' because "the future is a multilingual and multiethnic one, regardless of attempts to suppress that reality."[32]

It is an undeniable fact, that prior to British invasion in 1788, there were over 250+ distinct First Nations cultural groups on the Australian continent and surrounding islands. According to both First Nations knowledges and western scientific records, First Nations Peoples have practiced culture on the continent for at least 50,000 years.[33] This is at least 42,000 years, or 1,050 generations, before other human societies across the globe were beginning to indicate traits of 'civilisation' in line with contemporary society (permanent geographical basis, creation of tools for agricultural/food production, artistic expressions, and clothing).[34] Imagine as a thought experiment, one of your descendants, 1,000 times removed, was told your existence and way of life was a myth or unproven. Or, that the stories about your life, the things you experienced, and your legacy needed to be proved by some type of modern technology. You might consider such a reality an absurdity given you are a living and conscious being reading these words, right now. However, this is precisely the reductive narrative about First Nations Peoples being conveyed to over four million students in Australian schools today. Even though there has been increased recognition and representation of First Nations perspectives within the History curriculum, and a somewhat hyper-focus on *Indigenising* – putting more First Nations content into the curriculum – and development of supporting resources, little change has occurred to the larger meta/narrative of white supremacy.[35] This narrative is exactly what the authors throughout this book have sought to trouble in their unpacking of the ways "that schools continue to function as part of the [settler]colonial project" which attempts to hide "issues of systemic racial and intersectional inequalities that continue to be part of the fabric of schooling,"[36] and fails to recognise adequately First Nations sovereignty in Australia's nation-making story.

While change has been called for, and actioned by, First Nations Peoples and non-Indigenous comrades for decades, the work of decolonising history in Australia appears to face ongoing operationalisation challenges. By this we mean, there remains an absence of information outlining how educators may actually *do* this work while wrestling with the multitude of mandated educational pressures and larger workforce challenges (teacher shortages).[37] The lack of systematic and sustained change has raised questions about how those born and/or raised within a settler-colonial system may be able to identify, let alone, speak back to such processes. As a result of the conditioning processes of formal education, the argument has been put forth that non-Indigenous educators have been indoctrinated into historical ways of thinking and doing, whether they are aware of it, or not.[38] We do not suggest that the understandings, insights, and critical skills developed by history educators, researchers, and stakeholders during their engagement with the 'history wars' debates should be disposed of or forgotten. Rather, we argue that the critical skills associated with examining binary dichotomies should be sustained while making room for new pedagogies which work with multiple knowledges to reflect the current socio-political realities that both educators and students face every day.

Actualising decoloniality in Australian history education

Along with other scholars,[39] we argue that undertaking decolonial processes troubles the very foundation of the "colonial system and pedagogies [and is a process that] requires an ethos of mutual respect and care."[40] By this we mean, decoloniality focuses on unveiling the unproblematic manner in which settler-colonial ways of being, thinking, and doing delegitimatise First Nations knowledges and are embedded in education processes. It is not a process of Indigenising or browning First Nations content so that it is wedged into existing learning and curriculum structures for the purposes of *ticking a box*,[41] for this only continues to maintain deficit discourses of First Nationhood. Rather, decoloniality tackles the implicit, unspoken, unquestioned, and assumed undercurrents of western ideologies woven into the fabric of Australian education.

Drawing on Yunkaporta and Shillingsworth's[42] work, operationalising decoloniality ought to be a process of respecting, connecting, reflecting, and directing. It requires endurance of a "terrifying process of critical engagement with the colonising system, and worse, self-reflexivity exposing the roles that colonial discourses have played in the construction of ... identities."[43] It is the spirit work of decoloniality that involves our hearts, our heads, and our limbs (hands and feet). Because of this, it can be "hell and many don't make it beyond the token level of basic 'cultural awareness' or 'cultural competency.'"[44] Yet, this is precisely the work espoused throughout this book. While the task may appear daunting, "the beginning point isn't as important as actually *beginning*."[45]

A beginning point taken throughout the book is the authors positioning of themselves in relational ways to the First Nations Countries and storying of the content to which they write. As described by Yunkaporta and Shillingsworth, this has been a moral/ethical undertaking where authors have taken up decolonial practices to state their "relationships to people, Law, and place"[46] and indicate the interconnectedness ways of being, thinking, and doing. Rather than "disseminating new narratives that serve the interest of those seeking control through simplicity",[47] the authors have not shied away from exposing the complexities and challenges, but also the elevating possibilities offered, by operationalising decoloniality.

Hearts

The foundational entrance for educators undertaking decolonial work in Australian history begins by examining the ethical and relational processes of which they are engaged. This requires tackling processes of settler-colonialism employed in education which seek to create the conditions by which people are disconnected from experiences for the purposes of learning predetermined content considered sufficient and appropriate for their roles as future citizens. Drawing on Yunkaporta and Shillingsworth's[48] framework, how educators think about the world in relation to themselves and the values and beliefs they hold about education shape their pedagogical practice. Simply put, the heart of individuals drives their decolonial practices.

Research highlights that individuals operate in the world as a result of their personal ideologies, beliefs, and values that have been accumulated over the lifespan, and for educators, these impact ways of thinking and enacting learning and teaching work. As discussed throughout this book, despite decades of educational policy directives to convey a more truthful telling of Australia's history, tokenistic teaching practices regarding First Nations perspectives continue to persist in mainstream schooling en masse. Weuffen (Chapter 5) makes the claim that perhaps this is due to the relationally devoid nature of western education, a system in which the next generation of teachers have been educated themselves. But, by adopting a critically self-reflexive and relational approach to education, they propose that traditional western-centric views of history begin to be interrogated which opens spaces to respect and make connections with the beautiful kaleidoscope of interconnected worldviews. In this sense, the argument is put forth that decolonial journeying begins with the self. Weuffen provides two questions–under the headings *Who am I? Where do I come from?*–to encourage educators to undertake intercultural[49] reflectivity with the aim of scaffolding and supporting this journey.

Affirming the notion that the root of decolonial education practices in history begins with the self is Briggs, Anderson, and Slater's (Chapter 6) account of their collecting learnings, unlearnings, and relearnings about Australian history. Speaking from their lived realities as a Boon Wurrung Elder (Briggs) and in-service early childhood educators (Anderson and Slater), they invite educators to share captivating narratives of their relational and pedagogical journey of respecting First Nations laws/lores while connecting with the nature of existence of Country in their local communities. Highlighting the importance of committing to a spirit of continual self-reflection while navigating western education systems, they bring forth the transformational opportunities afforded by truth-telling through decolonial pedagogies and practice, that is, by centring listening, reflecting, and being. They invite readers to "learn with the tree" and hear the narratives that emerge from critical evaluative and gracious storying.

Providing yet further affirmation that critical self-reflection and examination of one's ethical and relational approaches are the heart and spirit of operationalising decoloniality in Australian History, McKnight (Chapter 7) recounts storied memories of settler-colonial ideologies that have influenced their own learning and teaching practices over time. While acknowledging caution against congratulatory saviour narratives, they unpack how entrenched and unethical processes of knowledge production throughout their education experiences have swayed pedagogical decision-making and coloured memories of past practices. Far from a self-flagellating narrative, their chapter speaks to the importance of experiencing discomfort and vulnerability while being courageous with one's spirit in the undertaking decolonial work. McKnight demonstrates the reflective potential of vignettes, as the work of hearts, feet, and hands, by stepping out professional learning processes for memory writing aimed at stimulating new ways of thinking and doing beyond "merely ticking boxes."

Heads

Yunkaporta and Shillingsworth's[50] framework asserts the importance of intellectual processes that critique the nature of knowledge and knowing which shape pedagogical practice. As Keynes (Chapter 2) poignantly states, history education in Australia has a complex and chequered past which has been used as a tool for nation-building and legitimisation of settler-colonialism. This presents a paradox for educators who have been trained to interrogate multiple narratives but portray a constructed historical truth of superiority couched within western traditions espoused by official curricula and education policies. In this sense, Keynes argues that mobilisation of a decolonial mindset requires reflection on epistemological traditions of knowledge production, and perhaps, a flipping of the lens to consider how the story of the *Australian* state is but a chapter in the much larger and longer First Nations story. They argue that this may be achieved through critical resource selection and explorations that unsettle assumed normative understandings of key concepts such as nationhood, sovereignty, history, Australia, and Australianness.

Fricker (Chapter 4) describes how, what could be described as the prestigious intellectual work of the academically superior, history texts reinforce a cult of forgetfulness in the minds of students and educators. They describe a process of decolonial intellectualisation that seeks out the parasitic nature of settler-colonialist ideologies in Australian history education. They argue that by elevating the voices, works, representations, and perspectives of First Nations Peoples in the seemingly privileged written accounts of history, westernised powers are diluted and shifted towards a truth-telling agenda; a key component of decolonial work. Fricker suggests four key strategies that educators and publishers might employ when critically reflecting on the selection and development of Australian history resources.

Offering practical insight about the necessity of brain work in operationalising decoloniality in studies of Australian history, Hradsky (Chapter 3) provides first-hand evidence about the power of drama-based professional learning for shifting educators' pedagogical processing and practices. They highlight how the, sometimes challenging, but ultimately, empowering intellectual work undertaken can be viscerally transformational for addressing and working with notions of white guilt and shame. Hradsky suggests that drawing on "verbatim theatre as a pedagogy creates opportunities for learners to engage deeply with people and texts from historico-spatial contexts different to their own." Their detailed illustrations present a compelling argument for "exposing [the] poison" of settler-colonialism through embodied approaches and challenges History educators to be discomforted, push beyond their intellectual comfort zones, and start enacting "de/colonising possibilities" that holistically engage the brain, and heart, and limbs.

Limbs

Methods employed in operationalising decoloniality ought to be the outcome of one's understanding of their reality, the values and beliefs influencing decision-making, and ways in which knowledge and knowing is valued.[51] It is perhaps the most easily observed component of decolonial practice and one most familiar with normative practices of learning and teaching. It involves doing something and moving. On this point, Garrad (Chapter 9) recommends a framework for teaching that prioritises interculturality by *doing* intercultural history in ways that combines narration, conscientisation, and critical thinking. Rather than adhering to westernised knowledge processes that seek to augment the *nation-making* story which present rudimentary accounts of First Nationhood, the intercultural framework guides pedagogical practices towards celebrating difference and diversity. The actualising potential of Garrad's framework is demonstrated by deconstructing *Year 9 Australian Curriculum: History* content descriptors to expose the visual language of whitewashed timelines commonly found in textbooks; a critique that resonates with points made in Fricker's chapter.

The authors throughout this book allude to the reality that decoloniality in Australian History education is an emerging way of working; one where theories are being developed into practice and require time to determine impact. However, Harvie (Chapter 8) highlights the need for mechanisms that support History teachers now. They indicate that cultural unfamiliarity, under preparedness, and lack of resourcing are common disabling factors influencing the perpetual (re)inforcement of settler-colonial narratives in Australian history. Yet, recent scholarship argues that such factors are not insurmountable and are perhaps falsehoods perpetuated to avoid the comfortability of decolonial work. Harvie's chapter offers some clear directions for moving beyond these dilemmas, including the centring of Country, reflecting propositions by Briggs et al., to embed First Nations perspectives within curriculum programmes and whole-of-school culture via storying, deep listening, and knowledge sharing, as well as examining the temporality and historicity of educators' own educational memories. However, linking with McKnight's arguments, Harvie recommends care to be taken so as not remain stuck in a (re)colonising loop.

Decolonising history education in places where education and storytelling has been shared for over two thousand generations means centring First Nations Peoples ways of being, thinking, and doing. While Garrard explores decolonising and intercultural approaches as prompts to interrogating the diversity of historical actors and narratives, Cairns (Chapter 10) spotlights the potential of problematising western-centric knowledge production practices to augment competing invasion narratives of Asia-related history. They offer various analytical tools as methods to identifying distorted views of history and amplifying the diverse narratives, knowledges, voices, experiences, and perspectives of multiple actors. For Cairns, such pedagogies are critical to developing more nuanced understanding of sovereignty and possession.

Perhaps offering one of the most tangible and observable methods of decoloniality in practice, King (Chapter 11) presents a vivid account of combining traditional and contemporary pedagogies through the co-creation of a cinematic virtual reality film. For millennia, First Nations Peoples have used both oral and written methods of storying to convey messages and educate successive generations. While western societies have also used these methods, written accounts have been privileged, and now, in a digital age, audio-visual recordings have gained popularity as a means of recording history. King exposes the challenging but rewarding reality of *doing* decoloniality in Australian history by co-designing learning with First Nations stakeholders to tackle the assumed superiority of settler-colonialism, build alliances, and foreground First Nations stories and histories within localised contexts.

Envisioning a decolonial future

From the chapters presented in this book, it is evident that the future of decolonising History education is a multi-dimensional undertaking situated primarily with the individual; at least in the immediate future. That does not mean that educational institutions are absolved of responsibility to shift towards more authentic, relational, and decolonial policies and practices. We are aware that systemic changes take time, as they should, to ensure informed and careful transformation for the benefit of all, is positive, and above all sustainable. This is critical given research continues to show that cognitive growth is limited when learning is presented in disconnected and isolated ways.[52] But, when new knowledge is presented in approaches that draw upon individuals' experiences and require embodiment with their ways of thinking and doing, transformation occurs.[53] Through narrative storytelling the authors have sought to indicate how such changes may be envisioned by engaging in "dialogue, synergy, and innovation [with] respectful interaction of diverse systems"[54] of learning and knowledge production.

There is evidence of a new generation of educators and scholars reigniting energy and focus to affecting change about how Australian history is conveyed to students. They have responded to the calls of pathfinders, of those who have come before them, and are taking up decolonising approaches to elevate the voices and experiences of First Nations Peoples in narratives of Australian history. While we can only theorise, at least for the moment, what a decolonised education system might look like in Australia, new scholarship indicates that society cannot continue to get bogged down in adversarial discourses and divisive tropes associated with the 'history wars.' Yet, by problematising the present and undertaking critical inquiry into the past, we can begin to hypothesise solutions and ways forward. Given the scholarship discussed across the entirety of this book, we postulate that at the heart of a decolonial future is critical engagement with multiple versions of history and brave pedagogical practices that extend thinking about historical paradigms and consciousness.

Returning to our earlier statement, despite being grounded in problematic traditions, the discipline of History, more so than any other area, is one of the most opportune spaces for reconciliation, truth-telling, and decolonial approaches. Even if the purpose of history in schools continues to be contested, educators recognise that historical inquiry helps the development of "critically-informed and critically-literate citizens,"[55] and encourages investigation into the shadowy spaces, the things that are not being shown or said to bring them to the surface. As Ammert and colleagues observe, "we do not have to like the past, but we must try to interpret and understand it."[56] One way in which this may be achieved, and in line with the focus of decolonial approaches, is through examining the intersection of historical and moral consciousness to highlight "issues regarding painful pasts and contested moral judgements on history … it is not sufficient to remember, describe, and analyse historical events and processes."[57] In addition to analytical tools to examine external documentation, "it is necessary to also reflect on the personal as well as societal moral perceptions and experiences of them."[58] By constructing the past from a settler-colonial lens, the only logical outcome is a settler-colonial curriculum which (re)enforces a settler-colonial reality and future. Yet, by taking up the decolonial pedagogies and strategies outlined in this book, the authors highlight a negating of the socio-political hyper-attentiveness within debates about *who we are* as Australians and the *Country's soul*. The outcome of which is the promotion of a critical consciousness which we hypothesise will turn the tide of change to create a collective mass within the education system so that reconciliation, truth-telling, and voice may be actualised on a daily basis.

Conclusion

This book has sought to provide fresh perspectives from in-service educators and early-to-mid career scholars about Australia's history and how it gets taught. It is not a critique of what educators do, or do not do, in classroom practice, rather, a critique about the systemic pressures on delivering History education and ways in which decolonial approaches may be taken up. The book extends knowledge of decoloniality in Australian history with deep respect for the work that has been cited to this point, and champions movement beyond the entrenched racial adversarial discourses espoused by the 'history wars' tropes that have been at the centre of education debates for the past 30 years. The authors have spoken to the pervasive and ongoing impacts of how a settler-colonial education system entrenches white supremacy and inequitable opportunities for recognising, celebrating, and working with a more accurate reflection of Australia's historical narrative. The research-informed evidence provided by non-Indigenous and First Nations educators and scholars presents practical strategies and tips based on their experiences. However, we caution readers to not see these strategies as quick fixes that "can be dropped into the same old tired curriculum that deadens the souls of"[59] students. Rather, decoloniality requires just and mature adaptations to socio-political discourses that are constantly shifting in the Australian schooling landscape.

The study of Australian history is now at cross-roads when it comes to conveying a historical narrative to the next generation of citizens. So too is the entire education system as scholars have argued vehemently that there must be a "shifting culture of power [for] we cannot continue to act as if [settler-colonial knowledges and skills] will remain as our society changes."[60] In the wake of a growing, albeit a slight 40% minority, of societal support for elevating the voices of First Nations Peoples, and the past several decades of education research exposing the historical illiteracy and abject failure of successive government meddling in Australia's historical narrative, change is needed. Despite fervent crusading, it is clear the settler-colonial fallacy of a peaceful and uncontested takeover by *settlers/colonisers/pioneers* is cracking. For the moment, while discourses of Australian history are caught up in self-referential western ideologies that seek to (re)enforce power and control, by sitting in the discomfort of interrogating current practices and being "willing to contend with the sometimes problematic aspects of our communities,"[61] we can begin the process of envisioning and actualising a decolonial education future.

Notes

1. E.g. Cairns, R. (2022, Feb 17). The national history curriculum should not be used and abused as an election issue. *The Conversation.* https://theconversation.com/the-national-history-curriculum-should-not-be-used-and-abused-as-an-election-issue-176783; Carretero, M., Asensio, M., & Rodriguez-Moneo, M. (2014). *History education and the construction of national identities.* Information Age Publishing; Taylor, T. (2019). Historical consciousness in the Australian curriculum. In T. Allender, A. Clark, & R. Parkes (Eds.), *Historical thinking for history teachers: A new approach to engaging students and developing historical consciousness.* Allen & Unwin. pp. 3–17.
2. Australian Curriculum, Assessment and Reporting Authority (ACARA). (2023). *History 7-10.* https://v9.australiancurriculum.edu.au/f-10-curriculum/learning-areas/history-7-10/year-7_year-8_year-9_year-10?view=quick&detailed-content-descriptions=0&hide-ccp=0&hide-gc=0&side-by-side=1&strands-start-index=0&subjects-start-index=0
3. See Brett, P., Heggart, K. & Fento, S. (2021). No Minister. Examining recent commentary on the draft Australian History and Civics and Citizenship curriculum. *The Social Educator, 39*(3), 3–16; Clark, A. (2021, Oct 26). 10 things every politician should know about history. *The Conversation.* https://theconversation.com/10-things-every-politician-should-know-about-history-170626; Parkes, R. (2015). What paradigms inform the review of the Australian curriculum: History? What does this mean for the possibilities of critical and effective histories in Australian education? *Curriculum Perspectives, 35*(1), 52–54.
4. Parkes, R. J. (2007). Reading history curriculum as postcolonial text: Towards a curricular response to the history wars in Australia and beyond. *Curriculum Inquiry, 37*(4), 383–400. https://doi.org/10.1111/j.1467-873X.2007.00392.x
5. Ball, S. J., Braun, A., & Maguire, M. (2012). *How schools do policy: Policy enactments in secondary schools.* Routledge; Green, B. (2018). Knowledge, pedagogy, democracy: Reclaiming the Australian curriculum. In A. Reid, & D. Price (Eds.), *The Australian curriculum: Promises, problems and possibilities* (pp. 265–276). Australian Curriculum Studies Association; Maher, K. (2021). The Aboriginal and Torres Strait Islander histories and cultures cross curriculum priority: Pedagogical questions of Country, colonialism and whose knowledge counts. *Social Educator, 40*(2), 3–17.
6. Leach, M. (2023, Sep 22). The voice: How do other countries represent Indigenous voices in government? *The Conversation.* https://theconversation.com/the-voice-how-do-other-countries-represent-indigenous-voices-in-government-212875
7. Referendum Council. (2017). *Final report on the Referendum Council.* Commonwealth of Australia. https://ulurustatemdev.wpengine.com/wp-content/uploads/2022/01/Referendum_Council_Final_Report.pdf
8. ABC News. (2023). *Indigenous voice to parliament referendum.* https://www.abc.net.au/news/voice-to-parliament-referendum
9. Barolsky, C. (2022). Truth-telling about a settler-colonial ideology: Decolonising possibilities? *Postcolonial studies, 26*(4), 540–556. https://doi.org/10.1080/13688790.2022.2117872; Hradsky, D. (2022). Education for reconciliation? Understanding and acknowledging the history of teaching First Nations content in Victoria, Australia. *History of Education, 51*(1), 135–155. https://doi.org/10.1080/0046760X.2021.1942238; Maher (2021). The Aboriginal and Torres; Referendum Council. (2017). *Final report.*
10. Hradsky (2022). Education for reconciliation; Lowe, K., Moodie, N., & Weuffen S. (2021). Refusing reconciliation in Indigenous education. In B. Green, P. Roberts, & M. Brennan (Eds.), *Curriculum challenges and opportunities in a changing world: transnational perspectives in curriculum inquiry* (pp 71–86). Palgrave.

11 Rollo, T. (2022). Beyond curricula: Colonial pedagogies in public schooling. In S. D. Styres & A. Kempf (Eds.), *Troubling truth and reconciliation in Canadian education: Critical perspectives* (pp. 121–138). University of Alberta. p. 17.
12 A selection of political movements occurring since the 1980s in Australia include: the Aboriginal Land Rights Act 1976 (NT), the Royal Commission into Aboriginal Deaths in Custody (Australian Human Rights Commission, 1996), The Mabo vs Queensland case (1992), the Bringing them Home report (Australian Human Rights Commission, 1997), and the first National Sorry Day (Reconciliation Australia, 2013).
13 Clark, A. (2006). *Teaching the Nation: Politics and pedagogy in Australian schools*. Melbourne University Press; Ditchburn, G. (2012). A National Australian curriculum: In whose interests? *Asia Pacific Journal of Education, 32*(3), 259–269; Parkes (2007). Reading history curriculum.
14 Lowe et al. (2021). Refusing reconciliation; Hradsky (2022). Education for reconciliation; Rollo (2022). Beyond curricula; Weuffen, S., Lowe, K., Amazan, R., & Thompson, K. (2023). The need for First Nations pedagogical narratives: Epistemic inertia and complicity in (re)creating settler-colonial education. *Journal of Curriculum Studies, 56*(1), 58–72. https://doi.org/10.1080/00220272.2023.2294723
15 Lingard, B., & McGregor, L. (2014). Two contrasting Australian curriculum responses to globalisation: What students should learn or become. *The Curriculum Journal, 25*(1), 90–110. https://doi.org/10.1080/09585176.2013.872048
16 Kennedy, K. (2009). An idea of a national curriculum in Australia: What do Susan Ryan, John Dawkins and Julia Gillard have in common? *Curriculum Perspectives, 29*(1), 1–9. p. 6. http://www.acsa.edu.au/pages/page439.asp
17 Lowe et al. (2021). Refusing reconciliation.
18 Macintyre, S. (2019). Understanding the Australian Curriculum: History. In T. Allender, A. Clark, & R. Parkes (Eds.), *Historical thinking for history teachers* (p. 21). Allen & Unwin.
19 Ministerial Council on Education, Employment, Training and Youth Affairs (2008). *Melbourne declaration on educational goals for young Australians*. https://files.eric.ed.gov/fulltext/ED534449.pdf
20 Keane, J. (2018), *National identity and education in early twentieth century Australia*. Emerald Publishing Limited. https://doi.org/10.1108/978-1-78769-245-920181009; Weuffen, S., Lowe, K., Burgess, C., & Thompson, K. (2023). Sovereign and pseudo hosts: The politics of hospitality for negotiating culturally nourishing schools. *Australian Educational Researcher, 50*(1), 131–146. https://doi.org/10.1007/s13384-022-00599-0
21 Fozdar, F., & Martin, C. (2021). Making history: The Australian history curriculum and national identity. *Australian Journal of Politics & History, 67*(1), 130–149. https://doi.org/10.1111/ajph.12766; Guenther, J., Harrison, N., & Burgess, C. (2019). Special issue. Aboriginal voices: Systematic reviews of Indigenous education. *Australian Educational Researcher, 46*(1), 207–211. https://doi.org/10.1007/s13384-019-00316-4
22 Australian Curriculum, Assessment and Reporting Authority [ACARA]. (2023). *Aboriginal and Torres Strait Islander histories and cultures (Version 8.4)*. https://www.australiancurriculum.edu.au/f-10-curriculum/cross-curriculum-priorities/aboriginal-and-torres-strait-islander-histories-and-cultures/
23 ACARA. (2023). *History 7–10*.
24 Ibid; Braun, V., & Clarke, V. (2020). One size fits all?: What counts as quality practice in (reflective) thematic analysis? *Qualitative Research in Psychology, 18*(3), 328–352. https://doi.org/10.1080/14780887.2020.1769238; Nowell, L. S., Norris, J. M., White, D. E., & Moules, N. J. (2017). Thematic analysis: Striving to

meet the trustworthiness criteria. *International Journal of Qualitative Methods*, 16(1), 1–13. https://doi.org/10.1177/1609406917733847

25 Lowe & Galstaun (2020). *Ethical challenges*; Weuffen et al. (2023). Sovereign and pseudo; Weuffen, S., Lowe, K., Moodie, N., & Fricker, A. (2024). Doing decolonisation: Cultural reconnection as political resistance in schooling. *Australian Educational Researcher*, 50(1), 147–165. https://doi.org/10.1007/s13384-022-00603-7

26 Lowe et al. (2021). Refusing reconciliation; Hradsky (2022). Education for reconciliation; Maher (2021). The Aboriginal and Torres.

27 Rollo (2022). Beyond curricula, p. 12.

28 Green, B. (2018). *Engaging curriculum: Bridging the curriculum theory and English education divide*. Routledge. p. 33. https://doi.org/10.4324/9781315650944

29 Moreton-Robinson, A. (2015). *The white possessive: Property, power, and Indigenous sovereignty*. University of Minnesota Press. https://www.jstor.org/stable/10.5749/j.ctt155jmpf; Weuffen et al. (2023). Sovereign and pseudo.

30 Donnelly, K., & Wiltshire, K. (2014). *Review of the Australian Curriculum: Final report*. http://docs.education.gov.au/system/files/doc/other/review_of_the_national_curriculum_final_report.pdf; Parkes, R. (2015). What paradigms inform the Review of the Australian Curriculum: History? What does this mean for the possibilities of critical and effective histories in Australian Education? *Curriculum Perspectives*, 35(1), 52–54.

31 Moodie, N., Maxwell, J., & Rudoph, S. (2019). The impact of racism on the schooling experiences of Aboriginal and Torres Strait Islander students: A systematic review. *The Australian Educational Researcher*, 49(1), 273–295. https://doi.org/10.1007/s13384-019-00312-8

32 Alim, A. S., & Paris, D. (2017). What is culturally sustaining pedagogy and why does it matter? In D. Paris & H. S. Alim (Eds.), *Culturally sustaining pedagogies: Teaching and Learning for justice in a changing world* (pp 1–24). Teachers College Press. p. 6.

33 Jozuka, E. (2016, Sep 22). *Aboriginal Australians are earth's oldest civilisation: DNA study*. https://edition.cnn.com/2016/09/22/asia/indigenous-australians-earths-oldest-civilization/index.html; National Museum Australia. (2022). *Evidence of first peoples*. https://www.nma.gov.au/defining-moments/resources/evidence-of-first-peoples

34 Kennedy, L. (2019, Sep 27). *The prehistoric ages: How humans lived before written records*. https://www.history.com/news/prehistoric-ages-timeline

35 Lowe et al. (2021). Refusing reconciliation; Lowe & Galstaun (2020). *Ethical challenges*; Moreton-Robinson, A. (2015). *The white possessive*; Rollo (2022). Beyond curricula; Weuffen et al. (2023). The need for First Nations.

36 Alim & Paris (2017). What is culturally sustaining, p. 2.

37 Harvie, K. (2024). Acknowledging First Nations history and culture in primary schools. In Cairns, R., Fricker, A., & Weuffen, S. (Eds.) *Decolonising Australian history education: Fresh perspectives from beyond the 'history wars'*. Routledge.

38 Allender et al. (2019). Historical thinking; Lowe et al. (2021). Refusing reconciliation; Lowe & Galstaun (2020). *Ethical challenges*; Parkes (2007). Reading History Curriculum; Weuffen et al. (2023). The need for First Nations.

39 Barolsky (2022). Truth-telling; Tuck, E., & Yang, K. W. (Eds.). (2019). *Indigenous and decolonising studies in education*. Routledge; Weuffen et al. (2023). Doing decolonisation.

40 Rollo (2022). Beyond curricula, p. 17.

41 Fricker, A. (2017). Indigenous perspectives: Controversy in the history classroom? *Agora*, 52(4), 4–12.

42 Yunkaporta, T., & Shillingsworth, D. (2020). Relationally responsive standpoint. *Journal of Indigenous Research*, 8(1), 1–14. https://digitalcommons.usu.edu/kicjir/vol8/iss2020/4
43 Ibid., p. 9.
44 Ibid.
45 Weuffen et al. (2024). The need for First Nations.
46 Yunkaporta & Shillingsworth (2020). Relationally responsive standpoint, p. 1.
47 Ibid., p. 8.
48 Ibid.
49 The merging of First Nations and non-Indigenous viewpoints.
50 Yunkaporta & Shillingsworth (2020). Relationally responsive standpoint.
51 Ibid.
52 Alim & Paris (2017). What is culturally sustaining; Broughton. A. (2019). *Evidence-based approaches to becoming a culturally responsive educator: Emerging research and opportunities*. IGI Global.; Lowe & Galstaun (2020). *Ethical challenges*; Maher (2021). The Aboriginal and Torres; Tien (2019). *Teaching identity*.
53 Ellis, E., Farmer, T., & Newman, J. (2005). Big ideas about teaching big ideas. *Teaching Exceptional Children*, 38(1), 34–41. https://doi.org/10.1177/004005990503800107; Riveros, A. (2017). Beyond collaboration: Embodied teacher learning and the discourse of collaboration in education reform. *Studies in Philosophy and Education*, 31(6), 603–612. https://doi.org/10.1007/s11217-012-9323-6
54 Yunkaporta & Shillingsworth (2020). Relationally responsive standpoint, p. 10.
55 Yates, L., Woelert, P., Millar, V., & O'Connor, K. (2016). *Knowledge at the crossroads?: Physics and history in the changing world of schools and universities*. Springer. p. 98.
56 Ammert, N., Edling, S., Löfström, J., & Sharp, J. (2022). *Historical and moral consciousness in education learning ethics for democratic citizenship education*. Routledge. p. 2.
57 Ibid., p. 4.
58 Ibid.
59 Alim & Paris (2017). What is culturally sustaining, p. 12.
60 Ibid., p. 6.
61 Ibid., p. 12.

Index

Pages in *italics* refer to figures and pages in **bold** refer to tables.

Aboriginal and Torres Strait Islander cross-curriculum priority 17, 20, 56, 71, 123, 126–128, 132, 135, 165, 196, 198
Acknowledging Country 35–37, 77, 89, 95, 100, 107, 120, 186
Aotearoa New Zealand 5, 26, 127
Asia 22, 57, 160, 162–164, 169–170, *197*
Asia as method 8, 164–168, 173
Asia-related history 8, 161–163, 172, 204
Australian curriculum 5, 8, 17, 20, 53, 56, 126–127, 144, 159; history 2, 9, 11, 24, 65–66, 70, 77, 128, 144–145, 149–150, 163, 166–168, 180–182, 194, 196–198; review of 2–3, 10, 70, 128, 142, 194, 199
Australian education system 5, 7, 9, 20, 34, 40–43, 46, 54, 65, 69–70, 90, 93, 104, 107, 109, 112–117, 129–130, 141, 143–144, 206
Australian history education 32, 37–38, 45, 58, 120, 144, 165
Australian prime ministers 9–11, 34, 42, 45, 142

Balnarring Preschool 87–90, 92, 95, 100–102
black armband/white blindfold 2, 9–11, 116, 127
Boon Wurrung People and Country 7, 31, 33, 87–89, 95, 100, 102–104, 107, 141, 159, 193, 202; Boon Wurrung Tarrang (Tree) story 96–103, *98*, 202

Bunurong People and Country 3, 31, 33, 35, 107, 141

children 7, 20, 26, 34–35, 54, 63, 88–89, 91, 93–95, 99–104, 108–109, 116, 123, 131–132, 146
Chinese-Australian history 160, 166–172
cinematic virtual reality (CVR) 8, 178, 180–185, 188
Civil Rights Movement Australia 59, 62–64; United States 59, 62, 64
Clark, Anna 10, 127, 144
collaboration and relationships 33, 35, 47, 118, 120, 131, 135–136, 176–178, 185–189
colonial curriculum 126, 128, 130–131, 141, 143, 163–164, *197*, 198
colonial narrative 2, 8, 21, 53–55, 58, 93–94, 109, 118–119, 142–144, 150–151, 160, 163–164, 169, 172, 178–179, 184, 194, 196–198
colonisation 4, 6, 12, 22–23, 25, 32, 38, 47, 54–55, 57–58, 62–63, 75, 77, 88, 90, 96, 100, 123–124, 126, 128, 130, 132–133, 137, 143, 146, 149–150, 153, 159, 163–164, **166**, 172, 177–179, 185–186, *197*, 198
counter-narrative 46, 155, 185, 198–199
Country 4, 7, 35, 40, 56, 71, 79, 88–89, 93–97, *99*, 100, 103–104, 117–120, 125, 128, 135–136, 142, 159, 171–172, 185, 187–188, 202, 204
Critical Race Theory 62
critical self-reflection 6–7, 46, 59–60, 70, 74–79, 90, 92, 99, 117–119, 136–137, 160, 201–202

cultural competence 110, 120, 200
cultural safety 112, 120, 135, 187

Dadirri 7, 126, 133–136
Deakin, Alfred 161–162
decoloniality 4, 6, 9, 73, 105, 194–195, 200–201, 203–204, 206
decolonial praxis/practices 6–7, 69, 72–80
decolonial process 3–4, 7, 12, 53, 57–64
decolonisation definition 3–4, 23–24, 37, 58–59, 73, 108–111, 126, 153, 160, 176, 200–201; liberal perspectives 21–24
decolonising curriculum 4–5, 25, 32, 109, 111, 126–127, 133, 135, 137, 143–144, 160, 187, 189
decolonising history 5, 9, 11–12, 57, 92, 109, 143–146, 153, 160, 165, 168–169, 176–189, 200, 204–205
decolonising publishing 55–58, 65, 203
decolonising strategies 3–5, 23–26, 35, 47–48, 65–66, 78–80, 103–105, 119–121, 135, 149–156, 165–166, 173, 189, 206
deimperialisation 160, 165, **165**, 173
Dja Dja Wurrung People and Country 1, 31, 53, 57, 60, 168–169, 194
drama 32–33, 45, 47–48, 135, 203; *ethnodrama* 33

early childhood 7, 71, 87–105, 202
Eastern Maar People and Country 35, 161
epistemic inertia 70–71, 74, 79–80
Eurocentrism 8–9, 74, 79, 109, 129–130, 132, 143–145, 151–153, 160, 163

Fanon, Franz 4, 57
First Nations and Indigenous scholarship 4–5, 11, 19–20, 23–24, 26, 45, 57–58, 60, 63, 160, 195
First Nations authors 62–65, 94–96, 136, 179–180
First Nations content 40, 43, 53, 56–57, 59, 61, 63–65, 181, 199–200
First Nations educators and teachings 1, 69, 88–93, 100, 102, 206
First Nations histories and cultures 1–2, 11–12, 18, 35, 63, 65, 109, 118, 124, 130, 132, 134, 164, 176–177, 180, 189, 199

First Nations Peoples perspectives 2–3, 11–12, 22, 25, 46, 60, 70–71, 75, 89, 120, 124–125, 135–136, 160, 178, 196
First Nations stories 6, 12, 47, 56, 59, 63, 88–89, 91–92, 94–96, 99–100, 102–105, 117, 153, 159, 176–177, 185–187
First Nations students 53, 128, 136, 177, 194
First Nations ways of knowing and being 92, 94, 96–100, 125, 134, 168–169, 178
frontier myth 178–179
Frontier Wars 58, 132–133, 149, 156, 178–179
future 5–7, 9, 17, 19, 21, 25, 48, 62, 80, 95–96, 103, 105, 108–109, 111, 126, 129, 131, 135, 137, 160, 193–195, 199, 201, 204–206

Ganma 7, 126, 133–136
Goodes, Adam 94, 132
Great Australian Silence 53, 56, 65, 142
Gundijtmara Peoples and Country 1, 69, 193

historical consciousness 142, 146–147, 149
historical empathy 8, 46, 150, 178, 180–185, 189
historical narratives 8–9, 17, 19, 22, 24, 59, 61, 71, 141–143, 145–150, 153–155, 159–160, 163–164, **165–166**, 167, 171–173, 178–181, 188, 195–196, 198–199, 201, 204–206; *see* counter-narrative
historical sources 8, 60, 63–64, 150, 160, 167–172–171, 181, 184, 187–188
historical thinking 25–26, 146, 148, 153, 181
History curriculum 2, 5–7, 11, 24, 65, 70, 109, 111, 124, 126, 128, 143–144, 147–149, 159–160, 188–189, 196, 198–199
history education 1, 4–5, 8–9, 16–17, 20–21, 24–26, 32, 47, 111–112, 119, 141–142, 144, 153, 159, 169, 172, 181, 202, 204–206
History, the discipline of 4, 6, 8, 20, 24, 70–71, 77, 160–161, 164, 173, 194–195, 205

Index

'history wars' 2–3, 5, 7, 9–12, 26, 48, 65, 70, 79, 107–110, 119–120, 127, 141–142, 159, 195–196, 199–200, 205
human rights 17, 21–22, 24, 108, 120

identity 34, *39*, 41, 72–75, 78, 96, 119, 134, 143, 150, 152, 168, 171, 177
imperialism 10, 55, 71, 76–77, 163–164, **165–166**, 171, 195–198
indigenising 59, 63, 199–200
intercultural history 8, 141–156, 203
interculturality 141, 144–145, 148, 152, 154, 203
Intercultural Understanding (ICU) Capability 145–146, 148, 155–156
invasion 18, 26, 89, 94, 102, 109, 127–128, 132, 141, 143, 150, 152–153, 156, 160, 195, 198–199; Asian invasion 159, 169–170; Invasion Day 142, 145, 169; invasion narratives 8, 147, 159–160, 162, 169, 204

Kirrae Wuurong People and Country 176, 179, 186–187

language 7, 34, 78–79, 100, 112, 117–118, 128, 133, 135–136, 141, 148–150, 155–156, 170, 179
language conventions/protocols 64, 112, 118, 124, 131, 137, 161
local communities and contexts 7–8, 66, 96, 120, 124–127, 133, 135–136, 160, 182
local history 8, 108, 127, 176–189
Lowe, Kevin 72, 117, 120, 177
Lowe, Uncle Rob 8, 176, 178, 183, 185

Macintyre, Stuart 5, 10
Maroondah Framework 7, 133–134, 137
memory 7, 97, 107–108, 110–112, 119–121, 130–132, 134, 178, 187, 202, 204; memoryscapes 187–188
metanarrative 195, 198–199
Moreton-Robinson, Aileen 160, 162, 168–169, 171–172

neo-colonial 4, 6–9, 53, 55–56, 58, 60, 65, 194

non-Indigenous contexts 8, 58, 65
non-Indigenous educators/non-Indigenous History teachers 1, 6–7, 56, 59, 65, 69–71, 74–77, 79–80, 87–89, 91–92, 109–110, 123–125, 129, 132, 145, 169, 177, 182, 187, 200, 206
non-Indigenous people/non-Indigenous Australians 6–7, 23, 31, 33–34, 40, 46, 59–60, 63, 69, 73, 76–77, 123, 126, 132, 134, 161, 168–169, 176, 185–186, 193, 195, 200

Peek Wuurong People and Country 8, 176–177, 179, 186–187
pedagogy 1, 17, 20, 33, 35, *36*, 45, 47, 70–72, 74–75, 78, 80, 88–93, 95, 100, 105
politics of history 3, 5–6, 9–11, 19, 22, 25, 41–42, 53, 70–71, 79, 109, 117, 131, 142, 147, 194–196, 206
positionality 4, 69–70, 72–80, 161
possession narratives/possessive logics 8, 26, 159–161, 168–171, 173, 198
pre-service teachers 123–125, 141, 149–150, 152–153, 161
primary education 7, 20, 32, 53, 123–137, 161
professional learning 32–33, 78, 108, 119, 121, 125, 129, 131, 133, 135, 202–203

racism 2, 10, 33, 60, 64, 73, 107, 109–112, 117–118, 120, 124, 132, 137, 160, 167, 182–184, 188
reciprocity 134, 185–187, 189
reconciliation 6, 17–22, 32–33, 35, 37, 59, 71–72, 88, 90, 95, 108–109, 126, 128, 195, 205–206
Reid-Loynes, Priscilla 91–92, 103
relationality 1, 72, 74, 76–79, 88, 131, 143, 165, 185–187, 189, 201–202, 205
relational standpoint 200–201
resources 6, 8, 32, 56, 63–66, 71, 94, 96, 103, 105, 120, 124–126, 129–130, 135–137, 143, 153–154, 156, 167–170, 172–173, 176–179, 186, 199, 203

self-determination 19, 24–25, 59–60, 127, 160
settler colonialism/settler-colonial 1–2, 5, 17–19, 21, 23, 54–55, 69, 71–79, 109–110, 119–121, 132, 159–161, 165, 169–170, 172, 186, 188–189, 193–195, 198–206
Shillingworth, Doris 9, 75, 201–202
sovereignty 3–4, 19, 23–26, 58–61, 156, 159–161, 168–169, 171–172, 195, 200, 202, 204
Stanner, W.E.H. 53, 56, 142
Stolen Generations 10, 19–21, 24, 116, 178
storytelling 8, 46, 89, 94–96, *101*, 101–104, 133, 148, 188, 204–205

terra nullius 22, 58, 89–90, 94, 146–148, 155–156, 171, 177–178
textbooks 53, 56, 58–65, 203
threshold concepts 6, 72–74
tokenism 70–72, 110, 144
transitional justice 17–19, 21, 23
treaty/treaty making 3, 16–17, 19, 22, 24, 58; *see* Voice, Treaty, Truth
truth commissions 16–21, 23
truth telling 2, 6–7, 9, 11, 16–21, 23–25, 71, 73, 89, 91, 103, 105, 109, 119, 124, 127–128, 156, 184–185, 189, 194–195, 201–203, 205–206
Tuck & Yang 4, 23, 58, 144, 160
Tudge, Alan (Minister) 10, 129, 142, 199

Uluru Statement from the Heart 2, 16–17, 21, 26, 156, 172

verbatim theatre 6, 32, 47, 203
Voice to Parliament referendum 2–3, 5–6, 10–11, 16, 142, 194, 206
Voice, Treaty, Truth 2, 10, 16, 194

Wadawurrung People and Country 1, 31, 69, 159, 161, 169, 193
Warrnambool 69, 177–180, 193
Westerncentrism 4, 71, 76, 160, 162–163, 196, 204
Western/ised 6, 10, 17–18, 21–23, 25–26, 73–74, 76–77, 79–80, 109, 129, 142, 144, 146, 162–164, **165**, 172, 194–196, 199–204, 206
Whiteness 33, 54, 59, 75, 110, 118, 152–153, 171, 198
Wurundjeri People and Country 1, 3, 16, 31, 33, 35, 96, 107–108, 119, 123, 133, 135–136, 159, 161, 193

yarning 7, 35, 103, 124, 126, 133–136, 185, 188–189
YARNS tool 64–65, 96, 118
Yoorook Justice Commission 16–17, 21
Yunkporta, Tyson 9, 75, 110, 117, 201–202

For Product Safety Concerns and Information please contact our EU
representative GPSR@taylorandfrancis.com
Taylor & Francis Verlag GmbH, Kaufingerstraße 24, 80331 München, Germany

www.ingramcontent.com/pod-product-compliance
Lightning Source LLC
Chambersburg PA
CBHW050534300426
44113CB00012B/2084